RENUNCIATION THROUGH *Wisdom*

RENUNCIATION THROUGH Wisdom

by

His Divine Grace A.C. Bhaktivedanta Swami Prabhupāda
Founder-Ācārya of the International Society for Krishna Consciousness

THE BHAKTIVEDANTA BOOK TRUST

Readers interested in the subject matter of this book are invited by the International Society for Krishna Consciousness to correspond with its secretary at one of the following addresses.

International Society for Krishna Consciousness
P.O. Box 262
Botany, NSW 2019
Australia

International Society for Krishna Consciousness
3764 Watseka Ave.
Los Angeles, California 90034
USA

International Society for Krishna Consciousness
P.O. Box 324
Borehamwood, Herts, WD6 1NB
England

First printing, 1992: 50,000

National Library of Australia Cataloguing-in-Publication Data:

A.C. Bhaktivedanta Swami Prabhupada, 1896-1977.
[Vairagya vidya. English]. Renunciation Through Wisdom

Includes index.
ISBN 0 947259 04 X.

1. Bhagavada-gita - Criticism, interpretation, etc.
2. Soul (Hinduism). 3. God (Hinduism).
4. Krishna (Hindu diety). I. Title II. Title:
Vairagya vidya. English

294.5924

Contents

Topics of Spiritual Science

The Deluded Thinkers

The Highest Use of Intelligence

Appendixes

Introduction

The International Society for Krishna Consciousness (ISKCON) has become well known for its large body of Vedic literature—books on *bhakti-yoga* that include the *Bhagavad-gītā*, the *Śrīnad-Bhāgavatam*, and the *Caitanya-caritāmṛta*. These three works by the movement's founder and spiritual guide, His Divine Grace A.C. Bhaktivedanta Swami Prabhupāda, are voluminous commented English translations of Sanskrit and Bengali classics. Remarkably, Śrīla Prabhupāda wrote these and many other, smaller works in the span of twelve years, from 1966 to 1977, while traveling widely and overseeing the growth of the Kṛṣṇa consciousness movement.

What many people may not know, however, is that during the years before he came to the West Śrīla Prabhupāda wrote extensively on Kṛṣṇa consciousness in his native language, Bengali. In 1976, soon after I joined the Hare Kṛṣṇa movement, I discovered some of Śrīla Prabhupāda's early Bengali writings. They were serialized essays that had appeared in a monthly magazine he edited called *Gauḍīya Patrika.*

One of these lengthy essays, entitled *"Bhagavāner-kathā"* (*"Knowledge of the Supreme"*) ran in the *Gauḍīya Patrika* in 1948 and 1949, soon after India won its independence. I decided that it would make a wonderful booklet for Śrīla Prabhupāda's growing number of followers in his native Bengal. When I presented Śrīla Prabhupāda that newly printed booklet in early 1977 in Calcutta, he was extremely pleased. He looked at me with his face shining brilliantly, and with a broad smile he said, "Thank you, thank you very much. Please keep printing my books."

I was so encouraged that I soon collected as many of Śrīla Prabhupāda's Bengali writings from the *Gauḍīya Patrika* as I could and printed them as booklets under the titles *"Bhakti*

Katha" (*The Science of Devotion*), *"Jñāna Katha"* (*Topics of Spiritual Science*), *"Muni-gānera Mati-bhrama"* (*The Deluded Thinkers*) and "*Buddhi-yoga*" (*The Highest Use of Intelligence*). Finally, I compiled all the booklets into a hardbound book called *Vairagya Vidyā*, which has now been translated in English and titled *Renunciation through Wisdom.*

My close friend and Godbrother Sarvabhavana dāsa did the translation, and he has done a very good job. In each of the original Bengali essays Śrīla Prabhupāda's profound spiritual wisdom shines through, and Sarvabhavana Prabhu has expertly conveyed this wisdom in his translation.

When Śrīla Prabhupāda wrote these essays, he was a family man playing the part of an insignificant devotee in the Gauḍīya Maṭha, the Kṛṣṇa consciousness society founded by his spiritual master, Śrīla Bhaktisiddhānta Sarasvatī Ṭhākura. Yet despite the humble position Śrīla Prabhupāda was taking at the time, his writings mark him unmistakably as a pure devotee. Anyone with an open mind and a gracious heart will see from his writings that Śrīla Prabhupāda was a self-realized soul all along.

Like his spiritual master, Śrīla Prabhupāda strictly followed the teachings of Śrī Caitanya Mahāprabhu in his presentation of Kṛṣṇa consciousness. Those teachings are summarized in the phrase *vairāgya-vidya-nija-bhakti-yoga,* which means "renunciation through the wisdom that comes from practicing devotional service." This line from a famous verse by Śrīla Sārvabhauma Bhaṭṭācārya, one of Lord Caitanya's intimate disciples, has inspired the title of the present book, *Renunciation Through Wisdom.*

What is this wisdom which produces renunciation? It is one of the fruits of devotional service to Kṛṣṇa. When one experiences the nectar of devotional service and becomes steeped in the knowledge of the Vedic literature, one naturally becomes averse to sense gratification and attains freedom from material bondage. Lord Kṛṣṇa spoke the essence of Vedic wisdom in the *Bhagavad-gītā.* As the *Gītā-māhātmya,* "the Glory of the *Bhagavad-gītā*" says in this poetic analogy:

> the cowherd boy Kṛṣṇa milked the cow of the *Upaniṣads* [the philosophical essence of the *Vedas*] for the sake of the calf Arjuna, and the milk that came forth is the *Bhagavad-*

> *gītā.* Saintly persons seriously concerned about their spiritual welfare will drink and relish that wondrous nectarean milk.

In *Renunciation Through Wisdom,* Śrīla Prabhupāda has simplified the teachings of the *Bhagavad-gītā* for our understanding. If we drink this nectar, very soon the brilliant sunshine of transcendental knowledge will dispel the darkness of ignorance caused by our unwanted material desires, and then love for Kṛṣṇa will dawn in our hearts.

Transcendental knowledge is eternal; it never becomes dated or outmoded but is always relevant, in all times and places. Therefore, *Renunciation Through Wisdom,* though written forty or more years ago in the context of modern Indian history, can enlighten anyone, in any part of the world. Actually, this wisdom is for everyone, for all time.

Bhakti Caru Swami
New York, July 1991

Bhagavāner-kathā

Knowledge of the Supreme

This Material Nature Is Full of Miseries

The editor of the daily *Amrita Bazar Patrika*, published from Allahabad, began the editorial the other day on a rather sad note:

> The nation's week began with memories of "Jalhianwallah-Bagh,"* and political serfdom no longer troubles us. But our troubles are far from being at an end. In the dispensation of providence, mankind cannot have any rest. If one kind of trouble goes, another quickly follows. India, politically free, is faced with difficulties that are no less serious than the troubles under foreign rule.

Now, if one consults the accounts ledger of India's serfdom and freedom, and views the contents from a spiritual perspective, the conclusion will be as follows: the four *yugas,* or ages, namely Satya, Tretā, Dvāpara, and Kali, add up to 4,320,000 years. Kali-yuga, which lasts 432,000 years, began from the time of Mahārāja Parīkṣit's rule, some five thousand years ago. For approximately one thousand of these five thousand years—i.e., since the invasion of Mohammad Ghori in A.D. 1050—India has been experiencing foreign rule. In other words, when we calculate according to scripture, India has exercised absolute sovereignty over the entire planet Earth for a period of 3,888,000 years, till Mahārāja Parīkṣit's rule. Hence the

* On 13 April 1919, 1516 people were killed or wounded at Jalhianwallah-Bagh, India, by the British army. This unprovoked attack on a prayer meeting caused outrage and was considered the turning point in Anglo-Indian relations. Indian leaders, including Gandhi, finally realized that the British would not easily give up their dominance of the country.

meager thousand years of foreign subjugation are not such a lamentable thing. Neither in the past nor at present has India's political serfdom or freedom been the prime concern of India's greatest thinkers and philosophers, who well knew the actual value of such things. The kings of India up to Mahārāja Parīkṣit were able to rule the entire world, and not for a mere couple of centuries but for hundreds of thousands of years. The reason for their rule was not a political one.

India's wise men of yore easily realized that the threefold miseries we humans are condemned to suffer can never be mitigated by the political condition controlling the country—whether foreign rule or freedom from it. At the dawn of modern history, the Armageddon fought in India over a political question lasted only eighteen days. On that historic battlefield the problem of human suffering and its permanent solution was discussed, and this discussion was compiled in the form of the *Bhagavad-gītā*.

Thus millennia ago the *Bhagavad-gītā* comprehensively discussed the same topic the editor of *Amrita Bazar Patrika* writes about in a despondent mood: "If one kind of trouble goes, another quickly follows." In the *Gītā* (7.14) Lord Kṛṣṇa says, "This divine energy of Mine, consisting of the three modes of material nature, is difficult to overcome." The Sanskrit words *daivī māyā* used here can be translated into modern terms as "nature's law." This natural law is so stringent that it is impossible to overcome it, in spite of our prolific articles in the newspapers or our big conferences tabling motions that run into volumes. Our advanced technological and scientific efforts aimed at protecting us from the clutches of nature's law are futile because they are all controlled by the very same nature's law, or *daivī māyā*. Therefore trying to utilize mundane science to overpower nature's law is like creating a Frankenstein. Efforts to extirpate human suffering through advanced technology and bring about lasting happiness have brought us to the Atomic Age. Western thinkers have become gravely concerned about the extent of destruction an atomic explosion can cause. Some leaders are trying to calm the alarm with platitudes about how atomic energy is to be used solely for peaceful purposes, but this is another form of deception caused by *daivī māyā*, or nature's law.

It is impossible for anyone to surmount the two-pronged attack of *daivī māyā*—that is, her covering potency and her throwing potency. The more we try to conquer this divine energy, the more powerfully we are defeated by her exciting us through the mode of passion and punishing us with the threefold miseries, culminating in all-devouring death. This struggle between the divine energy and the evil forces is eternal. Our inability to understand this struggle has led us to lament, "In the dispensation of providence, mankind cannot have any rest."

Despite repeatedly tasting defeat at the hands of the divine energy, the evil forces cannot understand why "mankind cannot have any rest." Yet in the *Bhagavad-gītā* the Supreme Personality of Godhead clearly explains this. At first He sternly warns the evil forces with these words, *daivī hy eṣā guṇa-mayī mama māyā duratyayā:* "This divine energy of Mine, consisting of the three modes of material nature, is difficult to overcome"; and then in the next line He tells them how to overcome this divine energy, *mām eva ye prapadyante māyām etāṁ taranti te:* "But those who have surrendered unto Me can easily cross beyond it."

The Cause of Suffering

Mahiṣāsura*, the most powerful demon, who was the personification of the forces of evil, was in fact endowed with intelligence, education, wealth, the ability to perform severe penances and attract large followings, and so on. His present-day followers, possessing identical qualifications, are no less enterprising and expert in exploiting the divine energy. They carry out elaborate scientific research, misspending huge amounts of money, time, energy, intelligence, men, and so on. But instead of peace and joy, what they discover through these

---

* Mahiṣāsura's father, Rambha, received a boon from the sun-god that his son could never be defeated. By this boon Mahiṣāsura gained sovereignty over all. The demigods sought protection from Viṣṇu who informed them that only a female could cause his defeat. The Lord appeared in a female form (called Devi) and killed the demon in a fierce battle.

researches ends up producing untold misery for humanity. This is a perfect example of *daivī māyā's* throwing agency in action. All these evil activities bring great losses to human society. As a result of this evil, the mundane scientists incur grievous sin, which destroys their real intelligence. And this loss of intelligence turns them away from God and robs them of their chance to surrender to Him. Thus in the *Bhagavad-gītā* (7.15) the Supreme Lord says:

na māṁ duṣkṛtino mūḍhāḥ
prapadyante narādhamāḥ
māyayāpahṛta-jñānā
āsuraṁ bhāvam āśritāḥ

> Those miscreants who are grossly foolish, who are lowest among mankind, whose knowledge is stolen by illusion, and who partake of the atheistic nature of demons do not surrender unto Me.

In the *Bhagavad-gītā* (16.7–20) the Supreme Lord has exhaustively described the nature of such atheistic demons:

> Those who are demoniac do not know what is to be done and what is not to be done. Neither cleanliness nor proper behavior nor truth is found in them. They say that this world is unreal, with no foundation, no God in control. They say it is produced of sex desire and has no cause other than lust. Following such conclusions, the demoniac, who are lost to themselves and who have no intelligence, engage in unbeneficial, horrible works meant to destroy the world. Taking shelter of insatiable lust and absorbed in the conceit of pride and false prestige, the demoniac, thus illusioned, are always sworn to unclean work, attracted by the impermanent.
>
> They believe that to gratify the senses is the prime necessity of human civilization. Thus until the end of life their anxiety is immeasurable. Bound by a network of hundreds and thousands of desires and absorbed in lust and anger, they secure money by illegal means for sense gratification. The demoniac person thinks, 'So much wealth do I have today, and I will gain more according to my schemes. So much is mine now, and it will increase in the future, more and more. He is my enemy, and I have killed him, and my other enemies will also be killed. I am the lord of everything. I am

> the enjoyer. I am perfect, powerful, and happy. I am the richest man, surrounded by aristocratic relatives. There is none so powerful and happy as I am. I shall perform sacrifices, I shall give some charity, and thus I shall rejoice.' In this way such persons are deluded by ignorance. Thus perplexed by various anxieties and bound by a network of illusions, they become too strongly attached to sense enjoyment and fall down into hell.
>
> Self-complacent and always impudent, deluded by wealth and false prestige, they sometimes proudly perform sacrifices in name only, without following any rules or regulations. Bewildered by false ego, strength, pride, lust, and anger, the demons become envious of the Supreme Personality of Godhead, who is situated in their own bodies and in the bodies of others, and blaspheme against the real religion. Those who are envious and mischievous, who are the lowest among men, I perpetually cast into the ocean of material existence, into various demoniac species of life. Attaining repeated birth amongst the species of demoniac life, O son of Kuntī, such persons can never approach Me. Gradually they sink down to the most abominable type of existence.

These verses from the *Gītā* aptly describe the demoniac nature.

There have always existed two types of men, the devotee and the demon. Long ago there lived a big demon named Rāvaṇa*, who disguised himself as a *sannyāsī,* a renounced mendicant, and tried to steal the wife of the Supreme Lord, Rāmacandra. She was the goddess of fortune, Sītā-devī. In this way the demon brought about his own destruction.

But now, in modern times, Rāvaṇa's dynasty has multiplied into millions. This has given rise to many different opinions, which have made the demons inimical toward one another. Thus they are all competing tooth and nail, trying to kidnap the goddess of fortune, Sītā-devī. Each one is thinking, "I am the most cunning, and so I will enjoy Sītā-devī all by myself." But like Rāvaṇa, all these demons, along with their entire

---

* Ravana was the king of the demons who opposed the Supreme Lord Ramacandra. This history is related in the *Ramayana* attributed to the sage Valmiki.

families, are being destroyed. So many powerful leaders like Hitler have come, but enamored by the illusion of enjoying and exploiting the Supreme Lord's energy and consort—Sītā-devī, the goddess of fortune—all of them have been thwarted and crushed in the past, are being thwarted and crushed in the present, and will be thwarted and crushed in the future. The root cause of the aforementioned lament—"In the dispensation of providence, mankind cannot have any rest"—is this demoniac mentality of exploiting and enjoying the Lord's divine energy.

The demons do not know when or where to renounce, nor do they know when or where to accept or receive. When diagnosing a patient, one has to properly judge this accepting and rejecting principle. So, in order to cure the demoniac mentality in human society, which causes the Rāvaṇa syndrome of trying to steal Sītā-devī, it is essential that the demoniac nature be transformed. For any treatment, two important factors are that the patient be in clean surroundings and that his medicine and food be administered punctually. Similarly, to transform the demoniac mentality, people have to be clean, disciplined, and truthful. This end is not served by advocating the theory of *yata mat, tata path*—that "there are as many ways to salvation as there are opinions"—for in this way one confuses and deceives the populace. By bringing the clean and the unclean, the disciplined and undisciplined, the truthful and the untruthful on to the same level, one will find it impossible to cure or even treat any patient.

The Godless Demons

The grossly materialistic demons are so completely bereft of spiritual knowledge that although at every moment they perceive the transience of the material body, all their activities center on the body. They are unable to understand that the soul within the body is the permanent and essential substance and that the body is mutable and temporary. Becoming first enamored of and then deluded by *vivartavāda* (the theory of evolution), they conclude that the entire cosmic body also lacks a soul. Since the fallacious theory they apply to their own physical existence leads them to reject any research into the existence of a soul residing within the body, they fail to perceive the presence of the Supersoul within the gigantic body of the cosmic manifestation. They falsely conclude that the body is everything, that there is nothing beyond it; similarly, they think that the material creation, which is the universal body, is factually governed only by the laws of nature. Any discussion on this subject is invariably put to premature death by their insistence that nature is the be-all and end-all. The more intelligent among them carry this discussion a little further and postulate that impersonalism is the quintessence of everything. But far beyond this realm of manifest and unmanifest material nature is the transcendental and eternal state. The atheists, however, are characteristically unable to believe in its existence.

In this way, with their perverted minds bereft of farsightedness, demoniac men perform activities that bring only misery to the people. And as a result of many such unwanted activities, the atom bomb was discovered. The endless plans these demoniac men chalk out can never bode well for humanity. In the past, Rāvaṇa attempted to build a stairway to heaven, claiming this was for humanity's benefit. Actually, he was trying to cheat the Supreme Lord, Rāmacandra. But he was unsuccessful. History repeats itself, for now we find that Rāvaṇa's descendants are attempting to cheat the Lord in the name of planning to benefit society. The thing to take note of is that no demon will compliment other demons' plans. Every demon will declare that since his plan is the most wonderful, all others must vote for him. Then an opponent will say that in actuality *his* plan is the best and hence he should rightfully be given all the votes. In this age of votes, the fighting over who is to actually get the votes has untimely broken all the stairways to heaven. If one calmly considers the facts, one will easily conclude that all these plans manufactured by the perverted brains of the demons, with their myopic vision, can never bring peace in the world. Of course, in one matter all the demons readily agree, and that is to surreptitiously enjoy Lakṣmī, the goddess of fortune and eternal consort of the Supreme Lord, without the knowledge of the Lord Himself.

Every demon is vainly proud, thinking no one is more intelligent and esteemed than himself. Therefore the overpowering desires that urge him on to perform various activities are, according to him, ultimately beneficial for human society. In the end, of course, it is inevitably revealed that all his aspirations were illusory and unrealistic. Yet despite this revelation, the demons continue to influence the populace through manipulations and lies.

There are no limits to the imagination of these unclean and deluded demons. They pose as self-styled leaders and endlessly worry about the welfare of society. They worry, for example, about where to lodge the people who come to purchase in the marketplace. What they actually think about is how to make foolproof arrangements to secure their own long-lasting enjoyment, along with their children's, their grandchildren's, and their great-grandchildren's enjoyment, up to the final dissolution of the world. But when they experience suffering instead of pleasure, the demons revert to violence against their fellow men to accumulate wealth. Their material desires are insatiable, and so even billions of dollars cannot appease them. Whoever is expert in illegally amassing huge fortunes becomes the top dog. The demons are full of hate, greed, anger, lust, and so on and they are tireless in their efforts to illicitly amass great wealth merely to gratify their sensual urges. On the other hand, their competitors are no less expert in cheating them of their black wealth. How can such ruthless competition aimed at stealing one another's illegally-earned money bring about peace and prosperity? Hence the demons can never help the person who laments, "In the dispensation of providence, man cannot have any rest."

The demon is always ruminating on how to increase his bank balance: "Today the stocks have gone up, and so also have my profits. Tomorrow, if these other commodities become dearer, my bank balance will further increase. And so my future looks bright and prosperous." The demon continues to think, but now on a slightly different subject: "One of my enemies has already been destroyed, and another one is soon to meet his end. This puts me in a more secure position. So now that I have become adept at eliminating my enemies, I am God Almighty. Why must you look in search of God? Hundreds of 'Gods' are floating right before your eyes." Such thoughts and actions make the demons more and more atheistic, and thus they refuse to hear the transcendental message of God. They proudly declare, "Who is God? Why, I am God! When I can illegally manipulate funds and become so wealthy that I can enjoy everything in this world, then I am indeed Almighty God. I am strong and happy and accomplished. Those who are weaklings, without money and means, must respect me as God. What is the use of crying after any other God?"

The demons are under the impression that no one is more wealthy and popular than themselves. They think that their wealth will somehow be protected by some spirit, and in this way they are deluded. Their final destination is hell.

The few religious deeds that the demons perform are merely a show; they are meant only to flatter their false ego and bring them more recognition and respect. They perform them only for their own sense enjoyment and are invariably acts of violence. The demons engage in these rituals without following the scriptural injunctions, merely to appease their vainglory.

Strutting with false pride, strength, anger, lust, and so on the demons become totally absorbed in bodily consciousness, thinking "This is my body. I am Indian, Bengali, and so on. He is a Muslim; he is a Hindu; he is a German". In this way they perpetrate acts of violence on others. The Supreme Lord repeatedly puts these most abominable, wretched sinners into the most distressful conditions, constantly punishing them with His stringent laws of nature, or *daivī māyā*. Thus taking repeated births as demons, these reprobates can never appreciate the transcendental pastimes, names, beauty, and so on, of the Supreme Lord. Gradually cultivating the impersonal knowledge of the Absolute, they are destined to suffer the worst possible life.

The Cause of the Demoniac Mentality

There are numerous causes of the demoniac mentality, but in this essay we shall broadly delve into only three: lust, anger, and greed. In the *Bhagavad-gītā* (16.21) Lord Kṛṣṇa describes these three characteristics as destroyers of the self—portals leading to hell.

The Supreme Personality of Godhead is the sole proprietor and enjoyer of everything. When the living entities forget this fact, they develop an intense desire to enjoy this phenomenal world. But they cannot be fully satisfied by such endeavors, and thus anger develops. Anger causes frustration, as in the story of the unsuccessful fox and the "sour grapes." The living entity is then forced to pretend to be a renouncer. But at the bottom of such renunciation burns the great flame of greed and the desire for enjoyment. This is only another stage of material desire. Therefore, unless one transcends this stage of acceptance and rejection of physical pleasures and becomes situated on the platform of the eternal self, one cannot understand the sublime message of the Lord. And without this understanding, one will continue to cultivate the demoniac mentality.

The only method by which one can elevate oneself from the depths of demoniac depravity to the path of self-realization is to learn the injunctions of the scriptures and act accordingly. Chaotic and undisciplined activities contrary to scriptural instructions are actions performed out of lust. It is not possible to eradicate anger and greed through such acts of lust; nor is it possible to experience true happiness and divine elevation. Therefore if we wish to find the path to spiritual upliftment and eternal peace—the need for which is expressed in the lament "In the dispensation of providence, mankind cannot have any rest"—revealed scriptures are our only guide. Simply by executing the injunctions of the scriptures, we can become free from acts of lust and chaotic living.

At present we are living in the thick of Kali-yuga*. The people of this age are mostly short-lived, misguided, unfortunate, and always tormented by disease and distress. Therefore it is not easy for them to appreciate the words of the scriptures. The followers of the world's various religions—Hindus, Muslims, Christians, Buddhists, and so on—are transgressing the scriptural injunctions of their own faiths to varying degrees and living as they like. Many people, far from following scriptural injunctions, ridicule the sacred texts and thus gradually slide down to a demoniac life of unrestricted sense enjoyment. The Supreme Lord and His devotees are very much concerned about the deliverance of these conditioned souls afflicted by the ill influence of Kali-yuga. The devotees, or

* Kali-yuga—the present historical age (fourth and last in a perpetually repeating cycle of four progressively degenerate ages).

Vaiṣṇavas, are the most compassionate, saintly souls, and thus they ardently desire to deliver the fallen living entities. The Supreme Lord always responds to the desires of these Vaiṣṇavas, and so He answers their prayers for the salvation of these suffering souls of Kali-yuga.

Seeing the miserable condition of the living entities in the Kali-yuga, Lord Caitanya, the savior of the fallen souls, has expounded a method for their salvation. This method is taken from the scriptures and is applicable to everyone. In previous ages, one could study the *Vedas* and purify oneself by living according to those instructions. But it is impossible for the present population to properly execute these Vedic injunctions, which include strictly following vows of celibacy. One who is extremely degraded and sinful cannot find the accurate path to realization by studying the *Vedas.* It is a waste of time even to explain the meaning of the *Vedas* to such persons, who are devoid of a proper up-bringing and discipline. Lord Caitanya has indeed showered His mercy upon these Kali-yuga people. So there is no doubt that those who are unable even to receive this mercy from Lord Caitanya are forever bereft of saving grace. As for those fortunate souls who, after realizing the greatness of Lord Caitanya's mercy, have accepted it—they have escaped the punishments of *māyā,* or "the dispensation of providence." But for those who have agreed to come under the influence of the cycle of karmic reactions and are being pummeled about by *māyā,* the Supreme Lord has arranged the process of *karma-yoga,* or fruitive activities with the aim of sacrifice to the Supreme Lord.

The learned sages say that the living entities go through 8,400,000 species of life. There are 900,000 aquatic species; 2,000,000 plants, mountains, and other nonmoving species; 1,100,000 insects and worm species; 1,000,000 bird species; 3,000,000 animal species; and 400,000 human species. After passing through all these species, the soul is finally born as a human being in Bhārata-varṣa, India. He achieves this birth by gradually awakening his consciousness. Many millions of years flash by as the soul goes through each of the above-mentioned species of life. So, even after all this, if the soul, despite being born as a human being in India, continues to be subjugated by *māyā* and goes round in the whirlpool of "the dispensation of providence," then there is no limit to his misfortune. Śrīla Kṛṣṇadāsa Kavirāja has therefore written,

bhārata-bhūmite haila manuṣya-janma yāra
janma sārthaka kari' kara para-upakāra

One who has taken his birth as a human being in the land of India (Bhārata-varṣa) should make his life successful and work for the benefit of all other people.

Human beings can perfect their lives by following in the footsteps of those great sages of India who have all along shown the proper path. The reason for this is simple: nowhere else can we find an example of the manner in which the sages of India have endeavored to find absolute cessation of *māyā's* attack and to become an eternal dust particle of the supreme Lord's lotus feet. In other countries, especially in the Occident, tremendous progress has been a made in the various fields of material science—but it is all based on the material mind and body, which are creations of *māyā,* the illusory potency. It is for this reason that the Westerners lament, "In the dispensation of providence, man cannot have any rest." At present, the Indians have similarly taken to the path of self-destruction by aping the Western ways. They have discarded and desecrated their own culture and have become beggars at another's door. They are now flying their flag of independence, but this is also a dispensation of *māyā.* Factually, they cannot gain anything from it. The Occident has never delved into the three stages in the development of the eternal relationship between the infinitesimal soul and the infinite Supreme Whole. These stages are, first, the initial contact with the Supreme Lord and the reawakening of one's relationship with Him; second, the execution of the means to achieve one's eternal relationship with Him; and finally, the blossoming of that relationship into one of love and total dependence of the soul upon the Lord.

Although Western people have brilliantly developed in mundane matters, they are tossed about in a sea of despair and listlessness. Similarly, the Indians, although trying to feel grateful for their mundane development, are experiencing the same listlessness and dissatisfaction. Strangely enough, now the Western thinkers are looking toward India to find peace and calm. We can safely harbor the firm conviction that soon the message of peace will reach their ears.

The Formula for Peace

Lord Kṛṣṇa, seeing the distressful condition of the living entities and forseeing their bleak future, spoke the scripture known as *Bhagavad-gītā,* which contains unequivocal instructions for mankind. These instructions are like the cooling showers of peace on the blazing forest fire of material existence. Ordinary human activities are quite different from the activities recommended in the *Śrīmad Bhagavad-gītā;* understanding this difference is essential for us. In our times we find many fruitive workers who claim to be *karma-yogīs* but in fact are seen to enjoy the fruits of their labor. What is needed is not this false *karma-yoga* but genuine *buddhi-yoga,* which Lord Kṛṣṇa several times explains in the *Bhagavad-gītā. Buddhi-yoga* means "devotion to the Supreme Lord." The Lord says in the *Gītā* (10.10), "To those who are constantly devoted to serving Me with love, I give the understanding by which they can come to Me." Elsewhere in the *Gītā* (18.56) the Lord says, "One can understand Me as I am, as the Supreme Personality of Godhead, only by devotional service." Therefore, since *buddhi-yoga* is the means to attain the Supreme Lord, then *buddhi-yoga* is nothing other than devotional service. The Supreme Lord is attained through loving devotional service. This fact is well known. Hence the Lord is also known as *bhakta-vatsala,* "He who is especially inclined toward His devotees."

The course of action one chooses through executing *buddhi-yoga* is the very means for mankind to attain lasting peace. Such a course of action will enable man to find rest "in the dispensation of providence". We can clearly understand the essence of *buddhi-yoga* from the *Bhagavad-gītā* (Chapter 2. 39–40):

> Thus far I have described this knowledge to you through analytical study. Now listen as I explain it in terms of working without fruitive results. O son of Pṛthā, when you act in such knowledge you can free yourself from the bondage of works. In this endeavor there is no loss or diminution, and a little advancement on this path can protect one from the most dangerous type of fear.

The attainment of peace through the process of *sāṅkhya-yoga* is for the modern man almost impossible. But peace is easily available through the process of *buddhi-yoga,* or loving devotional service to the Supreme Lord. And this peace is of the highest nature: it far exceeds the happiness experienced through any other process. Activities that are directly connected to devotional service blossom and develop unhindered by anything external. The amount of devotional activity one performs always remains intact; it is a permanent spiritual gain for the performer, never to be rendered futile. Even a little execution of devotional service is enough to save one from the greatest type of fear.

The process of pure devotional service is one. At the same time, the *Gītā* points out how to execute *buddhi-yoga* through *jñāna,* or analytical study, and *karma,* or fruitive action. When *buddhi-yoga* is executed in conjunction with fruitive activity, it is known as *karma-yoga.* Similarly, when it is executed in conjunction with analytical study, then it is called *jñāna-yoga.* And when *buddhi-yoga,* or devotional service, transcends both *karma-yoga* and *jñāna-yoga* and becomes completely unalloyed, that devotion is called pure *bhakti-yoga,* or loving devotional service to the Supreme Lord.

The fruitive activities one performs in this world, whether according to social norms or Vedic standards, give different results. Again, by experiencing the fruits of those labors, one creates new sets of activities and their concomitant results, which in turn give rise to newer sets of activities and *their* results. All these activities and their results cannot automatically be labeled *karma-yoga.* We can see that the process of performing fruitive actions and experiencing their results is like a mammoth tree sprouting endless branches and twigs. Can the performer of actions who experiences the endless fruits of that mammoth tree ever enjoy peace and benediction? No. Therefore it is said, "In the dispensation of providence, mankind cannot have any rest". Even in this lifetime, one who performs fruitive work is totally entangled in the cycle of *karma* as he sits on the tree of material existence. As a result, the soul must enter the 8,400.000 species and suffer the threefold miseries, never finding any rest or peace.

Yet people find it impossible to renounce fruitive activities. Even the so-called *sannyāsīs* who make a show of renouncing such activities must still perform many activities, at least to relieve their hunger. Śrīpāda Śaṅkarācārya, seeing the condition of the *sannyāsīs* during his time, commented, "One takes on many different garbs just to fill one's stomach." And trying to give up all activities is no solution. When Śrī Arjuna, a warrior, wanted to forsake his duty of fighting a war, the Supreme Lord, Kṛṣṇa, advised him, "Perform your prescribed duty, for doing so is better than not working. One cannot even maintain one's physical body without work." (*Bhāgavad-gītā* 3.8)

A person should never give up his prescribed duty without scriptural authorization, for this will cause chaos in the world. Since it is impossible to maintain the body without activities, it is impossible to totally renounce activities. On the other hand, the tree of material entanglement, which thrives on fruitive activities and their results, can never bring forth any hope for peace. It is for this reason that the Supreme Lord has explained how one is to perform activities:

> Work done as a sacrifice for Viṣṇu has to be performed; otherwise causes bondage to this material world. Therefore, O son of Kuntī, perform your prescribed duties for His satisfaction, and in this way you will always remain free from bondage. (Bhagavad-gītā 3.9)

It is another kind of "dispensation of providence" when the fruits of actions do not bind one. To perform all activities only as a sacrifice for the satisfaction of Lord Viṣṇu is true freedom from the results of activities, or the real art of *karma-yoga*. Through this process of *karma-yoga* one is freed from the shackles of fruitive results and one's inherent eternal loving devotion for the Supreme Lord gradually manifests. This type of *karma-yoga* is also referred to as desireless actions, or *naiṣkarmya*, or in other words activities performed without expectation of any sense gratification. One who works in this way offers all the results of his actions to the Supreme Lord instead of enjoying them himself.

All of us must try to earn whatever money is required to maintain ourselves and our family. Money buys food, and food maintains our body. Without sufficient food, the body becomes weak and useless, and then it cannot generate further means for its sustenance. Which is the cause and which is the effect is very difficult to establish. Such is the cycle of fruitive activities. Our material existence birth after birth consists of going round the great cycle of fruitive activity. If, by the mercy of the Supreme Lord or His pure representative, a fortunate soul caught in the midst of this turning wheel can understand his distressful condition, he begins to perform activities that will free him from this bondage.

Life's Only Goal

Our objective is not the temporary peace and happiness available in the material world. As living entities we are eternal, and hence the desire for permanent happiness should be our prime motive. Yet we souls change millions of bodies, going up and down the fourteen material planetary systems, chasing after illusory peace and pleasures, expending huge amounts of blood and energy. The permanent peace and happiness we demonically run after eludes us constantly; we do not know where real peace and happiness are available. As Prahlāda Mahārāja says in the *Śrīmad-Bhāgavatam* (7.9.25),

> In this material world, every living entity desires some future happiness, which is exactly like a mirage in the desert. Where is water in the desert, or, in other words, where is happiness in this material world?

In search of truth we become deviated and, taking shelter of the boat of the material body and mind, travel aimlessly in the ocean of material existence, with no land in sight. Mercilessly tossed about, we brood, "In the dispensation of providence, man cannot have any rest." If only we knew that our ultimate destination is Lord Viṣṇu, the Supreme Personality of Godhead! Then we could end our suffering. To dispel our ignorance about this fact, Lord Kṛṣṇa has informed us that we must perform all activities as a sacrifice for Lord Viṣṇu's satisfaction. The *Ṛg Veda* confirms this: "Lord Viṣṇu is the supreme shelter of everything. All the demigods are constantly meditating on Him." Thus we see that the demigods also consider Lord Viṣṇu's lotus feet their supreme destination, and they become liberated simply by performing all activities for His pleasure. One who wants release from the vicious karmic cycle must have Lord Viṣṇu's lotus feet as his final objective. Otherwise, he will have to become demoniac.

The followers of the *varṇāśrama* way of life, or *sanātana-dharma,* are now being called Hindus. Their forefathers, especially those who belonged to the upper castes—the *brāhmaṇas, kṣatriyas,* and *vaiśyas*—centred their lives on Lord Viṣṇu. In every stage of life, especially in the householder stage, people worshiped Lord Viṣṇu in their homes, performing devotional service for His satisfaction. A few very devoted souls continue to do so even today. They collect money only for the Lord's service. The money buys grains and vegetables, which they cook with devotion and then offer to Lord Viṣṇu. Later the devotees honor this *prasādam,* the Lord's mercy in the form of food, by eating it. In all these activities Lord Viṣṇu is the enjoyer, and one seeks to please Him. In the past, the times were conducive to such activities, and even now they are practiced in many places. Actually, such devotional service is applicable to everyone, to all places, and to all times.

Lord Viṣṇu is the Supreme Personality of Godhead, the goal of everything. Performing all works for His satisfaction is the only way to open up the path of liberation from the cycle of fruitive action, or *karma.* It is recommended that all progressive and beneficial activities be executed for the pleasure of the Supreme Lord, Viṣṇu. Echoing the words of the scriptures, the learned sages proclaim "the attainment of Lord Viṣṇu's lotus feet is the same as becoming liberated." The final step in the *karma-yoga* process is to satisfy Lord Viṣṇu, at which point one's own desires are automatically fulfilled. While delineating this point, Lord Kṛṣṇa says that if work is not performed for His satisfaction, then all activities are tainted with sin and result in sinful reactions, which create havoc in society. In the *Bhagavad-gītā* (3.13), Lord Kṛṣṇa says, "The devotees of the Lord are released from all kinds of sins because they eat food which is first offered for sacrifice. Others, who prepare food for personal sense enjoyment, verily eat only sin."

Preparing and eating food in the way just mentioned is service to the Supreme Lord, Viṣṇu. Sometimes it may appear that some sin is being committed in its execution, but if one takes and honors the remnants of the sacrifice, or offering to Lord Viṣṇu, then one is automatically exonerated from all binding reactions and becomes liberated. Though we may live very carefully, trying to avoid sins and strictly follow the path of nonviolence, still our lives are controlled by the cycle of karmic reactions. Hence, unwittingly we are forced to commit many kinds of sin. We commit so many sins in business transactions, common human dealings, daily chores, and especially political and administrative activities. It is fine to vociferously support nonviolence, but in actual life one is compelled to commit acts of violence. One may succeed in avoiding many kinds of sin, but it is impossible to escape committing the five great sins called *pañca-sūnā.* While walking on the street we may crush many ants to death against our wishes. While cleaning the house, we may squash many insects to death. While grinding food grains or lighting a fire, we destroy many tiny lives. In this way, while executing our ordinary, daily chores we are forced to commit violence and take many innocent lives. Willingly or unwillingly, we commit sins. Thus, when a religion fabricated by the human brain prompts one to embrace the path of nonviolence for its own sake, it inevitably gives advantage to one and difficulty to another.

It is impossible to be exempted from the adversities caused by mentally concocted beliefs. According to man-made laws, if one person murders another he is condemned to the gallows, but no action is taken against a man for killing animals. Such is not the law of providence. The law of God is such that it punishes the killers of both man and animals; both acts of murder are penalized. The atheists deny the existence of God because in this way they think they can commit sins unhindered. But all the revealed, authorized scriptures say that by killing innocent creatures, the householders commit many sins willingly or unwillingly while performing their normal daily activities. To get release from these sins, the householders are enjoined to perform certain sacrifices. Foremost of these is to eat and honor the remnants of food offered to Lord Viṣṇu. As for those selfish householders who cook food only for their own sensual pleasure and not for the service of Lord Viṣṇu, they have to suffer all the sinful reactions incurred while cooking and eating. This is the law of providence. Therefore, to get rid of these sins, the followers of the Vedic religion dedicate their household activities to Lord Viṣṇu's service.

The leaders of society are therefore advised to perform devotional service for Lord Viṣṇu's satisfaction—both for their own benefit and for the benefit of those they lead. As Lord Kṛṣṇa says to Śrī Arjuna in the *Bhagavad-gītā* (3.21), "Whatever action a great man performs, common men follow. And whatever standards he sets by exemplary acts, all the world pursues." Because everyone follows their example, the leaders are required to carefully study the process of devotional service to Lord Viṣṇu. This is their duty. Thus for the benefit of human society, there is a great need to construct universities that will impart knowledge of devotional service.

Alas! The times are such that those who are considered leaders and stalwarts of society are more viciously inimical to God than others. Therefore, what devotional service for Lord Viṣṇu's satisfaction can they perform? And if they cannot perform devotional service, then how will they gain release from their innumerable sins? If the stalwarts of society are not willing to declare that Lord Viṣṇu is the omnipresent Absolute Truth, and that He is all-pervasive due to His being both a person as well as formless, then what can the lesser man, the man on the street, understand about this esoteric subject matter? The Supreme Lord is the sole proprietor of everything. We cannot take the position of the enjoyer and proprietor of this material world. Whatever the Supreme Lord mercifully gives us as His remnants, that alone should we accept. We must never desire another's property. As the *Īśopaniṣad* states,

> Everything animate or inanimate that is within the universe is controlled and owned by the Lord. One should therefore accept only those things necessary for himself, which are set aside as his quota, and one should not accept other things, knowing well to whom they belong.

Only when the leaders of society center all their activities on the Supreme Lord, Viṣṇu, will these activities bring good fortune and benediction to the leaders themselves, as well as to their followers. But if the leaders avoid performing their activities for Lord Viṣṇu and instead pose as Lord Viṣṇu themselves—taking worship, wealth, and praise from their followers and returning the same to them as remnants—then others might become attracted by their pretentious renunciation and thus follow their path to doom. But nothing further will be achieved. Such leaders uselessly excite their ignorant sycophants, inducing them to perform many sinful activities. In this way such selfish leaders bring about their followers' doom simply to increase their own distinction, adoration, and wealth. Unfortunately, the leaders do not know that these minuscule portions of distinction, adoration, and wealth will be burned to ashes with their death. But the sinful methods used to acquire these temporary material advantages will beget results, which will then very subtly mix with their subtle body, namely mind, intelligence, and false ego. And these results will later become the seeds of further sinful activities, which will entangle the soul in the cycle of karmic reactions birth after birth, forcing him go through many different species of life.

How to Cure the Material Disease

The general populace simply follows the dictates and decisions of the leaders, who are bereft of any spiritual realization. Therefore it is advised that the leaders of society should act responsibly. The easy path to prosperity opens up when these leaders intelligently put into practice the precepts of *karma-yoga.* Without first becoming adept at curing one's own disease, why try to treat many patients? This is unreasonable. First a leader has to adopt the principles of *karma-yoga* in his own life; then he has to diagnose the disease of the people; then the medicine is to be prescribed and the proper diet given. Simply to offer the suffering people a sense-gratificatory cure that titillates their senses—this is not going to make them healthy. Rather, this will spread the disease further, and at one stage the doctor himself will be infected and finally die from it.

Forgetfulness of the Supreme Lord, Viṣṇu, is human society's real and original disease. So, if one does not treat this ailment but instead shows insincere and shallow concern for the patients, one might give them some momentary relief and pleasure, but ultimately such a course of action cannot cure them permanently. If the patient goes for proper medicine and diet but is instead administered bad medicine and diet, then he is certainly in the jaws of death.

The remnants of food offered to the Supreme Lord, *prasādam,* is the best diet for all patients. And to discuss and hear topics glorifying the Supreme Lord, to see the Lord's Deity form and offer worship to Him, and to completely surrender oneself to the Lord—these constitute the greatest medicine, the panacea. These activities are the only secure path to prosperity, whereas other activities will wreak disaster. The practices of devotional service to the Lord can never cause harm to society; rather, they can only usher in an age of opportunities and benedictions. Those who are opportunists and financial speculators should calmly consider these facts.

Stalwarts of society like Mahatma Gandhi tried in various ways to usher in an age of peace, but because such endeavors are not inspired or blessed by the spiritually evolved saints, they are not turning out successful, nor will they be fruitful in the future. The God of the monists, or Māyāvādīs, cannot eat, see, or hear. Such a concocted, formless God can never bring peace to the world. How can a God who has no sensory organs see the miseries of the people or hear their heartfelt prayers? To worship such a formless God in the name of searching for spiritual truth can only produce misfortune in the world, never good fortune. In the Māyāvāda school of philosophy, discussions on pure knowledge can throw some light on the real nature of the Absolute Truth, but they are unable to fully reveal the esoteric and personal aspects of the Supreme Absolute Being. These dry, empirical discussions fall far short of their objective: a complete understanding of the Absolute Truth. Therefore only if leaders like Mahatma Gandhi strive to realize the Supreme Absolute Person—not a formless energy—can they truly benefit human society.

Conditioned human beings are expert at dealing with this material body and mind. These gross materialists, who cannot see beyond materialistic activities, find it impossible to believe that besides our material universe, a spiritual universe exists. Completely identifying with the body, such materialists are like animals, simply eating, sleeping, mating, and defending. They are so captivated by these four animalistic propensities that they lose the power to discriminate between sinful and pious activities. They tirelessly endeavor for a little sense gratification, but all their efforts end in futility. Many modern scientists have taken up the role of priests facilitating such gross activities, which are unbeneficial and fatal. These scientists have made available a variety of products meant simply to titillate the senses, thus creating a deadly competitive mood among the materialists, which has in turn caused an obnoxious atmosphere in society. People think they become free and independent through such sensual activities, but factually they become more tightly bound up in chains. The greater their accumulated wealth, the greater their anxiety and depravity. As much as they try to usurp the Supreme Lord's position of being the only enjoyer, that much and more are they drawn into the jaws of a horrible death. And these activities make a herculean task out of such a simple and basic activity as sustaining the body, which needs a little nourishment only.

A grade higher than this mean class of gross materialists are those who believe in the transmigration of the soul. These are the fruitive workers who perform pious activities such as giving in charity, but their only motive is to ensure that their next life is one of luxury and sense enjoyment. Neither of these grades of fruitive workers realizes that both pious as well as sinful activities cause bondage. These materialists do not know that *karma-yoga,* activity performed without fruitive desire, is the best form of activity. Therefore they often think that the *karma-yogīs* are as attached to this material world as the gross materialists. The sole motive of the *karma-yogī,* however, is to instruct the members of society for their benefit. As Lord Kṛṣṇa, the Supreme Personality of Godhead, says in the *Bhagavad-gītā* (3.25): "As the ignorant perform their duties with attachment to results, the learned may similarly act, but without attachment, for the sake of leading people on the right path."

Like others, sages who are in knowledge of the Absolute Truth maintain their bodies, but the difference is that the goal of all their activities is to satisfy Lord Viṣṇu. Although the general mass of people may wrongly think that the sages' activities are the same as their own, in fact the sages are performing *karma-yoga,* not fruitive activity.

Present times have seen the widespread expansion of modern science and technology in our world in a variety of forms, which have entangled society more and more in the vicious cycle of *karma.* Huge factories, universities, hospitals, and so on are certain to entangle society further in the karmic cycle. Bygone ages never witnessed such huge, complex arrangements for gross materialistic activities. Wrong and simply bad association has tightly bound up the innocent populace in mean activities. But the learned man, the *karma-yogī*, can show society how to perform all these activities for the satisfaction of the Lord.

Previously, sages arranged for Lord Viṣṇu's Deity to be worshiped in practically every household, thereby creating the atmosphere for people to become *karma-yogīs*. Similarly, it is now urgent that similar arrangements be made to worship and serve Lord Viṣṇu in the huge factories, mercantile firms, hospitals, and so on. This can firmly establish true equality among men under a spiritual banner. Lord Nārāyaṇa is not poor; He is the Supreme Lord of lords. And hence attempts to say that the poor people are "Nārāyaṇas" is foolish. Rather, by widely organizing the worship and service of the Lord, one can greatly benefit everyone, including the poor. The Supreme Personality of Godhead manifests Himself in many forms, but generally the sages have chosen three of His multifarious forms to serve and worship as the Deity. They are Lakṣmī-Nārāyaṇa, Sītā-Rāma, and Rādhā-Kṛṣṇa. These three Deity couples are widely worshiped all over the Indian subcontinent. Therefore, we request the owners of large factories and business firms to establish the worship and service of any of these three Deities in their establishments. The owners can then distribute *prasādam*, offered food, to everyone. This practice will repair any disagreements between worker and owner, because both will become *karma-yogīs*.

Most factory workers and other laborers cannot maintain a good character and thus slide down to depravities. And if such derelicts increase in population, the world has no chance for a prosperous and fortunate future. But if the owners give their laborers and office staff *prasādam*, then both the givers and the receivers will gradually become purified and more attracted to the Supreme Lord. The whole society will become elevated, civilized, and united in harmony. On the other hand, by trying to achieve only their selfish interests, the owners create a situation in which any harmony or unity is not only fragile but dangerous. And when the owners fire these degraded laborers in pursuit of their crass self-interest, neither the owners themselves nor the laborers are benefited. Soon the workers automatically turn inimical toward their employers.

When laborers and bosses perform activities that are not intended to please Lord Viṣṇu and are in fact troublesome to the Lord, they end up arguing and fighting with each other, thus creating an awful situation in society. The Communists and Socialists are spending money, intelligence, and even lives propagating their "isms"; the Bolsheviks revolted, disrupting the entire land of Russia and promising to fulfill the people's dream of a prosperous household life on a mass scale; the workers' unions are constantly at odds with the employers. All these complicated problems have one simple solution: everyone should perform *karma-yoga,* or work meant to please the Supreme Lord.

The endeavors human beings have made to establish a close and harmonious relationship with one another have culminated in the United Nations. This organization is based on the concept of the family unit. The gradual expansion of the family unit to a large community, to a village, to a state, to a country, and finally to a continent has given the clue for the formation of the United Nations. The thing to be noted, however, is its center. What is the central attraction? If the process of expansion was reversed, we would end up with the human body as the basic unit. The senses are of prime importance in the body; more important than the senses is the mind, then intelligence, and finally the false ego. And more important than the false ego is the real self, a pure spiritual being that is part and parcel of the Supreme Lord, Viṣṇu. Therefore the conclusion is that the fountainhead of everything is Lord Viṣṇu. For this reason Prahlāda Mahārāja said,

> Persons who are strongly entrapped by the consciousness of enjoying material life, and who have therefore accepted as their leader or *guru* a similar blind man attached to external sense objects, cannot understand that the goal of life is to return home, back to Godhead, and engage in the service of Lord Viṣṇu.

Those who lose sight of the center and become attracted to the externals are shallow and misguided. These misguided persons are in a sense blind; hence the world cannot expect them to give any guidance toward enlightenment. However much these blind people may pretend to guide and benefit other blind people, factually they are fully controlled by the will of providence. We should make the effort to understand that the cause and source of everything is Lord Viṣṇu, the

Absolute Truth, and that the fullest manifestation of this Absolute Truth is Lord Kṛṣṇa, the source of even Lord Viṣṇu. As Lord Kṛṣṇa says in the *Bhagavad-gītā* (7.7), "O conqueror of wealth, [Arjuna], there is no truth superior to Me."

Thus the ultimate source of everything is indeed Lord Kṛṣṇa Himself, the all-attractive Supreme Personality of Godhead. After considerable deliberation, the sages in the past concluded that Lord Kṛṣṇa is the Supreme Being, the origin of all expansions and manifestations of the Supreme Absolute Truth. As the *Śrīmad-Bhāgavatam* (1.3.28) declares, "All of the abovementioned incarnations are either plenary portions or portions of the plenary portions of the Lord, but Lord Śrī Kṛṣṇa is the original Personality of Godhead..." Later we will discuss more thoroughly the subject of the expansions of Lord Viṣṇu, but for now let us establish that Lord Kṛṣṇa is the highest aspect of the Supreme. The *Brahma-saṁhitā* (5.1) confirms this: "Kṛṣṇa who is known as Govinda is the Supreme Godhead. He has an eternal blissful spiritual body. He is the origin of all. He has no other origin and He is the prime cause of all causes."

Thus if we can transcend the material body and its physical relationships and become connected with everyone through Lord Kṛṣṇa, the original Godhead, we can relate on a platform of truth and reality. Then the actual meaning of fraternity and equality will crystalize.

The Living Entities' Real Identity

A man's relationship with his sister's husband is based on his relationship with his sister. The brother-in-law, prior to his marriage with the sister, was a complete stranger to the man. And when their children become the man's nieces and nephews, his relationship with them is also based on his sister. Similar relationships grow up among races and nationalities, centering on the country of birth. Thus we have Indians, Bengalis, Punjabis, Germans, and so on. We also find relationships centering on religious beliefs. Thus there are Hindus, Muslims, Christians, and so on. But however much we might endeavor to adapt to such partial personalities of the self, and however we try to increase the number of these fractional identities, we will remain infinitesimal and partial. Being part and parcel of the Supreme Lord, if we do not aspire to serve Him, then we forego our actual identity and fall down into nescience. An appropriate parallel is the functioning of the body: if a limb refuses to execute its usual duty, it becomes useless to the body. Similarly, if our activities are not focused on Lord Kṛṣṇa, they are rendered impotent and valueless. The eternal constitutional position of the self is to serve the Supreme Lord, Kṛṣṇa. In fact, all our sufferings start from our refusal to act in our original capacity as Lord Kṛṣṇa's eternal servants. Therefore, the prime duty of all living entities is to become re-instated in their original, constitutional position. The first step toward that goal is to perform *karma-yoga.* In the *Caitanya-caritāmṛta* it is stated, "The living entity is bound around the neck by the chain of *māyā* because he has forgotten that he is eternally a servant of Kṛṣṇa."

People in general are ignorant and addicted to fruitive activities. Without disturbing their minds, the *karma-yogī* can benefit them by explaining the truth about man's eternal position as Lord Kṛṣṇa's servant. Thus in the *Bhagavad-gītā* (3.26) Lord Kṛṣṇa instructs,

> So as not to disrupt the minds of ignorant men attached to the fruitive results of prescribed duties, a learned person should not induce them to stop work. Rather, by working in the spirit of devotion, he should engage them in all sorts of activities [for the gradual development of Kṛṣṇa consciousness].

It is very difficult to convince those who adhere to fruitive activities that they should render devotional service to Lord Kṛṣṇa. The reason is that most fruitive workers are foolish, fallen, and impious. Therefore all their activities are whimsical and motivated by evil. Their intelligence and expertise are thus utilized in defiance of the Supreme Lord. They are totally in the grip of the illusory potency, *māyā,* and so they imagine themselves to be the Supreme Lord Himself, or at least His biggest competitor, like the demon Śiśupāla. They simply try to enjoy this material world in various ways. In fact, their hopes for enjoying this world are just make-believe, or *māyā,* and this make-believe yearning leaves them hopelessly cheated. Yet they cannot give up the hope to enjoy. And when they realize that fruitive activities are futile and are more or less forced to renounce them, then such renunciation becomes merely another illusory scheme for a greater enjoyment.

Those who hanker after the fruits of their actions undertake many hardships in executing their work, their imagination wanders like an untethered bull, and all the while their mind dictates to them that they are the actual enjoyers. Therefore, without disrupting the minds of these foolish, perverted *karmīs,* the intelligent person should engage them in doing what they are expert in and using the fruits in Lord Kṛṣṇa's service. Such a course of action will automatically uncover the fruitive workers' eternal relationship with Lord Kṛṣṇa. So, to instruct the people for their benefit, the servant of Kṛṣṇa, who is free from the reactions of fruitive activities, leads a life seemingly like that of the fruitive workers, but actually he is all along performing *karma-yoga.*

Had not Lord Kṛṣṇa mercifully instructed the process of *karma-yoga* to His devotee Śrī Arjuna, the ignorant souls would have suffered miserably for all time. These wretched *karmīs* have the noose of *māyā* constantly wrapped around their necks and are living from one distress to another, but because the Lord's deluding potency covers their intelligence, they cannot understand any of this. However much they might pretend to be the controllers, they are being continuously goaded by *māyā,* who leaves them helpless and impotent. Lord Kṛṣṇa has explained this in the *Bhagavad-gītā* (3.27), "The spirit soul bewildered by the influence of false ego thinks himself the doer of activities that are in actuality carried out by the three modes of material nature."

The foolish *karmī* cannot comprehend that because he has forgotten Lord Kṛṣṇa and is trying to usurp His position, the Lord's external potency, *māyā,* has tied a noose around his neck with the rope of the three modes of nature and is making him suffer excruciating pains. Although all of his activities are within the grip of the three modes of material nature and orchestrated by *māyā,* still the grossly foolish *karmī* believes that he is the master of his situation. Thus he busies himself with trying to make better arrangements for living in the world of duality.

Lord Kṛṣṇa instructs us that the living entities are His separated parts. The duty of the part is to serve the whole. A complete body has different parts and limbs, such as hands, legs, eyes, and ears. The hands and legs work the hardest, but they do not refuse to give food to the stomach, although the stomach does very little. On the other hand, if the hands and legs act contrarily and actually refuse to feed the stomach, then an impossible situation is created. There is no question of the hands and legs trying to enjoy in this situation, because the lack of food in the stomach will cause the hands and legs to become weak and useless. The book *Hitopadeśa* explains this point in detail in the story "*The Belly and the Senses.*"

Lord Kṛṣṇa is like the life air and the soul of the massive body of the entire cosmos. In several places in the *Bhagavad-gītā* Lord Kṛṣṇa makes this point—that He is the origin and cause of everything. Especially notable are 7.7, "There is no truth superior to Me," and 9.24, "I am the only enjoyer and master of all sacrifices." Therefore, how can there still be any doubt that Kṛṣṇa is the Supreme Lord and that the living beings are His eternal servitors? We have forgotten this simple truth, and thus instead of using our mind and senses in the Supreme Lord's service, we ourselves are posing as little Supreme Lords and utilizing our mind and senses to enjoy this material world. This is *māyā.*

Nowadays, different societies are shooting up like mushrooms. One such society that has made its presence felt claims to have started a movement for establishing the ideal kingdom of Lord Rāmacandra. But the kingdom of Rāma it is propagating seems to be without Lord Rāma. Lord Rāma's biggest competitor was a demon named Rāvaṇa, and present-day descendants of Rāvaṇa are also busy trying to kill Lord Rāma. So, where is the question of wanting to usher in the golden age of Lord Rāma? If one is sincere about establishing the ideal kingdom of Lord Rāma, then everything in the world should be engaged in Lord Rāma's service. But the attempt to reduce the position and prestige of Lord Rāma is in fact an attempt to establish the tyrannical rule of Rāvaṇa, the demon king. And if such a mistake is committed, then Hanumān, the valiant and invincible servant of Lord Rāma, will have to come and rectify the situation by destroying the entire race of demons. In order to avoid this mistake at the outset, we must follow the path of *karma-yoga* taught by Lord Kṛṣṇa.

The *karmīs* are foolish and ignorant, whereas the *karma-yogīs* are wise and learned. These wise men know that the nature of the material modes and material activities is exactly opposite to that of the soul. For this reason the *karma-yogīs* never engage in material activities under the modes of material nature, as the *karmīs* do, but rather perform *karma-yoga,* which is meant to satisfy Lord Viṣṇu. Such wise men always keep themselves aloof from close association with this phenomenal world, for they aspire to elevate the soul to its original spiritual position. They understand that the soul has come into contact with matter only by a freak arrangement. Therefore, although their ears, eyes, and other senses are involved in this phenomenal world, the sages refrain from material activities. As Lord Kṛṣṇa says in the *Bhagavad-gītā* (3.28),

> One who is in knowledge of the Absolute Truth, O mighty-armed one, does not engage himself in the senses and sense gratification, knowing well the differences between work in devotion and work for fruitive results.

Then in Chapter 3.30–31, Lord Kṛṣṇa describes the means for achieving such a liberated state,

> Therefore, O Arjuna, surrendering all your works unto Me, with full knowledge of Me, without desires for profit, with no claims to proprietorship, and free from lethargy, fight. Those persons who execute their duties according to My injunctions and who follow this teaching faithfully, without envy, become free from the bondage of fruitive actions.

Identifying the self with the material body and mind, or thinking that the soul is material, or thinking that everything in relation to the body belongs to oneself—such illusions keep a person ignorant and bereft of self-realization. Therefore Lord Kṛṣṇa advises us to be situated in knowledge of the self. When we become spiritually aware, we can understand that the "I," the self, is not the body or mind; we can realize that we are products of the superior, spiritual energy of the Supreme Lord and hence fully spiritual and eternal. With realization of these transcendental truths comes knowledge of the actual nature of the material energy in its pure form. And when these spiritual realizations gradually mature, one achieves a natural distance from the dualities of material nature. At this stage of spiritual development, the false ego is destroyed, all false identification and titles are removed, and we are liberated from the shackles of the illusory, material energy on the strength of our spiritual association with the Transcendence. No longer does *māyā* entangle us in material activities.

There are sufficient scriptural proofs to substantiate that Lord Kṛṣṇa is the Supreme Absolute Truth. Even scriptures like the Bible or the Koran, declare that the Absolute Truth is the all-powerful, all-knowing Supreme Person. Throughout the Vedic literature, that Supreme Person is declared to be Lord Kṛṣṇa. And in the *Bhagavad-gītā*, Lord Kṛṣṇa Himself says that He is the Absolute Truth. Thus simply by associating somehow with Lord Kṛṣṇa, we can become illuminated about the divine Self. When the sun rises in the morning, everything again becomes visible in the sunlight. Similarly, when the sun of Lord Kṛṣṇa rises on the horizon of the transcendental spiritual sky of our realization, the darkness of illusion is immediately extirpated. Then only does one become purified and radiant with pristine beauty.

These facts may sound exaggerated or mythical to a foolish man, but these are not fairy tales for little boys: they are the reality and the truth. Those who have taken shelter of Lord Kṛṣṇa or His devotee can appreciate and fathom this subject matter. The only ones who will not accept this truth are those who are inimical toward Lord Kṛṣṇa and who want to be the Supreme Lord themselves because of a perverted mind. As Lord Kṛṣṇa says in the *Bhagavad-gītā* (9.11), "Fools deride Me when I descend in the human form." Such men are envious of the Lord. The truth about Lord Kṛṣṇa and His transcendental position can never enter such confused and deluded brains.

In Praise of the Supreme Lord's Devotees

The pious and saintly Vaiṣṇavas understand the exact meaning of the *Bhagavad-gītā*. The simple message of the *Gītā* is self-illuminated like the sun. Its knowledge is not hidden under a gloomy shroud of impersonalism. There is actually no room for extracting some alternative meaning and then giving a so-called esoteric dissertation on it. The devotees of Lord Kṛṣṇa alone can fully take to heart the instructions of the *Gītā*, and by acting accordingly they are liberated from the awesome and eternal enslavement of the cycle of karma. Such persons are not restricted to a particular country, race, or society. The Lord's devotees belong to a class of their own—they form a spiritual society unhindered by geographical conditions. God is not the monopoly of any particular group. Therefore the message of the *Gītā*, being universal, can be followed by anyone and everyone. After all, it is in the *Gītā* (9.32) that Lord Kṛṣṇa has unconditionally declared,

> O son of Pṛthā, those who take shelter in Me, though they be of lower birth—women, *vaiśyas* [merchants], as well as *śūdras* [workers]—can attain the Supreme destination.

The demons misinterpret the words of Lord Kṛṣṇa concerning caste and social division, and they act capriciously on that basis. But this cannot blemish Lord Kṛṣṇa or His words. In the *Bhagavad-gītā* (4.13) Lord Kṛṣṇa clearly says,

> According to the three modes of material nature and the work associated with them, the four divisions of human society are created by Me. And, although I am the creator of this system, you should know that I am yet the nondoer, being unchangeable.

The four divisions of society—namely intellectuals, administrators, merchants, and laborers—should be determined not by birth but by merit, just as one becomes a doctor or a judge not by birthright but by merit alone. In this world of the three modes of material nature, social classes have always existed. Therefore a person's birth should never determine his caste or class in society. The four classes were created according to a person's qualifications.

Doctors are available in every country and society; similarly, the four classes of men are also present in every country and society. A son born to a doctor is not necessarily sure to grow up to be a doctor; similarly, the progeny of the four classes of society do not automatically fix their future career according to that of their parents. The scriptures describe in detail the divisions of society, with their inherent characteristics. Therefore we commit a serious mistake when we regard the different classes of men as belonging to particular countries or races. The Indian culture of today is restricted by the hereditary caste system and kept in the custody of narrow-minded people who are like frogs in a well. If, instead, India had spread the transcendental message of *Bhagavad-gītā* in the generous manner befitting a noble *brāhmaṇa,* then peace and tranquillity in this world would not be in such acutely short supply. By the propagation of brahminical culture, the world would have greatly prospered. Instead, the Vedic culture has been seriously maimed by the imposition of the hereditary caste system, and this has had grievously adverse effects on the world. The Supreme Lord in His incarnation as Lord Caitanya has opened many avenues to peaceful living by propagating the brahminical culture, which He calls the religion of the soul. Those who are fortunate can emulate His life, follow His divine teachings, and perfect their lives.

Varṇāśrama-dharma, the system of four spiritual orders and four social orders of life, is of two kinds: demoniac and transcendental. They have nothing in common. The divisions of society mentioned in the scriptures are present at all times and in all lands. If one with knowledge of the scriptures scrutinizes the different societies, he can easily discern the four classes. Persons possessing brahminical or priestly qualities in varying degrees are seen in practically every society. In modern terms they are called intellectuals. All the other classes are also present. Therefore it is an established fact that the four divisions of society, according to merit, are, were, and will be present everywhere.

Those who think that *brāhmaṇas* and the other three castes exist only in Indian society are sadly mistaken. The scriptures have declared that in Kali-yuga everyone is born a *śūdra,* or a menial laborer, a member of the fourth class. Still, India has many persons endowed with high, brahminical characteristics, and without doubt such persons are also seen in every other country. Every country has these four classes of men, determined according to merit. As a matter of fact, even those who are less than *śūdras*—the *caṇḍālas,* or dog-eaters—are eligible to perform devotional service. If a *caṇḍāla* becomes an elevated devotee of the Lord, then on the basis of his merit he should be respected by all other classes. There is much scriptural evidence in this regard: the *Hari-bhakti-vilāsa* (10.91) states, "A devotee *caṇḍāla* achieves the same spiritual success as the devotee *brāhmaṇa.*" And in the *Bhāgavatam* (7.9.10), Prahlāda

Mahārāja says, "A devotee *caṇḍāla* is many times more elevated than an ordinary ritualistic *brāhmaṇa.*" Indeed, such a devotee *caṇḍāla* can be the *guru* of the *brāhmaṇas;* this has been shown throughout history by many spiritual preceptors who were born in a low caste but who initiated persons of higher castes. So, the castes are classified according to merit and activity, but a pure devotee of the Lord is beyond all these classifications. He is transcendental to everything material. How can a person who is elevated beyond all castes, a saint, be adequately worshiped if he is worshiped only as a *brāhmaṇa*? Therefore one who has taken shelter of the Supreme Personality of Godhead is the recipient of all good fortune in all countries and at all times. The *Bhagavad-gītā* mentions this in several places.

Whatever part of this world a person belongs to, if he follows the instructions of the Supreme Lord in the *Bhagavad-gītā,* then he attains the transcendental platform and can become even more elevated than a *brāhmaṇa.* As Lord Kṛṣṇa says in the *Gītā* (4.24),

> A person who is fully absorbed in Kṛṣṇa consciousness is sure to attain the spiritual kingdom because of his full contribution to spiritual activities, in which the consummation is absolute and that which is offered is of the same spiritual nature.

This verse explains how one can attain spiritual knowledge by performing activities that please the Supreme Lord.

Śrīpāda Śaṅkarācārya propounded the impersonal theory, citing phrases like *sarvaṁ khalv idaṁ brahma:* "By nature everything is Brahman, spirit." Śaṅkarācārya's theory has caused great confusion about established scriptural conclusions, but this phrase clearly supports the *Gītā* verse quoted above.

At this point it is urgent that we discuss how one can perform devotional service for the Supreme Lord's pleasure. In this regard it is also noteworthy how saintly leaders like King Janaka executed *karma-yoga,* or devotional service, by performing sacrifice. The aim of all sacrifices should be to please the Supreme Lord, Viṣṇu or Kṛṣṇa. Contact with matter is unavoidable in our present conditioned state, because while performing activities to sustain the body and to accomplish other purposes, we become intimate with material nature. But if we can spiritualize these activities by performing every one of them as a service to Brahman, the Supreme Absolute Truth, then these activities become *yajña*, or sacrifice. When the Vedic phrase *sarvaṁ khalv idaṁ brahma* is interpreted in this way, it is acceptable. In other words, when one invokes the spiritual or transcendental or absolute in everything, then matter loses its mundaneness, and then only can one realize the perfect meaning of the phrase *sarvaṁ khalv idaṁ brahma*. The Vaiṣṇavas say that anything connected with the Lord in devotional service is transcendental. In other words, it is nondifferent from the Supreme Lord Himself, Mādhava. Just as iron in long and constant touch with fire loses the characteristics of iron and becomes fiery, so everything offered in sacrifice to the Absolute, or the Transcendence, becomes absolute, or transcendental.

In the *Bhagavad-gītā* (14.27) Lord Kṛṣṇa says, "And I am the basis of the impersonal Brahman, which is immortal, imperishable and eternal and is the constitutional position of ultimate happiness." This verse unequivocally declares that Brahman is Lord Kṛṣṇa's bodily effulgence. Since Lord Kṛṣṇa is the source of Brahman, devotional service to Lord Kṛṣṇa establishes the true meaning of *sarvaṁ khalv idaṁ brahma*. A sacrifice is properly performed only when all the sacrificial ingredients—the offerings, the fire, the ghee, and so on—become spiritualized, or reach the stage of Brahman, by their contact with Lord Kṛṣṇa. And since the performance of sacrifice culminates in the manifestation of real love for Lord Viṣṇu, loving devotional service to Lord Viṣṇu is the very best form of sacrifice. Such a stage can be also described as total absorption in Brahman.

Persons who act in this way become progressively detached from matter and attached to Lord Kṛṣṇa's devotional service. Thus they are able to purify the mirror of their hearts, extinguish the forest fire of material existence, and become situated in their original, spiritual position. They exist at a level of realization far above the impersonal realization of the Absolute, for they are free from the contamination of vainly trying to merge with the Supreme and usurping His Absolute position. They never fall from this stage of consciousness. Fully absorbed in their own transcendental identity, they are the complete masters of their senses. They are the perfect persons to rule this universe, if they so desire, and they alone bring good fortune to everyone. The conditioned souls, however, are unable to benefit the world in any way. The purified, rare souls continuously perform *karma-yoga* and are always in a liberated state. In the *Bhagavad-gītā* (5.7) it is stated,

> One who works in devotion, who is a pure soul, and who controls his mind and senses is dear to everyone, and everyone is dear to him. Though always working, such a man is never entangled.

There are those who live and act in a manner exactly opposite to that of the pure souls, who are constantly acting in *karma-yoga*. Such fruitive workers have no connection with the Supreme Lord, Kṛṣṇa. Therefore, they cannot cleanse their heart of material contamination. They are slaves of their sensual urges, spending their time in gratifying their senses according to their whims. Yet they shamelessly say that all their actions are prompted by the Supreme Lord. Being cheaters and atheists, they speak like this so that their impious acts may be acceptable, and thus they inflict untold misfortunes and calamities on the world. By contrast, the pure, self-realized souls are constantly absorbed in serving Lord Kṛṣṇa's lotus feet with their body, mind, and words. They never associate with atheistic people. These saintly persons know that although the spirit soul is infinitesimal, it is nevertheless endowed with minute free will at all times. The Supreme Lord is absolutely independent and can exercise absolute free will over all; because the spirit soul is qualitatively the same as the Supreme Lord, the Lord does not annul his minute free will.

The spirit soul unfortunately misuses this God-given minute free will and falls into the dark well of nescience and illusion. Once the spirit soul takes shelter of *māyā*, the illusory material energy, he develops the material qualities of goodness, passion, and ignorance. The spirit soul loses his original characteristics and develops a new nature, which is controlled by the three modes of material nature, and this continues until such time as he transcends them. His actions are prompted accordingly. If it happened in any other way, then material variegatedness would not be visible in this phenomenal world. So if a person fails to inform himself about the very subtle laws and workings of material nature, and at the same time he argues that all activities are sanctioned and inspired by the

Supreme Lord, then he is reducing the Supreme Lord's position and making Him out to be partial and unjust. The Lord never favors one and discriminates against another. Factually, He advises everyone to give up all material activities, which are by nature unstable and temporary. Because of forgetfulness of God, a man becomes an eternal victim of ignorance, which then colors all his actions. The *Bhagavad-gītā* (5.14) says,

> The embodied spirit, master of the city of his body, does not create activities, nor does he induce people to act, nor does he create the fruits of action. All this is enacted by the modes of material nature.

Therefore all activities except those performed as a sacrifice to Lord Viṣṇu are whimsical actions done of one's own volition. They are not performed under the Supreme Lord's direction or sanction. Since such activities stem from the material modes of nature, they are automatically under nature's total control. The Supreme Lord is merely an impartial and silent witness to such activities.

The actions of the *karma-yogī,* or devotee, are always connected with the Absolute Truth. Hence the devotee remains situated on the transcendental platform, far beyond the mundane sphere. In such a realized position, he does not see this material creation as separate from the Supreme Lord but as a transformation of His energy. Such perceptions are unhindered by the material modes of nature. Indeed, the *karma-yogī's* realization of everything's inherent connection with Lord Kṛṣṇa is equipoised and transcendental. The *Gītā* (5.18) states, "The humble sages, by virtue of true knowledge, see with equal vision a learned and gentle *brāhmaṇa,* a cow, an elephant, a dog and a dog-eater [outcaste]."

The *brāhmaṇa* endowed with such learning is primarily in the material mode of goodness. Among the animals, the cow is also in the mode of goodness; elephants, lions, and so on, are situated primarily in the mode of passion; dogs and some humans (such as the *caṇḍālas* and other outcastes) are in the mode of ignorance. The *karma-yogīs,* who are always meditating on the Supreme, never see these outer coverings of the soul, but rather the pure soul proper. This is true equal vision in relation to the Supreme. The *karma-yogīs* perceive that all elements and objects in this world are materials for the Supreme Lord's worship and that all living entities are eternal servitors of Lord Kṛṣṇa. One attains the purest stage of equal vision when one ceases to take into consideration the outer covering of the soul, the body, but rather is established in the soul's innate nature of serving the Lord. In this stage one engages all things in devotional service to the Supreme Lord by using them as ingredients for sacrifice to please Lord Viṣṇu.

The *karma-yogī* knows that Lord Kṛṣṇa is the only enjoyer and exploiter of all material objects and that He is the only Lord and master of all living entities. Forgetful of this relationship with Lord Kṛṣṇa, the living entity falls into the clutches of *māyā*, or illusion. Under the influence of *māyā*, he tries in vain to act the part of an enjoyer or a renouncer—but this is all a mere fantasy. In fact, the real affliction of the living entity is the pretense that he is the enjoyer or renouncer. All types of good and pious activities—like *yoga*, the cultivation of knowledge, austerity, and renunciation—are misapplied labor if they cannot kindle in the heart the flame of loving attraction for topics relating to the Supreme Lord. As Lord Kṛṣṇa declares in the *Bhagavad-gītā* (5.29),

> A person in full consciousness of Me, knowing Me to be the ultimate beneficiary of all sacrifices and austerities, the Supreme Lord of all planets and demigods, and the benefactor and well-wisher of all living entities, attains peace from the pangs of material miseries.

Earlier in this book we discussed the need for performing work as sacrifice, and now from this verse the truth that Lord Kṛṣṇa is the original Supreme Person, the enjoyer of all sacrifices, comes out with clarity. It must be understood that the results of sacrifice performed by the *karma-yogīs*, as well as the austerities of the knowledge-seekers, are all meant to be enjoyed by Lord Kṛṣṇa alone. The object of the *yogīs*' meditation, the Supersoul within the heart, is actually a partial expansion of Lord Kṛṣṇa. We will discuss this subject matter in detail later in this book.

Lord Kṛṣṇa is the well-wisher of the followers of all the different disciplines—*karma-yoga, jñāna-yoga, aṣṭāṅga-yoga* (meditation), and *bhakti-yoga*. And because Lord Kṛṣṇa is the well-wisher of everyone, He sends His close associates to the world to establish proper religious teachings in every millennium.

Lord Kṛṣṇa is the supreme master of all the planets, the original Lord, and the cause of all causes. The only path to peace is the path of gradual elevation in *karma-yoga*, leading to realization of the Absolute Truth, Lord Kṛṣṇa.

Those who are already executing their work for the satisfaction of Lord Kṛṣṇa are not required to separately perform sacrifices, austerities, or meditation, that are not on the platform of pure Kṛṣṇa consciousness. Previously we explained that a pure *karma-yogī* is automatically a *brāhmaṇa, sannyāsī,* and a *yogī.* Like a *karmī,* or fruitive worker, he is expert in performing sacrifices and executing his duties; like a *jñānī,* or seeker of knowledge, he is renounced and austere; and like a *yogī,* he is also detached from the fruits of his work and has brought his senses under control. One who is completely detached from all fruitive work and has become attracted to the Supreme Lord and His loving devotional service is simultaneously ornamented with all good qualities. As Lord Kṛṣṇa says in the *Bhagavad-gītā* (6.1),

> One who is unattached to the fruits of his work and who works as he is obligated is in the renounced order of life, and he is the true mystic, not he who lights no fire and performs no duty.

Since the *karma-yogī* knows that the ultimate enjoyer of the fruits of all his activities is Lord Kṛṣṇa, he does not hanker after those fruits and is fully detached from them. He always thinks of doing everything for Lord Kṛṣṇa. Such an unattached *karma-yogī* never thinks that action in Kṛṣṇa consciousness is meant for enjoying sense pleasure or avoiding pain. The *sannyāsī* renounces everything, including activities prescribed by the scriptures, in favor of cultivating knowledge of the Absolute. The *yogī* retires from active service and, desiring to see the Supersoul within his heart, spends his days in meditation with half-closed eyes. But he whose work is a sacrifice for the satisfaction of the Supreme makes no endeavors for his physical requirements. Since he is engaged in devotional service to the Supreme Lord, he is not required to execute the ritualistic activities recommended in the scriptures. Such a detached *karma-yogī* is superior to one who is merely unattached to the fruits of his work. The *karma-yogī* is automatically accomplished in the knowledge of the Absolute that the *sannyāsī* seeks and the eight mystic perfections that the meditating *yogī* aspires for.

The real *karma-yogīs* are in fact devotees of the Supreme Lord. Since they have attained perfection, they do not hanker for profit, adoration, or distinction. In their state of perfection, all knowledge and mystic powers automatically embellish them. With everything desirable available to them, why should they need anything else?

Following the eightfold path of Patañjali, the meditative *yogīs* gradually elevate themselves, mastering the different stages until they reach *samādhi*, or the state of absorption in the Supersoul. In their desire to reach perfection, they tolerate all sorts of adversities and sufferings and remain fixed on their goal. Ultimately they attain a state of consciousness that cannot be compared to anything in this material world. In this state of mystic perfection, no suffering—not even death—seems formidable. Lord Kṛṣṇa's comment about such *yogīs* has been recorded in the *Bhagavad-gītā* (6.22),

> Established thus, one never departs from the truth, and upon gaining this he thinks there is no greater gain. Being situated in such a position, one is never shaken, even in the midst of greatest difficulty.

In his purport to this verse, Śrīla Bhaktivinoda Ṭhākura says that when one detaches oneself from the sensual world and becomes situated in *samādhi*, complete absorption in the Absolute Truth, one perceives the pure spiritual self and is rewarded with intense bliss. Such a *yogī* never deviates his concentration from the Absolute Truth, the object of his meditation. The eight mystic perfections—*aṇimā, laghimā, prāpti, prākāmya,* and so on*—which the *yogī* acquires during his discipline, are by-products of his *yoga* practice. In *samādhi* the

---

* The eight mystic perfections are described by Lord Kṛṣṇa to Uddhava in the *Śrīmad-Bhāgavatam* 11.15.4-5. They are: *aṇimā*—becoming smaller than the smallest; *mahimā*—becoming greater than the greatest; *laghimā*—becoming lighter than the lightest; *prāpti*—aquiring whatever one desires; *prākāmya*—experiencing any enjoyable object, either in this world or the next; *īśitā*—manipulating the subpotencies of *māyā*; *vaśitā*—being unimpeded by the three modes of nature; *kāmāvasāyitā*—obtaining anything from anywhere, to the highest possible limit.

yogī regards all these mystic perfections as insignificant. Many *yogīs*, after mastering a few of these mystic perfections, pretend to have mastered them all, and because of a restless mind they deviate from the goal of permanent *samādhi*. On the other hand, for the *karma-yogī*, the devotee of the Lord, there is no such possibility: his heart and concentration remain fixed on his goal because he always works for the pleasure of Lord Kṛṣṇa. He is always in *samādhi*, the *yogī's* ultimate destination. In the Lord's devotional service, the devotee experiences ever-fresh emotions, and as his perfections become more mature, the transcendental bliss he relishes is inexplicable and inconceivable to mundane mercenaries.

What to speak of *karma-yoga*, even in the lesser discipline of eightfold *yoga*, whatever progress the *yogī* makes on the path toward the goal of *samādhi* does not go in vain, although he may not reach the ultimate goal in one lifetime. In his next life he will continue his progress. By contrast, when the fruitive worker dies, whatever wealth and education he has acquired, along with the endeavor that went into acquiring them, all become null and void. As for the pure *karma-yogī*, or devotee, his devotional activities are all beyond the level of mind and body. They are related to the soul and the Supreme Soul, and hence his activities become the wealth of his pure, eternal soul. Just as the soul is never destroyed with the disintegration of the body, so this wealth of devotional service is never devalued. Thus the *Bhagavad-gītā* says that the *karma-yogī* always works for the benefit and elevation of his soul, and that this endeavor and its results remain permanent spiritual assets in this life and the next. These spiritual assets are never liquidated. As Lord Kṛṣṇa says in the *Bhagavad-gītā* (6.40),

> Son of Pṛthā, a transcendentalist engaged in auspicious activities does not meet with destruction, either in this world or in the spiritual world; one who does good, My friend, is never overcome by evil.

Human beings are divided into two categories: the law-abiders and the law-breakers. Those who care only about satisfying their senses and do not submit to discipline and law are like animals, completely uncontrolled. Whether such an uncontrolled person is cultured or uncultured, educated or uneducated, weak or strong, his actions are always bestial. They can never benefit anyone.

The law-abiding human beings are further divided into three groups: the *karmīs,* or fruitive workers; the *jñānīs,* or knowledge-seekers; and the *bhaktas,* or devotees. The *karmīs* are divided into two sections: the *sakāma-karmīs,* or fruitive workers who want to enjoy the results of their labor, and the *niṣkāma-karmīs,* who renounce the fruits of action. The *sakāma-karmīs* are greedy after insignificant, transient happiness. They make progress in their mundane activities and enjoy the heavenly planets in the life hereafter, but all that enjoyment is temporary. Therefore the soul's real benefit evades them.

To attain true, eternal happiness, which comes only after the dissipation of material bondage, is the real benefit for the soul. Thus any path that does not lead the soul to strive for this supreme goal—eternal transcendental bliss—is considered useless. When eternal bliss is the goal of ritualistic activities (*karma-kāṇḍa*), then they are transformed into *karma-yoga.* Through the practice of *karma-yoga,* the heart is purified of material contamination and one gains knowledge of the Absolute. Thereafter one becomes situated in meditation on the Absolute, and finally one attains *bhakti,* pure devotional service. In the process of *karma-kāṇḍa,* it is recommended that one renounce physical pleasures for a time; so a *karmī* may sometimes be called an ascetic. Yet however much penance a *karmī* may perform, ultimately this penance is another form of sensual enjoyment, since that is its ultimate goal. The demons also perform penance to increase their powers, but it is all simply to enjoy their senses. Once the living entity can transcend the stage of hankering after sensual pleasures, he comes easily to the stage of *karma-yoga,* which is in all respects good. Only such a person can benefit society.

The spiritual progress the *karma-yogī* makes in this lifetime remains intact, and he continues in his next life from that point. In the *Bhagavad-gītā* (6.43), Lord Kṛṣṇa comments, "On taking such a birth, he revives the divine consciousness of his previous life, and he again tries to make further progress in order to achieve complete success, O son of Kuru." In his next life the unsuccessful *yogī* may be born in the family of a pious *brāhmaṇa* or wealthy merchant. When we talk of failure in *yoga,* we refer to *karma-yogīs, dhyāna-yogīs,* and *jñāna-yogīs.* Among the followers of these paths, the *karma-yogī* is closest to becoming a pure devotee, since he has dedicated his activities to the Supreme Lord's service. Gradually, acting in this manner, he becomes a *bhakti-yogī.* Such a *yogī* is in the highest order, and he is fit to instruct all other *yogīs.*

In the *Bhagavad-gītā* (6.47) Lord Kṛṣṇa says,

> And of all *yogīs,* the one with great faith who always abides in Me, thinks of Me within himself, and renders transcendental loving service to Me—he is the most intimately united with Me in *yoga* and is the highest of all. That is My opinion.

The fruitive workers cannot be counted among the *yogīs.* The actual *yogīs* are the *karma-yogīs,* the *jñāna-yogīs,* the *aṣṭāṅga-yogīs,* and the *bhakti-yogīs.* Factually they are the same, although named differently. The yogic process is like a ladder one ascends gradually toward the final goal of the Absolute Truth. *Niṣkāma-karma,* or renunciation of the fruits of one's labor, is the first step on this ladder. When knowledge and austerity are added to it, it becomes *jñāna-yoga,* the second step in this ladder. And when meditation on the Supreme is added to *jñāna-yoga,* the third step is reached, namely *aṣṭāṅga-yoga.* Finally, when loving devotional service to the Supreme Lord is practiced along with *aṣṭāṅga-yoga,* it is transformed into *bhakti-yoga.* This entire successive process is *yoga.* For an exact and clear delineation of the subject of *yoga,* all four steps need to be explained separately. Those who desire the best for humanity take to the path of *yoga.* The process for progressing in *yoga* requires, first, determination and strict execution of discipline at each stage. When a person is firmly situated at one stage, he then has to relinquish attachment and adherence to the practices of that stage in order to elevate himself to the next higher stage. Those who cannot reach the top for some reason and get stuck at any one of the four stages acquire the designation of that particular stage. Thus there are *karma-yogīs, jñāna-yogīs, aṣṭāṅga-yogīs,* and *bhakti-yogīs.* Lord Kṛṣṇa instructs Arjuna that one who renders loving devotional service to Him, the Supreme Lord, is the highest among all *yogīs,* and that Arjuna should thus strive to become such a *bhakti-yogī.*

The successive, step-by-step spiritual path is not the same as step-by-step progress in the material world. In the mundane process the rules of progress are strict and cannot be transgressed. If one wants to acquire a doctorate at a university, he has to begin from the elementary school level and gradually work upwards. It is impossible to go directly to the university without prior schooling. In spiritual life, however, although there are strict regulations, by the Supreme Lord's grace one can bypass many intermediary stages and reach the top, or "doctorate" level. One can attain this divine grace by intimate and constant association with the Supreme Lord. And such intimate association with the Lord comes about through confidential exchanges with a pure devotee of the Supreme Lord. Every one of us is intimately and eternally related to the Supreme Lord, but due to the bad influence of *māyā* we have forgotten our relationship with Him.

The living entities are like sons of the Lord, and as such they are rightful heirs to the great wealth of their rich father. But because of the reactions to sins committed in previous lives, they are roaming about without a home, suffering acute poverty. That the living entities are suffering is quite clear to all. But they do not know who their wealthy father is or where they can go to reclaim their valuable inheritance. Without proper knowledge, they are trying in vain to escape from their poverty while aimlessly roaming about like poor beggars. They meet many who promise to help them, but in the end such helpers turn out to be beggars themselves. A few among these strangers seem rich and prosperous, but the directions they give do not lead to the father's house, and so the living entities' poverty knows no end. The wealthy strangers suggest many paths, such as *karma, jñāna,* or *dhyāna,* but the problem of poverty remains unsolved. The living entities can escape their poverty only by learning and practicing the science of devotional service to the Supreme Lord. Caitanya Mahāprabhu, the Supreme Personality of Godhead and the source of all incarnations, explained the science of devotional service to Śrīla Rūpa Gosvāmī at Prayāga (Allahabad). These instructions are the crest jewel of teachings for all humanity. In *Śrī Caitanya-caritāmṛta* (*Madhya* 19.151), the Lord says,

> According to their *karma,* all living entities are wandering throughout the entire universe. Some of them are being elevated to the upper planetary systems, and some are going down to the lower planetary systems. Out of many millions of wandering living entities, one who is very fortu-

> nate gets an opportunity to associate with a bona fide spiritual master by the grace of Lord Kṛṣṇa. By the mercy of both Lord Kṛṣṇa and the spiritual master, such a person receives the seed of the creeper of devotional service.

By the mercy of Lord Kṛṣṇa, this seed of devotion is available in the *Bhagavad-gītā*. Only one who is able to receive this devotional seed can understand the purport of the *Bhagavad-gītā*. Otherwise, simply repeatedly reading the *Bhagavad-gītā* and discussing its teachings will not produce any results.

In the *Bhagavad-gītā*, Lord Kṛṣṇa Himself reveals the truth about Himself. When an ordinary mortal writes an autobiography, he receives many accolades, but when the Supreme Lord writes about Himself, we unfortunately do not fully believe in His words. Furthermore, we overlook the cardinal issues in His writings and quibble over lesser subjects, trying to magnify them by giving them concocted connotations and meanings. This practice is stretched to such absurdity that the original meaning is lost and the lopsided conclusions attract only ridicule from readers. In the *Bhagavad-gītā* Lord Kṛṣṇa unequivocally declares that He is the Supreme Absolute Truth and that it is the duty of everyone to render Him loving devotional service. The *Bhagavad-gītā* was revealed for the sole purpose of explaining these two principal points. One who understands them is eligible to begin spiritual life as a neophyte devotee. *Śraddhā,* or faith, is the first prerequisite in spiritual life and is described as synonymous with neophyte devotion. Thus *Śrī Caitanya-caritāmṛta* (*Madhya* 22.62) says,

> By rendering transcendental loving service to Kṛṣṇa, one automatically performs all subsidiary activities. This confident, firm faith, favorable to the discharge of devotional service, is called *śraddhā*.

Bhakti kathā

The Science of Devotion

Everything Is Achieved by Serving Lord Kṛṣṇa

While instructing Śrīla Rūpa Gosvāmī on the science of devotional service, Lord Caitanya discussed in some detail the material world and the living entities. He pointed out that among the 8,400,000 species of life—900,000 species of aquatics, 2,000,000 kinds of plants, 1,100,000 varieties of insects, 1,000,000 species of birds, 3,000,000 kinds of beasts, and 400,000 species of humans—*Homo sapiens* are clearly in the minority. Furthermore, humans are subdivided into three categories, namely, the uncivilized, the half-civilized, and the civilized. Also, many who supposedly belong to the civilized group act without restraint and discipline, only for the purpose of enjoyment. In this way they create chaos for the rest. Their sole intention in life being to gratify their senses (their instruments of enjoyment), they always try to keep their senses in fit working condition. They even go to the extent of transplanting monkeys' organs into their bodies once they get too old to enjoy with the vigor of youth.

Such gross sense enjoyers do not understand that the mind is more subtle than the sense organs and superior to them. Superior to the mind is the intelligence, and behind the intelligence is the false ego, which is far superior to the intelligence and which covers the spirit soul. Philosophical inquiry into the existence of the soul will remain a subject beyond the reach of these gross materialists. The gross sense enjoyers are actually to be counted among the animals, because man has more serious matters to attend to than just titillating his senses. Hence he is considered the most advanced among all the living entities. And indeed we do find that some men comprehend the gravity of human life. They carefully reject chaotic living, emulate the exemplary lives of saintly persons, and direct their lives in such a way as to fulfill the purpose of human life.

Followers of various religions—such as the Christians, Hindus, Muslims, and Buddhists—all adhere to the rules of their faith according to the intensity of their belief and the circumstances in their respective countries. Lord Kṛṣṇa speaks of these persons in *Bhagavad-gītā* (7.3):

manuṣyāṇāṁ sahasreṣu
kaścid yatati siddhaye
yatatām api siddhānāṁ
kaścin māṁ vetti tattvataḥ

Out of many thousands among men, one may endeavor for perfection, and of those who have achieved perfection, hardly one knows Me in truth.

Since time immemorial, living entities have been going through many lower species of life, gradually rising through the evolutionary process and, due to some good fortune, receiving a human birth. In the lower species of life the spirit souls are densely covered by the material modes, and thus carnal appetites dominate their lives. Among the human species, some denounce sensual pleasures and are honored by the world as saints, *yogīs*, philosophers, scholars, and so on. They experience mental perceptions far superior to gross sensual experiences, and may reach even subtler levels of fine intellect. But even more subtle than the intellect is the spirit soul. So true spirituality, or the real religion of the living entity, means to be situated in the self.

Except for the religion of the self, all paths and religions are pseudo-spiritual exercises consisting only of eating, sleeping, mating, and defending oneself from danger. These are the primary activities of the animals. The lower species cannot elevate themselves by executing the religion of the self, or soul. But since human beings are inherently able to practice the religion of the self, some endeavor to reach perfection. Only as a human being can one make such inquiries as "Who am I?" and "Why do the threefold miseries always give me trouble?"

Human life alone affords one the chance to attain unending happiness. In this life one should think, "Although I do not want suffering, it nevertheless comes; although I do not desire death, it forcibly snatches away my life; although I detest old age, when my youth is finished I will surely begin to age; and although I try to be free from disease and disaster, they never leave me alone." Although he sees all this suffering, a fool works hard to make his life comfortable, whereas an intelligent person calmly considers his situation and thinks of the best means to end his distress once and for all. When such thoughts become frequent and sincere, his search leads him to inquire into the Absolute Truth. Such a person takes up the path of self-realization. He may have many duties, but because of his previous pious activities such a wise person will execute these duties and at the same time confront the realities of birth, death, old age, and disease.

The lower stratum of those who strive for perfection are the *karmīs,* or fruitive workers, who look to gratify their senses. Above them are the *jñānīs,* or seekers of knowledge, who restrain the urges of their senses and become situated on the subtle, mental plane. Superior to them are the *yogīs* who seek mystic perfection. Lord Caitanya has described all these persons as *aśānta,* restless. Among them, those who are free of all material designations and are rid of the false ego, and who are thus liberated beings situated in the self—they alone can understand Lord Kṛṣṇa, the Supreme Person, in truth. When they become fully conversant with the science of Kṛṣṇa consciousness, such saintly souls can act as spiritual masters for all humanity, regardless of any external designation. Lord Caitanya confirms this in the *Caitanya-caritāmṛta* (*Madhya* 8.128):

kibā vipra, kibā nyāsī, śūdra kene naya
yei kṛṣṇa-tattva-vettā, sei 'guru' haya

> Whether one is a *brāhmaṇa,* a *sannyāsī,* or a *śūdra*—regardless of what he is—he can become a spiritual master if he knows the science of Kṛṣṇa.

Therefore we can conclude that neither the *karmīs* nor the *jñānīs* can fathom the depths of the science of devotional service to Kṛṣṇa. Especially the foolish *karmīs* are disqualified, for they generally consider Lord Kṛṣṇa an ordinary mortal, and this disregard for the Lord leads them to misconstrue the meaning of His words in the *Bhagavad-gītā.*

Humanity, now in the grips of the evil influence of the age of Kali, has become callous to any spiritual culture. Thus people pass their time in the animalistic activities of eating, sleeping, mating, and defending. What to speak of cultivating spiritual knowledge about the Supreme Lord, Kṛṣṇa, they cannot even spare the time for religious rituals or the pursuit of transcendental knowledge. If one strictly follows the scriptural directions for cultivating *karma* and *jñāna*, one purifies his consciousness enough to understand the science of Kṛṣṇa to a certain degree. The final conclusion of *jñāna* is that once one attains the state of oneness with the Absolute, then the doors of an even higher state, that of devotional service to Lord Kṛṣṇa, open up. Since this state of oneness is practically impossible for the people of Kali-yuga to attain, in the *Bhagavad-gītā* Lord Kṛṣṇa Himself has taught the science of how to render devotional service to Himself. Then, knowing that the unfortunate human beings of this age would misunderstand even His own words, Lord Kṛṣṇa again appeared—this time in the form of Caitanya Mahāprabhu, a pure devotee of the Lord—to teach the world the essence of the *Bhagavad-gītā* through His personal example.

Lord Kṛṣṇa says in the *Bhagavad-gītā* that He is the source of everything, but envious and cunning people try to refute this fact. Thus He appeared as Lord Caitanya and taught that Lord Kṛṣṇa is the source of everything. There is no difference between the instructions of Lord Kṛṣṇa and those of Lord Caitanya. The object of worship is the same. Still, the unfortunate people of this age refuse to accept these teachings. Trying to give them Kṛṣṇa consciousness is, as the well-known expression goes, like "casting pearls before a herd of swine." The human beings afflicted by Kali-yuga are like a herd of swine. The Lord has shown them boundless mercy by widely teaching the science of devotional service to Kṛṣṇa, which is rarely attained even by Lord Brahmā. Yet because it has been so easy for them to come by this precious and rare commodity, they have abused the mercy shown them. This is another manifestation of their misfortune. By teaching them the science of self-realization, Lord Kṛṣṇa has twice personally tried to save the people of this age from groveling in carnal pleasures, and both times they have converted those divine instructions into a means and an excuse for pursuing sense gratification.

When presented with a colorful glass doll and a diamond, a child will naturally be attracted to the doll and not the priceless jewel. Similarly, the people of Kali-yuga, endowed as they are with limited intelligence, have rejected the priceless diamond of devotional service to Kṛṣṇa and instead chosen the cheap doll of fruitive activity and dry speculation. Just as the child cannot comprehend that the invaluable diamond can purchase many thousands of cheap glass dolls, so the less intelligent people of Kali-yuga cannot understand that *kṛṣṇe bhakti kaile sarva-karma-kṛta haya:* "By rendering transcendental devotional service to Lord Kṛṣṇa, one automatically performs all subsidiary activities."

Those who know the science of Kṛṣṇa consciousness automatically know of subsidiary subjects like fruitive activity, speculative knowledge, *yoga,* charity, penance, austerity, and chanting *mantras.* Lord Kṛṣṇa confirms this in the *Śrīmad-Bhāgavatam:*

> By executing devotional service to Me, My devotees easily acquire everything that can be attained by performing penances, fruitive activity, philosophical speculation, renunciation, *yoga,* charity, religiosity, and other pious acts.

Lord Kṛṣṇa Is the Supreme Absolute Truth

The famous atheist Kapila propagated the Sāṅkhya philosophy. He concluded that the material world consists of twenty-four material elements, namely, earth, water, fire, air, and ether; form, taste, smell, sound, and touch; eyes, tongue, nose, ears, and skin; mouth, hands, legs, anus, and genitals; mind, intelligence, and false ego; and the unmanifested state of the three modes of nature (*pradhāna*). When Kapila was unable to perceive the unmanifested soul after analyzing the twenty-four elements, he concluded that God does not exist. Thus the devotee community regards Kapila as an atheist.

Lord Kapila, the son of Devahūti, is a different person from the atheistic Kapila. Lord Kapila is accepted as an empowered incarnation of the Supreme Godhead. In the *Bhagavad-gītā* Lord Kṛṣṇa refutes the atheist Kapila's Sāṅkhya philosophy and its contention that the unmanifested soul is nonexistent.

In the *Gītā* (7.4) Lord Kṛṣṇa also establishes that the material ingredients are all under His control and supervision:

bhūmir āpo 'nalo vāyuḥ
khaṁ mano buddhir eva ca
ahaṅkāra itīyaṁ me
bhinnā prakṛtir aṣṭadhā

Earth, water, fire, air, ether, mind, intelligence, and false ego—all together these eight constitute My separated material energies.

Who is Lord Kṛṣṇa, and what is His original form? Unless one knows about His opulence, potencies, fame, beauty, knowledge, and renunciation, one can never enter into the realm of pure devotional service. As stated in the *Caitanya-caritāmṛta* (*Ādi* 2.117):

siddhānta baliyā citte nā kara alasa
ihā ha-ite kṛṣṇe lāge sudṛḍha mānasa

A sincere student should not neglect the discussion of such philosophical conclusions, considering them controversial, for such discussions strengthen the mind. Thus one's mind becomes attached to Śrī Kṛṣṇa.

One who is situated in knowledge of Kṛṣṇa and acts accordingly is executing devotional service. In pursuing the process initiated by Kapila man failed to fathom the same for hundreds and thousands of years. The Supreme Lord Kṛṣṇa has, in a few words, lifted the shroud of mystery and revealed the truth.

Earth, water, fire, air, ether, mind, intelligence, and false ego—all together these eight constitute My separated material energies. Besides these, O might-armed Arjuna, there is another, superior energy of Mine, which comprises the living entities who are exploiting the resources of this material, inferior nature. All created beings have their source in these two natures. Of all that is material and all that is spiritual in this world, know for certain that I am both the origin and the dissolution.

Those who cannot understand this truth remain far from the science of devotional service, while those who do understand it are strengthened in their devotional life. Lord Kṛṣṇa is the Supreme Personality of Godhead, the supreme male. So, when the supreme male is present, automatically material nature, His female counterpart, is there to serve Him. Those who falsely pose as the Supreme Person claim to have the material nature at their disposal and conclude that nature is no longer at Lord Kṛṣṇa's beck and call. Naturally this is absurd, and only fools will make such a claim.

Similarly, those philosophical schools which propound that the Supreme Person is subservient to *prakṛti,* or nature, are also far from the truth. When one thinks about nature and nothing further, the thought is left incomplete. One has to inquire, "Whose nature is it?" Nature has to belong to someone; she cannot exist on her own. Thus what must be established is the identity of the Supreme Person, or *puruṣa*—the male factor. *Prakṛti* is the same as *śakti,* or energy. Through the energy, an intelligent person will seek out the possessor of the energy. The *Upaniṣads* and other Vedic scriptures clearly state that Brahman is the Absolute Truth and the possessor and source of multifarious energies. In the *Bhagavad-gītā* (14.27) this Brahman is said to be the bodily effulgence of Kṛṣṇa (*brahmaṇo hi pratiṣṭhāham*). This is confirmed in the *Brahma-saṁhitā* (5.40):

yasya prabhā prabhavato jagad-aṇḍa-koṭi-
koṭiṣv aśeṣa-vasudhādi-vibhūti-bhinnam
tad brahma niṣkalam anantam aśeṣa-bhūtaṁ
govindam ādi-puruṣaṁ tam ahaṁ bhajāmi

I worship Govinda, the primeval Lord, whose effulgence is the source of the nondifferentiated Brahman mentioned in the *Upaniṣads,* being differentiated from the infinity of glories of the mundane universe appears as the indivisible, infinite, limitless, truth.

Brahman exists as the all-pervading energy in this phenomenal world. Therefore the *Vedas* have defined Brahman as formless, impersonal, pure, and so on. But the source of Brahman is an eternal personality who has no material form but who has a transcendental form full of spiritual potencies and all divine qualities. He is the Supreme Personality of

Godhead, the embodiment of eternity, knowledge, and bliss. He possesses all six transcendental opulences to an infinite degree, He performs superexcellent divine pastimes, and He alone is to be searched out and known in all the scriptures. The materialistic, fruitive workers make the mistake of thinking that this supreme transcendental personality is mundane, and thus they become degraded into pseudo-devotees. And the dry speculators, having been repulsed by the material phenomena in their search for knowledge of the Absolute, think that the transcendental form of the Supreme Personality of Godhead is also repulsive, thus clearly proving that their ascending process of acquiring knowledge is insufficient and inferior. Both these groups are in a pathetic spiritual state. Therefore, to shower His causeless mercy upon them, the Supreme Lord has revealed the truth about Himself and His transcendental potencies in the *Bhagavad-gītā*.

The above-mentioned eight ingredients make up the material nature, or the Supreme Lord's external potency. These material ingredients—earth, water, fire, air, and so on—are devoid of any free will, and so they are known as the Lord's inferior energy. By contrast, the potency that activates the inferior energy is known as the Lord's superior energy, or spiritual potency. On principle the energy cannot be the enjoyer; nor can one energy enjoy another energy. Energy is the enjoyed, and the energetic is the enjoyer.

The living entities are a product of the Lord's superior, spiritual energy, and so they are superior to earth, water, fire, and so on, which are always devoid of volition. But that does not mean the living entities are on the same platform as the Supreme Lord, who is the absolute controlling principle. It is easy to discern the superiority of spirit over inert matter. The *jīva* principle is setting into motion and sustaining everything in this material world. And if the *jīvas* did not try to lord it over the material nature, then there would be no variegatedness in this phenomenal world. The material elements would have remained unchanged if the *jīvas* had not been inclined to control and enjoy them. Only through the material energies' connection with the conscious living entity can such substances as earth, wood, stone, and iron be orchestrated so as to give rise to huge, opulent buildings, factories, and cities. Matter cannot organize itself.

From the foregoing one can understand that this massive cosmic creation, with its innumerable planetary systems and heavenly bodies, has come about only through the interference of some superior and powerful consciousness. It is beyond doubt that matter is inert, incapable of voluntary action, and that consciousness has activated the twenty-four material ingredients so as to exhibit variegatedness in material nature. All this goes to prove the inherent insufficiency and imperfections in material nature. Thus transcendental happiness is possible only in spiritual variegatedness. In the *Bhagavad-gītā* (7.5) Lord Kṛṣṇa confirms that the *jīvas* belong to His superior energy:

apareyam itas tv anyāṁ
prakṛtiṁ viddhi me parām
jīva-bhūtāṁ mahā-bāho
yayedaṁ dhāryate jagat

> Besides these, O mighty armed Arjuna, there is another, superior energy of Mine, which comprises the living entities who are exploiting the resources of this material, inferior nature.

Because the spirit soul (*jīva*) is born of the Lord's superior, spiritual energy, it has little in common with the material energy, just as the aquatics have no affinity for the land and the land beasts are out of place in the water. The apparent close connection between the material energy and the spiritual energy is in fact illusory. The *jīvas,* being a product of the spiritual energy, try to exploit the material energy, but ultimately such attempts fail, because it is impossible for one energy to always exploit and lord it over another energy. The *jīvas* can, however, eternally serve the Supreme Energetic, Lord Kṛṣṇa. When the *jīva* exploits the material energy in his endeavor to serve the Lord, that activity is transcendental—the performance of sacrifice. Any other kind of activity amounts to nothing but materialistic, fruitive work.

In the *Viṣṇu Purāṇa* (6.7.61) one reads about the three kinds of energy:

viṣṇu-śaktiḥ parā proktā
kṣetra jñākhyā tathā parā

avidyā-karma-saṁjñānyā
tṛtīyā śaktir iṣyate

> The potency of Lord Viṣṇu is summarized in three categories—namely, the spiritual potency, the living entities, and ignorance. The spiritual potency is full of knowledge; the living entities, although belonging to the spiritual potency, are subject to bewilderment; and the third energy, which is full of ignorance, is always visible in fruitive activities.

Thus all phenomena in this material world are simply interactions of the Supreme Lord's superior, spiritual energy with His inferior, material energy. The material energy is known as the *kṣetra,* or field of activity, and the spiritual energy is known as the *kṣetra-jña,* or the knower of the field of activity. All the different species of living entities, with their varied characteristics, are produced by the interaction of the *kṣetra* and the *kṣetra-jña.* The energetic principle, the controller of both these energies, is the Supreme Personality of Godhead, Kṛṣṇa. He must be recognized as the ultimate cause of the creation, maintenance, and annihilation of this cosmic manifestation. As He says in the *Bhagavad-gītā* (7.6–7):

etad-yonīni bhūtāni
sarvāṇīty upadhāraya
ahaṁ kṛtsnasya jagataḥ
prabhavaḥ pralayas tathā

mattaḥ parataraṁ nānyat
kiñcid asti dhanañjaya
mayi sarvam idaṁ protaṁ
sūtre maṇi-gaṇā iva

> All created beings have their source in these two natures [the inferior and the superior energies of the Lord]. Of all that is material and all that is spiritual in this world, know for certain that I am both the origin and the dissolution. O conqueror of wealth, there is no truth superior to Me. Everything rests upon Me, as pearls are strung on a thread.

The various quotations we hear from the *Vedas* concerning Brahman—*ekam evādvitīyaṁ brahama:* "Brahman is one without a second"; *neha nānāsti kiñcana:* "Besides this, nothing exists"; *sarvaṁ khalv idam brahma:* "Everything and everywhere is Brahman"; *ahaṁ brahmāsmi:* "I am by nature Brahman", and so on—find their conclusion in the verses from the *Bhagavad-gītā* quoted above. The Supreme Lord, endowed with the six transcendental opulences to the absolute degree, is the highest governing principle. Thus no other personality is equal to or greater than Him. Lord Kṛṣṇa confirms this point by saying "There is no truth superior to Me," and then explaining how He is present everywhere and intimately connected with everything through His all-pervasive energies.

The material nature is the result of the transformation of the Lord's energies. Both the energies and the energetic are inconceivable, and they are simultaneously one and different. Hence the phrase *sarvaṁ khalv idaṁ brahma,* ("Everything is Brahman") in fact declares that everything consists of transformations of the Supreme Lord's material and spiritual energies. The transformation of His energies neither increases nor decreases the Supreme Absolute Truth; hence Brahman is described as changeless. And the inferior energy, being only the reflection of Brahman, is *nirākāra*, impersonal.

Śrī Caitanya Mahāprabhu propagated the philosophy of the simultaneous oneness and difference of the Lord and His energies. The highest esoteric truth is that Lord Kṛṣṇa is the Supreme Absolute Truth and that both the living entities and the material world are His subordinate energies. Those who fail to understand this principle are materialists, while those who do understand it and are trying to re-establish their relationship with Lord Kṛṣṇa are liberated souls, devotees of the Lord. Lord Kṛṣṇa explains this in the *Bhagavad-gītā* (7.13–14):

tribhir guṇa-mayair bhāvair
ebhiḥ sarvam idaṁ jagat
mohitaṁ nābhijānāti
mām ebhyaḥ param avyayam

daivī hy eṣā guṇa-mayī
mama māyā duratyayā
mām eva ye prapadyante
māyām etāṁ taranti te

Deluded by the three modes [goodness, passion, and ignorance], the whole world does not know Me, who am above

> the modes and inexhaustible. This divine energy of Mine, consisting of the three modes of material nature, is difficult to overcome. But those who have surrendered unto Me can easily cross beyond it.

The dualities of like and dislike, good and bad, are all due to the three modes of material nature—goodness, passion, and ignorance. These modes hold all conditioned living entities under their sway. Therefore it is difficult for conditioned souls to understand that the Supreme Lord, being absolutely spiritual, is above the three modes and thus *param avyayam,* absolutely inexhaustible. The reason the Lord uses these words *param avyayam* is that although He permeates everything by means of His transcendental energies, He remains eternally unchanged and the complete whole. One should avoid making the mistake of thinking that because Brahman, the Supreme Absolute Truth, pervades the entire cosmic manifestation, therefore He cannot possess a definitive form or personality. The heat radiating from a fire spreads in all directions, yet the fire remains unchanged. Similarly, the sun has been emanating light and heat since time immemorial, yet it has not lost any of its potency. And the sun possesses but a minuscule fraction of the Supreme Lord's inexhaustible potency. So what question is there of the Lord's potency being either transformed or decreased? The Lord's energies, like a fire's heat and light, spread everywhere, yet His energies can never diminish at any time. Thus in the *Bhagavad-gītā* He describes Himself as *param avyayam,* inexhaustible, the supreme energetic principle. The *Vedas* describe Him in the following way:

pūrṇasya pūrṇam ādāya
pūrṇam evāvaśiṣyate

> Whatever is produced of the complete whole is also complete in itself. Because He is the complete whole, even though so many complete units emanate from Him, He remains the complete balance. (*Īśopaniṣad,* Invocation)

Like the Supreme Lord Himself, the process for freeing oneself from the mesmerizing grip of the material energy and coming closer to the Lord is also one without a second. As the only way to see the sun is by the help of sunlight, so the only way to see the Supreme Personality, Lord Kṛṣṇa, is by the illumination of sunlike Kṛṣṇa Himself. Only by surrendering to His lotus feet and rendering Him loving devotional service can one approach Him. Neither fruitive activity through physical strain nor speculative knowledge through mental gymnastics can help one attain the highest perfection of God consciousness. Only through *bhakti,* or devotion, can the Supreme Lord be achieved. Speculative knowledge and mystic *yoga* can at best accord one a partial realization of the Absolute Truth—namely, realization of Brahman and Paramātmā (the Supersoul), respectively. It is through the singular means of *bhakti* that one can perceive face to face the Supreme Personality of Godhead, Kṛṣṇa, the embodiment of eternity, knowledge, and bliss. When the rising sun chases away the blackness of night, everything becomes clearly visible. Similarly, when the sun of Kṛṣṇa rises above the horizon of one's consciousness, the stygian gloom of *māyā,* the illusory energy, is driven away, and the original form of every object comes into distinct focus. Thus full knowledge and realization of the Absolute Truth come exclusively through devotion to the Supreme Lord.

However, the path to this perfect realization is fraught with hindrances caused by *māyā,* the insurmountable material energy. In this regard one may ask, "If by serving Lord Kṛṣṇa one can automatically discharge all subsidiary duties, then why doesn't everyone in the world surrender to Lord Kṛṣṇa and worship Him as the supreme absolute being? Almost everyone in the world more or less agrees that there is only one God, not two or more. Yet when that one and only Supreme Personality, Lord Kṛṣṇa, comes personally to declare this truth, why do people still refuse to surrender to Him? Perhaps it is understandable that those who are illiterate and ignorant cannot accept Lord Kṛṣṇa's supremacy and therefore do not surrender to Him. But there are many erudite scholars, philosophers, and leaders of society who extensively discuss the scriptures yet still do not take shelter of Lord Kṛṣṇa's lotus feet. Why?" The Lord Himself answers this question in His *Bhagavad-gītā* (7.15):

na māṁ duṣkṛtino mūḍhāḥ
prapadyante narādhamāḥ

māyayāpahṛta-jñānā
āsuraṁ bhāvam āśritāḥ

Those miscreants who are grossly foolish, who are the lowest among mankind, whose knowledge is stolen by illusion, and who partake of the atheistic nature of demons do not surrender unto Me.

People with demoniac mentalities never surrender to the Supreme Lord. There have always existed two kinds of men: the good, pious men and the impious reprobates. These two types of people are always present in every country and at every period in history. Pious men obey God's laws and are gradually elevated to perfection. The impious, on the other hand, capriciously flaunt God's laws and try to be independent. The racial strife, civil wars, violent revolutions, and world wars so common in the modern age are all caused by the whimsical and selfish nature of impious men.

Pious people can live in any country and adhere to the instructions of their scripture, or they can associate with other pious men from another country and exchange knowledge and realizations. As a result, these seekers of the Absolute Truth can certainly perceive that Lord Kṛṣṇa is the Supreme Personality of Godhead. On the other hand, sinful persons have one interest: to satisfy their egoistic cravings. They may make a show of being vanguards of religion, but behind this façade they continue their reprehensible activities. They vilify the sanctity of the religion of their birth and go against their own country's interest. Their self-centered lives preclude their following even the common etiquette of human behavior, what to speak of dedicating their lives to Lord Kṛṣṇa's devotional service. Such demoniac persons are more dangerous than poisonous snakes.

Generally, the gross fools and the ignorant fruitive workers do not surrender to the Supreme Lord. Such people never enquire into the Absolute Truth. They never ask such questions as "Who is God?" "What is the world?" "Who am I?" "Why am I working like an ass my whole life?" or "What is the result of my endeavors?" The ass slaves his whole life carrying the washerman's burden, just for a handful of grass. Similarly, the *karmīs* (fruitive workers) toil tirelessly simply to secure a supply of food and other necessities. The ass is a symbol of foolishness, for he works hard only to fill his belly and copulate with a she-ass. So also do the asinine *karmīs* toil tirelessly out of affection and attachment, struggling to maintain their homes and, beyond that, the land of their birth, which they consider worshippable. In the home, the *karmī's* sole source of enjoyment is his wife, who cooks for him and provides pleasure for his misery-ridden senses. The short-sighted *karmīs* do not want to know of any broader issues concerning themselves or their world; they are simply tethered to their home and bodily cares. And those leaders who foster the people's sensual lives are bigger fools and rascals than the ordinary *karmīs*. Therefore they never come in contact with the *Bhagavad-gītā* or Lord Kṛṣṇa. The word *surrender* means nothing to them.

People who do not surrender to the Supreme Lord are called *narādhama,* "the lowest of men." Such men fritter away their human lives, behaving like animals. In other words, when a person does not use this rare human birth to achieve its actual purpose but wastes it in degraded activities, he is called a *narādhama.* When a beggar suddenly finds a treasure yet continues to live like a beggar, he is surely a miser and a *narādhama.* Similarly, when someone receives the priceless gift of a human birth yet squanders it by living like an animal—simply eating, sleeping, mating, and defending—then such a person is a *narādhama.* These fools do not realize that after many millions of births in lower species, the soul finally receives the rare human birth. And it is in this birth that the soul must sincerely endeavor to elevate himself to the transcendental platform, attain the Absolute Truth, and return to his original home in the spiritual world. If in this human life the soul makes no attempt to alleviate his situation, even after learning how horribly he has suffered in millions of previous lifetimes, then such a person is certainly a miserable miser and *narādhama.* But if one tries to utilize his rare human birth for self-realization by becoming elevated to the brahminical class, then his life is successful. *Brāhmaṇa* does not mean *brāhmaṇa* by birth. A *brāhmaṇa* is one who surrenders to Lord Kṛṣṇa, the Lord of the *brāhmaṇas.* A *narādhama* cannot do so. Therefore another meaning of *narādhama* is "one who rejects devotional service."

Another class of men who do not surrender to Lord Kṛṣṇa are the demons, those who are staunchly inimical to Him. Famous and powerful demon kings like Rāvaṇa, Hiraṇyakaśipu,

Jarāsandha, and Kaṁsa acquired many powers through learning and severe austerities. But because they always challenged the various incarnations of the Supreme Lord, such as Lord Rāma, Lord Nṛsiṁhadeva, Lord Viṣṇu, and Lord Kṛṣṇa, they are known as demons. Often the demons do not lack education or intelligence, but because of their fiendish mentality toward the Supreme Lord, their learning and brain capacity come to naught. Their abilities, being fully in the grip of material nature, are ultimately taken from them. The reason for the demons' failure has been stated earlier: if one does not surrender to Lord Kṛṣṇa, it is impossible to surmount material nature.

Torturing the devotees of Kṛṣṇa is the preoccupation of the demons, who think that Lord Rāma and Lord Kṛṣṇa cannot punish them because They are ordinary mortals. Thus the demons conclude that they themselves are as learned and intelligent as Lord Rāma and Lord Kṛṣṇa. The atheistic students of Navadvīpa thought Lord Caitanya was an ordinary human being, and thus to win their respect the Lord accepted the renounced and austere *sannyāsa* order of life. In this way the Lord showed Himself to be the personification of divine magnanimity. The demons invariably confuse matters: they worship humans as gods and call God a human being. In the *Bhagavad-gītā* (9.11) the Lord fittingly describes such grossly foolish persons: *avajānanti māṁ mūḍhā mānuṣīṁ tanum āśritam.* "Fools deride Me when I descend in the human form." The demons' learning, intelligence, and titles are like the gems that glitter on a poisonous snake's hood. The presence of a priceless gem on a snake's hood does not decrease his venom. Similarly, a demon's erudition, intelligence, and titles do not make him less of a demon, and thus he is as horrendous as a venomous snake.

Decorating a dead body and taking it to the funeral pyre with pomp is certainly nothing but a flagrant display for entertainment only. The public is similarly cheated when accolades and scholarly degrees are piled on a demon who is an arrant competitor of the Supreme Lord. The atheistic, demoniac education imparted to the young in modern universities is simply producing a bunch of demons with titles. Proof of this is the recent incident in which Principal Garg of Aligarh University was murdered by some students. The whole state of Uttar

Pradesh is shocked and has opened a probe into this vicious act. The governor has called for a conference of the leaders and teachers, but in the past all such conferences have met with the same frustrating fate: no solution. We think the present conference will also fail. The only means to eradicate the demoniac mentality in society is to teach the science of Kṛṣṇa consciousness. Having taken note of all the disaster and corruption wreaked by the demons, it is the moral responsibility of every citizen in the world to learn and teach the science of Kṛṣṇa consciousness.

Dr. Ane's Comment on the System of Education

We were pleased to hear Dr. Ane's address at the Calcutta University convocation on January 12, 1957. Dr. Ane is presently the honorable governor of the state of Bihar. An excerpt from his speech follows:

> Our youth are being brought up in a tradition of veiled contempt for religion and everything religious. Spiritualists and religious devotees are the laughing-stock of the educated youth, and as the general masses are religious-minded and have great respect and reverence for such devotees and spiritualists, they feel generally disgusted with the attitude of the educated class and have no regard for them. The educated class has also no affection for the masses, whose way of life is mostly molded by religious ideas. The result is that the educated classes have not been able to produce a sufficient number of servants to work with a real missionary spirit for the amelioration of the suffering of the masses.

Dr. Ane goes on to say that the existing academic courses in schools and colleges exclude classes on religion.

We have included this portion of Dr. Ane's speech, taken from a local newspaper, because we want to impress upon the reader the urgent need for introducing religious studies into the universities. Because in the past strong objections were raised against including religious classes in the schools, they have been excluded, and now severe reactions are being seen in today's youth. I think that excluding spiritual studies from education thwarts all chances for the human mind to awaken and blossom. Because of a lack of spiritual education, today's youth are undisciplined. Students who do not pray or meditate in the early morning, and again in the evening, gradually become agnostics, and their minds float about aimlessly without purpose. They reject religious ideas and ethics and instead embrace logic and argument as supreme. Often they fall into the vicious grip of some unscrupulous politician. The exclusion of religious courses from the universities is the main reason one does not see nowadays a pure and sublime relationship between student and teacher. Many educators feel the need for religious education today.

A few months ago (on January 18, 1957) we had the opportunity of meeting Dr. Ane at the Government House in Patna, and we had some discussions. Being a pious man, he could appreciate our spiritual topics and offered us full support for our missionary activities which are aimed at eradicating the demoniac mentality on a wide scale. His recent speech gives us hope of improvement.

Possessed of perverted intelligence, the demons, rascals, and fools can never surrender to Lord Kṛṣṇa. Similarly, Lord Kṛṣṇa never shows them His mercy. The most munificent incarnation of Godhead, Lord Caitanya, repudiated the sinner Gopāla Cāpala because he was envious of the Lord's devotee. In this regard, the Supreme Lord states His opinion in the *Bhagavad-gītā* (4.11): *ye yathā māṁ prapadyante tāṁs tathaiva bhajāmy aham.* "As all surrender unto Me, I reward them accordingly." Thus the Lord arranges for the demons to slide lower and lower into degraded species of life and suffer hell for many millions of births. In the Chapter 16 (19–20) the Lord says:

tān ahaṁ dviṣataḥ krūrān
saṁsāreṣu narādhamān
kṣipāmy ajasram aśubhān
āsurīṣv eva yoniṣu

āsurīṁ yonim āpannā
mūḍhā janmani janmani
mām aprāpyaiva kaunteya
tato yānty adhamāṁ gatim

> Those who are envious and mischievous, who are the lowest among men, I perpetually cast into the ocean of material existence, into various demoniac species of life. Attaining repeated birth amongst the demoniac species of life, O son of Kuntī, such persons can never approach Me. Gradually they sink down to the most abominable type of existence.

Yet the Supreme Lord's devotees, being more merciful than the Lord Himself, are compassionate toward even the lowest demons like us.

The Lord's devotees can save even those whom the Lord Himself rejects. This is their unique character. Therefore the devotees of the Lord arrange various means to save the fallen, reprobate souls from perdition. In fact, they live among these spiritual derelicts to encourage them toward spiritual perfection, using any means at hand—even tricks. His Divine Grace Śrīla Bhaktisiddhānta Sarasvatī Ṭhākura Prabhupāda wanted to open a students' hostel in London, the logic being that it was necessary to give sugar-coated pills, in the form of a little sense gratification, to those debauched students in order to attract them to join the path of God-realization.

If they so desire, powerful spiritual masters, or pure devotees of the Lord, can instantly deliver the entire universe and take everyone to the shelter of the Supreme Lord's lotus feet. Śrīla Vāsudeva Datta declared to Lord Caitanya that he was prepared to take on all the sinful reactions of every living entity in the universe and suffer eternally in hell if the Lord was willing to liberate all the living entities at one time. The pure devotees are so magnanimous that they are always concerned about the spiritual well-being of every soul. The only way to receive the Supreme Lord's mercy is to bathe oneself in the dust of the lotus feet of such unalloyed devotees.

The devotees of the Lord understand that it is *māyā's* influence that has spoiled the people and made them demoniac. Thus the inherently noble disposition of the devotees leads them to think only of the demons' benefit, without a tinge of envy. The devotees are therefore known as *patita-pāvana,* "the saviors of the fallen." In fact, the devotees are more compassionate than the Supreme Lord Himself. Of course, it is the Supreme Lord's grace alone that makes them more compassionate than the Lord. And by the mercy of such devotees, the lowest sinful men and women can attain the lotus feet of the Lord.

On the other hand, offending such pure devotees finishes all possibility of salvation. If one offends the Supreme Lord, only His pure devotees can save the offender, but if one offends the pure devotee, then even the Supreme Lord will not save the offender from doom. For this reason alone, pure devotees never feel offended. When Jesus Christ was being crucified, he did not blame anyone for it. Haridāsa Ṭhākura was severely lashed in twenty-two marketplaces by the Muslim Kazi's sentries. Still he prayed to the Lord not to punish his tormentors. Lord Nityānanda was wounded by the two rascals Jagāi and Mādhāi, yet the Lord stood His ground, bleeding profusely. He delivered the two notorious brothers and thus brilliantly exemplified the title *patita-pāvana.* Such is the profound compassion of the pure devotees.

Therefore the reprobates' only means of attaining any piety is through the association of devotees. We are looking forward to that time when the stalwart disciples of that illustrious crest jewel of all Vaiṣṇavas, His Divine Grace Bhaktisiddhānta Sarasvatī Ṭhākura Prabhupāda, having received the blessings of their spiritual master, will come together again for the benediction of the whole world and, without wasting any more time, preach the message of Śrīla Rūpa Gosvāmī and Śrīla Raghunātha dāsa Gosvāmī. Śrīla Gaurakiśora dāsa Bābājī always tried to dissuade his disciple, Śrīla Bhaktisiddhānta Sarasvatī Ṭhākura, from going to Calcutta, which he considered a bastion of Kali-yuga. Yet though some might think Śrīla Bhaktisiddhānta Sarasvatī Ṭhākura disobeyed his *guru's* order, he preached not only in Calcutta but in other capitals of Kali-yuga, such as London, Berlin, Bombay, Madras, and Delhi. He vehemently opposed the idea of constructing a temple in some quiet spot and leading a passive and uneventful life in the monastery. He represented perfectly the ideal of utilizing 100 percent of one's energy in God's service for the spiritual upliftment of humanity. A certain Gujarati friend offered to build him a temple in Ville Parle, a quiet and remote section of Bombay. He immediately refused. We had the greatest good fortune of seeing him act and preach in this way. And now it is our ill fate that after the passing away of Śrīla Bhaktisiddhānta Sarasvatī Ṭhākura, the exemplar of *patita-pāvana,* we have returned to our lowly, fallen ways. Is there a glimmer of hope for our deliverance?

From the ocean of loving compassion, which had been completely dammed up, Lord Nityānanda cut a canal of love of Godhead and flooded the entire world. And then some persons called caste Gosvāmīs, claiming to be the Lord's descendants, again dammed up that ocean of mercy with their malpractices of fruitive activities and rituals. Śrīla Bhaktisiddhānta Sarasvatī Ṭhākura once more cut open the canal of love of Godhead and brought in the flood waters. And now are we, of all persons, trying once more to dam it up like the caste Gosvāmīs? By the influence of the good association of the Lord's devotees, even a fool and rascal like me, possessed of a destructive, demoniac mentality, can accumulate enough piety to become inspired to serve the Supreme Lord.

By nature children are restless and playful, so in the kindergarten they are given toys and games to interest them in learning. Similarly, a neophyte is trained to perform activities in the mood of sacrifice, and he is encouraged to worship the Deities according to the scriptural injunctions. The expert Vaiṣṇava preceptor then gradually draws him toward the platform of pure devotion by narrating the spiritually potent topics of Kṛṣṇa consciousness and giving him the remnants of food offered to the Supreme Lord. These two aspects of devotional life act like medicine on the neophyte, who, like the rest of the world, is affected by the material disease. Devotional service to Lord Kṛṣṇa is the living entity's eternal birthright; it is not a new subject fabricated by the human mind. A base fool thinks that devotion to Lord Kṛṣṇa is merely a mundane psychological state of mind. But in truth devotional service is our eternal spiritual substance—"the essential spiritual reality" (*vāstava-vastu*), according to the *Śrīmad-Bhāgavatam* (1.1.2). Devotion to Lord Kṛṣṇa can be invoked naturally in the purified hearts of devotees. When a disease is cured, the patient feels hungry; similarly, when a neophyte accrues sufficient piety by associating with devotees, he feels attraction for devotional service within his heart.

Four kinds of pious men establish a relationship with the Supreme Lord, Kṛṣṇa. As the Lord states in the *Bhagavad-gītā* (7:16):

catur-vidhā bhajante māṁ
janāḥ sukṛtino 'rjuna

ārto jijñāsur arthārthī
jñānī ca bharatarṣabha

O best among the Bhāratas, four kinds of pious men begin to render devotional service unto Me—the distressed, the desirer of wealth, the inquisitive, and he who is searching for knowledge of the Absolute.

One obtains another kind of piety by strictly executing his duties under the system of *varṇāśrama-dharma,* a social system containing four spiritual orders and four social orders. Learned sages have long propagated this system. As the *Viṣṇu Purāṇa* (3.8.9) states:

varṇāśramācāravatā
puruṣeṇa paraḥ pumān
viṣṇur ārādhyate panthā
nānyat tat-toṣa-kāraṇam

The Supreme Personality of Godhead, Lord Viṣṇu, is worshipped by the proper execution of prescribed duties in the system of *varṇa* and *āśrama.* There is no other way to satisfy the Supreme Personality of Godhead. One must be situated in the institution of the four *varnas* and *āśramas.*

The *brāhmaṇas* (the intellectual, priestly class), the *kṣatriyas* (kings and administrators), the *vaiśyas* (the mercantile community), and the *śūdras* (menial workers) are the four social orders, or *varṇas.* If they live according to the scriptural injunctions pertaining to their particular *varṇa,* then they can accrue piety. Similarly, if the members of the four *āśramas*—namely, the *brahmacārīs* (celibate students), *gṛhasthas* (householders), *vānaprasthas* (pilgrims), and *sannyāsīs* (renunciants)—also act in conformity with the scriptural edicts, they too acquire immense piety. But when the ill influence of Kali-yuga corrupts this *varṇāśrama* system, human society is beset by all sorts of degradations. As a result, the living entities are punished by a variety of natural calamities caused by the illusory potency of the Lord. When the citizens abide by the rules of the king, the kingdom runs smoothly and everyone is prosperous and content. But when the demoniac population of thieves, rogues and criminals steadily increases, the kingdom is filled with chaos and terror.

In Search of the Supreme Lord

Varṇāśrama religion cannot be practiced in an atmosphere of such chaos and violence. The system now being called *varṇāśrama* is actually ungodly, demoniac religion in disguise. To wear the holy thread and go through the purificatory process within this demoniac system does not result in piety. Discarding all purificatory processes and religious rites, the men of Kali-yuga vie with each other to become the biggest and the strongest. A person becomes a *"brāhmaṇa"* just by slipping a holy thread over his head—indeed, such has been predicted in the scriptures—but this does not earn him any piety. Lord Caitanya rejected this kind of cheating *varṇāśrama* system. Foreseeing the degraded condition of Kali-yuga, Lord Kṛṣṇa hardly discusses *varṇāśrama* religion in the *Bhagavad-gītā* and instead stresses the performance of work as sacrifice. Hence it is clearly understood that by the performance of sacrifice for Lord Viṣṇu, the Supreme Person, He becomes satisfied and all ill effects are eradicated.

Persons afflicted by disease or other miseries are known as *ārta,* "the distressed." Commonly, a sick person depends on a doctor and medicine to cure his disease. But far-sighted scholars say that suffering of any kind is a result of sinful activities performed in the past. Ordinary people do not understand that sinful reactions result from ignorance. This ignorance exists in manifest (*prārabdha*), unmanifest (*aprārabdha*) and latent (*kuṭashta*) form.

There is no material means of counteracting these sinful reactions. Administering a pain-killer provides temporary relief but cannot remove the root cause of a disease. Similarly, no materialistic effort aimed at counteracting sinful reactions can provide ultimate relief. One obtains maximum benefit only by surrendering to the Supreme Lord. The *Bhakti-rasāmṛta-sindhu* [*The Nectar of Devotion*] supplies us with numerous proofs of how devotional service to the Lord destroys sinful reactions, the seeds of sinful reactions, and ignorance, the root of all sin. Hence we see that pious men depend solely on the Supreme Lord in moments of distress.

It is not the prime duty of human beings to try to relieve their present sufferings. The search in life is for that medicine—that panacea—which will cure the material disease altogether. This disease manifests itself in countless ways, such as birth, old age, disease, and death. The pious person seeks the association of saintly persons and follows the scriptures, and in this way he endeavors for his greatest good. The beginning of devotional service is the development of faith in the scriptures and the words of the saints. This faith destroys all unwanted desires in the heart and increases one's surrender to the Supreme Lord's will.

Innocent enquirers are known as *jijñāsu*, "those who are inquisitive." These innocent enquirers are society's hope for the future. Most intelligent and innocent young children are inquisitive: they question their parents about many things and remember the answers. When these bright young boys and girls receive proper guidance from parents and teachers who can lucidly answer their queries, they easily understand each point and gradually develop fine brains. From among these intelligent souls, those who are especially pious begin to keenly enquire about God and other spiritual topics. Others, who pursue ignoble material knowledge, cannot become successful in life and end up beating the chaff. Those who are inquisitive about the self and the Absolute Truth, Brahman, quickly surrender to Lord Kṛṣṇa and His devotees. Such surrender proves their good measure of piety brought over from their previous births. Beginning with fundamental enquiries about Brahman, they swiftly become elevated, understand the statement of Lord Kṛṣṇa in *Bhagavad-gītā* (14.27) that He is the basis of the impersonal Brahman, and begin to worship Him.

A person with meager piety, however, can never become a devotee of the Supreme Lord. As the scripture states:

mahā-prasāde govinde
nāma-brahmaṇi vaiṣṇave
svalpa-puṇyavatāṁ rājan
viśvāso naiva jāyate

> O king! A person with little piety can never develop faith in Lord Govinda, His mercy, His holy name, or His pure devotees.

Most householders desire material gain. Nowadays especially, everyone is feeling the pinch of poverty. The ordinary man thirsts for money solely to enjoy his senses. Once a person falls into the useless company of sense gratifiers, he spends his wealth on fineries, gold, and women. With more wealth, he seeks adoration and distinction, and along with these he gets mansions, cars, and so on. There is only one interest in this endeavor, and that is to enjoy the senses. Persons whose only goal in life is to gratify the senses were referred to earlier as the less intelligent fruitive workers, or *karmīs.* If any among them happen to have some piety, then these select individuals will not merely fritter away all their time in titillating their senses, but will spend some time worshipping the Supreme Lord. Although these elite *karmīs* do not associate with the pure devotees of the Lord, they call themselves spiritualists. Actually, they harbor the desire to gratify their carnal desires. They fail to comprehend that the Supreme Lord is known as Hṛṣīkeśa, "the supreme master of the senses." Sometimes a *jñānī* (a seeker of knowledge) or a practitioner of mystic *yoga* will also worship the Lord, but they also are merely interested ultimately in sensual pleasures. The only way these adulterated devotees can become pure devotees is if they read Śrīla Rūpa Gosvāmī's *Bhakti-rasāmṛta-sindhu.* This book is an authority on the science of devotional service.

Genuine *jñānīs* know how everything is connected to Brahman, the Absolute Truth. They are humble, unassuming, clean, brahminical, and reverent toward the *guru,* and they possess many other good qualities. Most often they take to the renounced order (*sannyāsa*) and lead a pure and saintly life. Yet frequently these *sannyāsīs* develop one major fault: they consider themselves God. They misinterpret the meaning of the Vedic phrase *ahaṁ brahmāsmi,* "I am Brahman," and thus they cannot realize pure knowledge of Brahman. They end up deifying the process of negation, and that finally leads to absolute monism. In this way, many *jñānīs* who want to know the Absolute Truth, the Supreme Brahman, get somehow misled by the illusory potency, *māyā. Māyā* prepares her last fatal trap, liberation, by which she keeps the monists stranded in the ocean of material existence. She deludes them into thinking "I am that," "I am He," as if they were in a drunken daze.

If by some chance the Māyāvādī *sannyāsīs* can earn a little piety and then be graced by a pure Vaiṣṇava devotee—as the

Māyāvādīs of Benares were by Lord Caitanya—then they can easily realize that knowledge of the impersonal Brahman or the Supersoul is incomplete. Then they can be enlightened with the transcendental knowledge of the Supreme Personality of Godhead. Many sages in the past, like the great Sanaka Ṛṣi, and many self-realized renunciates, like the famous Śukadeva Gosvāmī, got a taste for knowledge of the Supreme Personality of Godhead after practicing their impersonal disciplines. Then they relished indescribable bliss by hearing the Supreme Lord's transcendental pastimes. In the *Śrīmad-Bhāgavatam* (2.1.9), Śukadeva Gosvāmī says:

pariniṣṭhito 'pi nairguṇya
uttama-śloka-līlayā
gṛhīta-cetā rājarṣe
ākhyānaṁ yad adhītavān

> O saintly King [Parikṣit], I was certainly situated in transcendence, yet I was still attracted by the delineation of the pastimes of the Lord, who is described by enlightened verses.

One of the stalwarts in the spiritual line of Gauḍīya Vaiṣṇavas, Śrīla Viśvanātha Cakravartī Ṭhākura, has given his opinion on the four types of pious men who approach the Lord—namely, the distressed, those desiring material gain, the inquisitive, and those who know things as they are. He says,

> The distressed, those in need of material gain, and the inquisitive—these three are neophyte fruitive devotees. Their devotion is mixed with fruitive desires. All of them want to fulfill their desires according to their specific qualities. Finally, when they become purified, they desire to reach the divine abode of the Supreme Lord—the Vaikuṇṭha planets. They are not like the *karmīs,* or fruitive workers, who want to attain to the heavenly planets. As Kṛṣṇa says in the *Bhagavad-gītā* (9. 25) *yānti mad-yājino 'pi mām:* "One who worships Me attains My supreme abode." The *jñānī,* or one who knows things as they are, is the fourth type of pious man, and he is superior to the other three kinds. He attains a higher result because his devotion is mixed with knowledge. Like Sanaka Ṛṣi, he attains the devotional mellow of neutrality. Moreover, because the Lord and His pure devo-

tees shower their causeless mercy upon him, a *jñānī* devotee can also achieve pure love of Godhead, as in the case of Śukadeva Gosvāmī. When devotion mixed with fruitive desires becomes free from those fruitive desires, it is automatically transformed into devotion mixed with knowledge. The result of practicing this devotion mixed with knowledge is mentioned above.

Sometimes, when devotees belonging to the categories of mixed devotion develop a taste for the devotional mellow of servitude and practice it, they attain devotion in servitude mixed with awe and reverence. When their devotion becomes more purified, they attain pure devotion in the mellow of servitude, friendship, and so on., and due to their love for the Lord they become His eternal associates. All this is clearly delineated in the *Śrīmad-Bhāgavatam.* Here we have discussed only a few points for reference.

Lord Kṛṣṇa Alone Is the Supreme Godhead; Everyone Else Is His Servant

Generally the tendency of the *jñānīs* is to veer toward impersonal monistic thought. Their idea of monism is this: having experienced the transience and bitterness of material existence and recognized the futility of fruitive activity, they now realize that they are the Self, Brahman, the Absolute Truth. In fact, when realization of the transcendence is perfectly complete, one perceives the personal aspect of the Absolute Truth in the highest spiritual abode. And when the perception of the personal aspect of the Supreme Godhead deepens, one becomes naturally attracted to the absolute transcendental beauty of Lord Kṛṣṇa. As the Lord says in the *Bhagavad-gītā* (7.19):

bahūnāṁ janmanām ante
jñāna-vān māṁ prapadyate
vāsudevaḥ sarvam iti
sa mahātmā su-durlabhaḥ

After many births and deaths, he who is actually in knowledge surrenders unto Me, knowing Me to be the cause of all causes and all that is. Such a great soul is very rare.

One who fully understands Lord Kṛṣṇa never experiences any bitterness anywhere in the entire material existence. He thrives on the knowledge of His eternal relationship with the Lord; indeed, he sees everything in the world, and the world itself, in relation to Kṛṣṇa. In this way he is unlike the impersonalistic salvationists, who regard this world as merely evanescent matter. Such a wise devotee realizes that everything is engaged in Lord Kṛṣṇa's service, that nothing can exist outside this relationship, independent of Lord Kṛṣṇa. In other words, for the devotee this world becomes transformed, surcharged with the existence of Kṛṣṇa in everything. The illusory potency recedes into oblivion, and this world takes on the characteristics of the spiritual world, Vaikuṇṭha. Such a pure devotee of Kṛṣṇa is not selfish, thinking he alone will enjoy the benefits of surrendering to Lord Kṛṣṇa's lotus feet. Rather, he tries to attract everyone in the world to Lord Kṛṣṇa, and by this effort he becomes known as a *mahātmā,* a magnanimous soul. Such magnanimous souls are truly rare.

It is seen that many so-called *mahātmās,* without first realizing that this entire world is pervaded with Lord Kṛṣṇa's presence, want to become the Lord and master themselves and be served in that capacity. In this way they become fully imprisoned by His illusory potency. They become hounded and bombarded by endless desires, which finally force them to begin worshipping demigods, who are inferior to the Supreme Lord. As Kṛṣṇa says in the *Bhagavad-gītā* (7.20):

kāmais tais tair hṛta-jñānāḥ
prapadyante 'nya-devatāḥ
taṁ taṁ niyamam āsthāya
prakṛtyā niyatāḥ svayā

> Those whose intelligence has been stolen by material desires surrender unto demigods and follow the particular rules and regulations of worship according to their own natures.

Persons who are thus constantly tormented by unlimited desires suffer much distress, which spoils their intelligence. That is why Kṛṣṇa calls them *hṛta-jñānāḥ,* "men with lost intelligence." They become polytheists and hasten to worship various demigods. Polytheists cannot comprehend that *kṛṣṇe bhakti kaile sarva-karma kṛta haya:* "By worshipping Lord Kṛṣṇa, one automatically takes care of all other, subsidiary duties." Polytheists think that demigods like the sun-god are equal to the Supreme Lord, Kṛṣṇa. Such men of distorted intelligence can never take shelter of Lord Kṛṣṇa's lotus feet. On the other hand, lofty-minded persons with incisive intelligence are convinced that Lord Kṛṣṇa is the Supreme Being. If somehow they harbor some material desires, they immediately approach Lord Kṛṣṇa and pray to Him. In the *Śrīmad-Bhāgavatam* (2.3.10) we find this verse:

akāmaḥ sarva-kāmo vā
mokṣa-kāma udāra-dhīḥ
tīvreṇa bhakti-yogena
yajeta puruṣaṁ param

> A person who has broader intelligence, whether he be full of all material desire, without any material desire, or desiring liberation, must by all means worship the Supreme Whole, the Personality of Godhead.

Whatever desire a person may have, to fulfill it he must serve Lord Kṛṣṇa, the Supreme Personality of Godhead, with intense and unfaltering devotion. (This point was discussed earlier by Śrīla Viśvanātha Cakravartī Ṭhākura.) If this injunction is followed, then even those who have an aversion to Lord Kṛṣṇa will eventually decide to surrender to Him.

Lord Kṛṣṇa is the supreme controller and the Supreme Absolute Being, yet He never forces His will upon the infinitesimal living entities. Rather, it is to the living entity's own benefit to recognize that Lord Kṛṣṇa alone is the Supreme Personality of Godhead and that everyone else is His servitor. The sun-god and other demigods perform their duties according to Lord Kṛṣṇa's wishes; indeed, this is why they are called demigods. And since a devotee of the Supreme Lord also follows His wishes, he is also known as a *sura,* or demigod. Conversely, those who oppose the Lord's wishes are known as *asuras,* demons.

The demigods do not possess any independent powers. In fact, they do not wield enough power even to invoke respect for themselves. That is done by the Supreme Lord. Lord

Kṛṣṇa's partial expansion, the Supersoul, resides in everyone's heart, and it is He who instills within one's heart faith and respect for the various demigods. The extraordinary powers seen in the sun-god and other demigods are in fact the Supreme Lord's powers. Once attracted to these extraordinary powers, an intelligent person will gradually be drawn to the source of that power, the Supreme Energetic, Lord Kṛṣṇa. Worship of demigods is indirect, inferior, and unsystematic worship of the Supreme Lord. Those who are too attached to fulfilling their material desires are naturally more attracted to the energy than to the energetic, the source of that energy. Hence in the *Bhagavad-gītā* (7.21–22) Lord Kṛṣṇa says:

yo yo yāṁ yāṁ tanuṁ bhaktaḥ
śraddhayārcitum icchati
tasya tasyācalāṁ śraddhāṁ
tām eva vidadhāmy aham

sa tayā śraddhayā yuktas
tasyārādhanam īhate
labhate ca tataḥ kāmān
mayaiva vihitān hi tān

> I am in everyone's heart as the Supersoul. As soon as one desires to worship some demigod, I make his faith steady so that he can devote himself to that particular deity. Endowed with such a faith, he endeavors to worship a particular demigod and obtain his desires. But in actuality these benefits are bestowed by Me alone.

The demigods' powers are like those of a king's officers. The demigods have no independent powers because they are *jīvas,* minute living entities. An officer of the king can bestow some favors because of the powers invested in him by the king. Similarly, a demigod can shower benefits upon his worshipper because the Supreme Lord has given the demigod some power. If the desire-filled demigod worshipper becomes a little enlightened about the fact that the demigod he worships is fulfilling his desires by the grace of Lord Kṛṣṇa, then with clear intelligence he will begin worshipping Lord Kṛṣṇa directly.

Different demigods have different powers. The sun-god has the power to cure diseases; the moon-god imbues plants with taste and nutritional or medicinal potency; Goddess Durgā gives strength and courage; Goddess Sarasvatī bestows learning; Goddess Lakṣmī grants wealth; Goddess Cāṇḍī offers one the opportunity to consume meat and intoxicants, and Gaṇeśa gives success in one's endeavors. But all these powers are invested in the demigods by the Supreme Lord, and thus only He, the complete whole, can bestow every kind of benediction. There is an immeasurable difference between a well and the ocean.

We have already touched on the point that everything in the world has been produced by the interaction of the Lord's *kṣetra-śakti* (His inferior energy, comprising the "field of action") and His *kṣetrajña-śakti* (His superior energy, which is "the knower of the field"). Therefore everything in this world is merely a transformation of Lord Kṛṣṇa's energies. In one sense the energy principle and the energetic principle are nondifferent, just as fire and its burning potency are inseparable and nondifferent. Unfortunately, the impersonalists, the monistic philosophers, have wreaked havoc in the world with their misguided opinions concerning transformation of the Lord's energy.

Demigods and all other living entities belong to the energy principle, as does the material nature itself. No one but the Lord and His plenary expansions are in the category of the energetic principle. Thus the energy and the energetic are one and different. A person who cannot grasp this subtle principle of simultaneous, inconceivable oneness and difference of the Lord and His energies will surely degenerate into an impersonalist, or Māyāvādī. He will be forced from the path of devotion and become silent. The Supreme Lord, the source of all opulence, is the energetic principle. If we consider Him to be impersonal, then we limit His absoluteness. The words "Supreme Absolute" are applicable to Lord Kṛṣṇa alone. The Lord is the Supreme Absolute Principle, unequalled and unsurpassed. Thus the *Vedas* say He is "one without a second." The Lord's energies are manifested in various forms, and those who become bewildered by these variegated manifestations end up becoming polytheists. It should be clear to all that whatever variegatedness we see in the universe is but a transformation of the Supreme Lord's diverse energies.

The Māyāvādīs reject the theory of transformation of energy and subscribe to the theory of the transformation of Brahman itself. Thus they become fixed in their belief that Brahman is impersonal. The Supreme Lord has described the specific situations in which He manifests Himself in His impersonal form. There are many quotes from the scriptures substantiating this point. The Supreme Lord, by manifesting both His personal and impersonal features, has firmly established the principle that the Supreme Absolute Person is inconceivably and simultaneously one with and different from His energies. This philosophical conclusion—called *acintya-bhedābheda-tattva*—has been explained by Lord Kṛṣṇa Himself in the *Bhagavad-gītā* (7.12): *matta eveti tān viddhi na tv ahaṁ teṣu te mayi.* "I am, in one sense, everything, but I am independent. I am not under the modes of material nature, for they, on the contrary, are within Me."

The Supreme Energetic is the source of all energies. Yet although all energies emanate from Him, He remains aloof from the workings of these energies. From this we can conclude that the demigods' extraordinary potencies are an intrinsic part of the Supreme Lord's potencies, but that the demigods are separate from the Lord. Hence the boons granted by demigods benefit the recipient only temporarily. Lord Kṛṣṇa confirms this fact in the *Bhagavad-gītā* (7.23):

anta-vat tu phalaṁ teṣāṁ
tad bhavaty alpa-medhasām
devān deva-yajo yānti
mad-bhaktā yānti mām api

> Men of small intelligence worship the demigods, and their fruits are limited and temporary. Those who worship the demigods go to the planets of the demigods, but My devotees ultimately reach My supreme planet.

We have already discussed that if fruitive workers filled with fruitive desires approach the Supreme Lord instead of going to the demigods, then the benedictions they receive from the Supreme Lord will be everlasting. They will automatically rise a step higher in the ladder of *yoga*—from fruitive activities to *jñāna-yoga*, or the path of absolute knowledge. This means that instead of being elevated to the heavenly planets within this material world, they will attain liberation in the Vaikuṇṭha planets, the Lord's spiritual abode beyond this material world. The demigod worshippers go to the planets of the demigods, the heavenly planets, which are temporary. Once a person's accrued piety is used up, he has to come back to earth. On the other hand, once the devotees of the Supreme Lord attain to Vaikuṇṭha, His supreme abode in the spiritual sky, they never have to return to this world of mortality.

Lord Kṛṣṇa Incarnates in Kali Yuga in the Form of His Holy Name

Persons with meagre intelligence worship the demigods for fleeting fortunes. So one may ask, "If by worshipping the Supreme Lord one can have all his desires fulfilled, why doesn't everyone worship Him?" Devarṣi Nārada once answered a similar question posed by Yudhiṣṭhira Mahārāja. The sage said:

mahā-prasāde govinde
nāma-brahmaṇi vaiṣṇave
svalpa-puṇya-vatāṁ rājan
viśvāso naiva jāyate

O king, a person with little piety can never develop faith in Lord Govinda, His mercy, His holy name, or His pure devotees.

Lord Kṛṣṇa has corroborated this in the *Bhagavad-gītā* (7.28):

yeṣāṁ tv anta-gataṁ pāpaṁ
janānāṁ puṇya-karmaṇām
te dvandva-moha-nirmuktā
bhajante māṁ dṛḍha-vratāḥ

Persons who have acted piously in previous lives and in this life and whose sinful actions are completely eradicated are freed from the dualities of delusion, and they engage themselves in My service with determination.

Persons with a demoniac mentality are steeped in sin; hence their understanding of the importance of spiritual knowledge is nil. Those who have been able to eradicate their sins by living according to the dictates of their social and spiritual order, and who have thus acquired sufficient piety, are qualified to practice *karma-yoga.* Gradually they progress to *jñāna-yoga,* and finally, in meditation, they realize the transcendental and supreme position of the Lord. Such highly fortunate realized souls can see in their hearts the eternal, transcendental, two-handed form of the Supreme Lord, known as Śyāmasundara, playing His flute. The description of the Lord in *Śrī Brahma-saṁhitā* (5.30) reads:

veṇuṁ kvaṇantam aravinda-dalāyatākṣaṁ
barhāvataṁsam asitāmbuda-sundarāṅgam
kandarpa-koṭi-kamanīya-viśeṣa-śobhaṁ
govindam ādi-puruṣaṁ tam ahaṁ bhajāmi

> I worship Govinda, the primeval Lord, who is adept at playing on His flute, with blooming eyes like lotus petals, with head decked with peacock's feather, with the figure of beauty tinged with the hue of blue clouds, and His unique loveliness charming millions of cupids.

Those who are committing sins like illicit sex, fault-finding, and unjustified violence rarely attain spiritual knowledge or realization. Sinful activities deepen the dark gloom of ignorance, while pious activities bring the light of transcendental knowledge into one's life. This knowledge culminates in realization of Kṛṣṇa. However, simply performing pious activities does not make one eligible for God-realization. Only when a person performs pious activities and associates with saintly persons does spiritual knowledge dawn on his consciousness. Then, when he transcends the platform of duality—especially when he no longer takes part in the controversy over the Absolute Truth's monistic or dualistic existence—he sees Lord Kṛṣṇa in his enlightenment and worships Him with determination as one without a second, matchless and supreme. In the perfected stage of pious activities, the mode of goodness dominates the consciousness, dissipating the darkness of nescience and illusion, which are products of the mode of ignorance. As soon as the mode of passion is fully subdued, spiritual realization illuminates the sky of one's consciousness.

The point to consider at this juncture is, does anyone in the present age, Kali-yuga, have the means to properly perform such pious activities as fire sacrifices, giving in charity, penances, or austerities? It is universally accepted that the unfortunate people of Kali-yuga are absolutely unable to undertake such extravagances. For this reason Lord Caitanya, the most munificent incarnation of Godhead and the savior of the Kali-yuga, has declared the truth of the following *mantra* from the *Bṛhan-nāradīya Purāṇa*:

harer nāma harer nāma
harer nāmaiva kevalam
kalau nāsty eva nāsty eva
nāsty evagatir anyathā

> In this age of quarrel and hypocrisy, the only means of deliverance is chanting the holy name of the Lord, chanting the holy name of the Lord, chanting the holy name of the Lord. There is no other way. There is no other way. There is no other way.

In the Age of Kali the only process for attaining perfection is to hear, chant, and remember the holy name of the Supreme Lord. Numerous quotes from the scriptures substantiate this. All inauspiciousness is destroyed by chanting the all-auspicious name of Lord Kṛṣṇa. The *Śrīmad-Bhāgavatam* (12.12.55) confirms this:

avismṛtiḥ kṛṣṇa-padāravindayoḥ
kṣiṇoty abhadrāṇi ca śaṁ tanoti
sattvasya śuddhiṁ paramātma-bhaktiṁ
jñānaṁ ca vijñāna-virāga-yuktam

> Remembrance of Lord Kṛṣṇa's lotus feet destroys everything inauspicious and awards the greatest good fortune. It purifies the heart and bestows devotion for the Supreme Soul, along with knowledge enriched with realization and renunciation.

Therefore, to remain beyond the reach of delusion and duality, one has to always remember and meditate on the beatific form of Lord Kṛṣṇa, who has a darkish complexion and is playing His flute. One must also remember and chant the holy name of Kṛṣṇa, which is nondifferent from Him, its nature being eternal, perfect, pure, and independent. In the *Bhagavad-gītā* (8.6–7) Lord Kṛṣṇa explains the importance of remembering Him always:

yaṁ yaṁ vāpi smaran bhāvaṁ
tyajaty ante kalevaram
taṁ tam evaiti kaunteya
sadā tad-bhāva-bhāvitaḥ

tasmāt sarveṣu kāleṣu
mām anusmara yudhya ca
mayy arpita-mano-buddhir
mām evaiṣyasy asaṁśayaḥ

> Whatever state of being one remembers when he quits his body, O son of Kuntī, that state he will attain without fail. Therefore, Arjuna, you should always think of Me in the form of Kṛṣṇa and at the same time carry out your prescribed duty of fighting. With your activities dedicated to Me and your mind and intelligence fixed on Me, you will attain Me without doubt.

At the time of death, our state of consciousness determines our next birth. Death destroys the body made up of the five gross elements, but the subtle body, consisting of mind, intelligence, and false ego, remains. As the air carries the scent of the place it blows over, so the soul carries a person's subtle body of mind, intelligence, and false ego, along with his state of consciousness, on to his next birth, and his body is determined accordingly. When a breeze blows over a garden, it carries the fragrance of flowers with it, but when it blows over a rubbish heap, the breeze is filled with the stench. Similarly, the activities a person performs during his lifetime continuously influence his mentality, and at the time of death the cumulative effect of these activities determines his state of consciousness. Thus the subtle body formed during one's lifetime is carried over to one's next birth and manifests as the soul's next gross body. Naturally, therefore, the gross body reflects one's state of consciousness. As the popular saying goes, "The face is the index of the mind."

And the mind is the product of the activities of one's present and previous lives. In other words, one's mind, intelligence, and false ego, which are influenced by one's habits in this and previous births, form the matrix that determines the type of body and mentality one will have in the next life. Hence the connection between one's previous, present, and future lives is the mind, intelligence, and false ego.

The activities of the day evoke dreams at night and induce emotions appropriate to those activities. Similarly, the activities performed in one's lifetime flash across one's mind at the moment of death and determine one's next life. Therefore, if one's present activities are directed toward chanting, hearing, and remembering the Supreme Lord's transcendental name, along with descriptions of His beauty, qualities, pastimes, associates, and paraphernalia, then one's consciousness at the moment one leaves one's body will automatically be attracted to the Lord. Such a spiritual state of consciousness at the moment of death ensures the soul's entry into the Supreme Lord's eternal abode in his very next birth. To awaken this spiritual consciousness is man's prime goal in life. We therefore find that Lord Kṛṣṇa, out of compassion for the conditioned souls, instructs Arjuna to fight and at the same time remember Him. This is called *karma-yoga.* Therefore devotees always remember Him in all their activities—in their endeavors for food and safety and even in the middle of the battlefield while fighting a war. Life being like a battlefield, in which one may die at any time, the devotees remember Him at every moment, and He willingly becomes the charioteer of their chariotlike bodies. The activities of their bodies, minds, and words are thus prompted by the Supreme Lord's will, and at the end, when they leave their gross and subtle bodies, they go directly to the spiritual sky.

The prime symptom of pure devotional service is constant chanting, hearing, and remembrance of the holy name. Mixed devotional service, as we have previously discussed, is devotional service adulterated by *karma* (fruitive desire) and *jñāna* (attachment to knowledge). Such devotional service is often impeded by the particular situation or association a person finds himself in. But there is never any impediment to pure devotional service. Perfect realization of the Supreme Lord does not occur until one is firmly situated in unalloyed devotional service. Lord Kṛṣṇa confirms this in the *Bhagavad-gītā* (18.55): *bhaktyā mām abhijānāti yāvān yaś cāsmi tattvataḥ.* "One can understand Me as I am, as the Supreme Personality of Godhead, only by pure devotional service." And in verse 8.14 the Lord mentions the primary characteristic of this pure devotional service:

ananya-cetāḥ satataṁ
yo māṁ smarati nityaśaḥ
tasyāhaṁ sulabhaḥ pārtha
nitya-yuktasya yoginaḥ

For one who always remembers Me without deviation, I am easy to obtain, O son of Pṛthā, because of his constant engagement in devotional service.

Undeviating concentration on the Supreme Lord is the first sign of pure devotion. In other words, a pure devotee is one who wards off all desires and thoughts not related to unflinching devotional service to the Supreme Lord. Many spiritual stalwarts have commented upon pure devotional service. For example, Śrīla Rūpa Gosvāmī, the foremost of the great spiritual preceptors in the time of Śrī Caitanya Mahāprabhu, wrote in his *Bhakti-rasāmṛta-sindhu* (1.1.11):

anyābhilāṣitā-śūnyaṁ
jñāna-karmādy-anāvṛtam
ānukūlyena kṛṣṇānu-
śīlanaṁ bhaktir uttamā

One should render transcendental loving service to the Supreme Lord Kṛṣṇa favorably and without desire for material profit or gain through fruitive activities or philosophical speculation. That is called pure devotional service.

People propitiate demigods to satisfy their material desires. Those neophyte devotees of Kṛṣṇa who try to appease demigods like the sun-god in order to escape ill health do so because they succumb to serious doubts about Lord Kṛṣṇa's supreme divinity. In analyzing the word *anyābhilāṣa* ("desires other than those directed toward serving Lord Kṛṣṇa"), we find that one fosters this type of perverted intelligence when one thinks that the sun-god, who is merely a manifestation of the Supreme Lord's potency, can protect one from ill health but that the Supreme Lord, Kṛṣṇa, cannot. Once these mind-clouding doubts disperse, one enters the doors of pure devotional service. *Karmīs* and *jñānīs* are also tainted by material desires—the desire to enjoy their senses and the desire for liberation, respectively. Pure devotional service is attained only when these material desires are dissipated and one renders unbroken, favorable devotional service to Lord Kṛṣṇa. The great sage Nārada has said:

sarvopādhi-vinirmuktaṁ
tat-paratvena nirmalam
hṛṣīkeṇa hṛṣīkeśa-
sevanaṁ bhaktir ucyate

Bhakti, or devotional service, means engaging all our senses in the service of the Lord, the Supreme Personality of Godhead, the master of all the senses. When the spirit soul renders service unto Him, there are two side effects—one is freed from all material designations, and, simply by being employed in the service of the Lord, one's senses are purified. (*Nārada Pañcarātra*)

The various identities a person adopts in relation to his mind and body are all material designations. The pure soul is unencumbered by such mundane designations, for the only identity he has is that of a servant and inseparable part of the Supreme Lord. Thus, with the shedding of all false designations, one enters a state of transcendence, and when one is firmly situated in transcendence, one becomes pure. Serving the Supreme Lord, the master of all senses, with such purified senses is unalloyed devotional service.

In *Bhagavad-gītā* 8.14, the two words *ananya-cetāḥ* ("without deviation") and *nitya-yukta* ("regularly") are very significant. One cannot become undeviating in devotional practice without being fixed in undeviating faith. When a person regularly serves the Supreme Lord with this faith, he automatically loses all desires for fruitive activity, speculative knowledge, worship of the demigods, and ritualistic pious activities, and he becomes undeviating in his devotional service. The word *satatam* ("always") must be understood to imply that devotional service is independent of time, place, circumstance, adversity, and so on. Everyone, regardless of race, caste, sex, or other material designations, can give up mental speculation, fruitive actions, and *yoga* practice and take complete shelter of Lord Kṛṣṇa's lotus feet without deviation. The word *nitya* means "daily," "regularly," or "constantly." Those who meditate constantly on Lord Kṛṣṇa's lotus feet can easily attain Him. As Lord Brahmā states in the *Brahma-saṁhitā* (5.33):

advaitam acyutam anādim ananta-rūpam
ādyaṁ purāṇa-puruṣaṁ nava-yauvanaṁ ca
vedeṣu durlabham adurlabham ātma-bhaktau
govindam ādi-puruṣaṁ tam ahaṁ bhajāmi

> I worship Govinda, the primeval Lord, who is inaccessible to the *Vedas,* but obtainable by pure unalloyed devotion of the soul, who is without a second, who is not subject to decay, is without a beginning, whose form is endless, who is the beginning, and the eternal *puruṣa,* yet He is a person possessing the beauty of blooming youth.

In the process of executing religious duties, performing fruitive activities, cultivating empiric knowledge, and practicing mystic *yoga,* much endeavor, time, and money is spent. One has to accept the sinful reactions along with the pious results of such activities. The only way to nullify these results and reactions is to worship the Supreme Lord, Kṛṣṇa. Thus worshipping and serving Lord Kṛṣṇa are the only advantageous activities for the entire world.

The Supreme Lord is the embodiment of eternal bliss and is always engaged in transcendental pastimes. The only thing required to worship Him is undeviating devotion—ostentation will not please Him. Devotional service to Lord Kṛṣṇa does not produce hate or envy; only the agnostic reprobates are strongly opposed to the Lord's devotional service and His devotees. One derives the greatest bliss in devotional service. Indeed, when one finally obtains the Lord, it is like being drowned in an ocean of unlimited ecstasy. Only the devotees of Lord Kṛṣṇa can taste this ecstasy and be always joyful.

Under Illusion of Māyā Man Has Forgotten Lord Kṛṣṇa

The *karmīs, jñānīs,* and *yogīs,* as well as the common politicians and anyone else who is working hard to make a comfortable and peaceful situation in this material world, must clearly realize that the world is transitory and full of misery. However much one may toil to make a permanent settlement in this world, at the end everyone is forced to leave. As long as one stays here, one must come to grips with the reality of suffering. Since time immemorial the soul has been coming and going. The Lord's devotees, however, not only live happily in this world, but after they leave here they enter the eternal and ever-blissful abode of the Lord. As the Lord says in the *Bhagavad-gītā* (8.15):

mām upetya punar janma
duḥkhālayam aśāśvatam
nāpnuvanti mahātmānaḥ
saṁsiddhiṁ paramāṁ gatāḥ

After attaining Me, the great souls, who are *yogīs* in devotion, never return to this temporary world, which is full of miseries, because they have attained the highest perfection.

According to the above verse, the devotees attain the highest perfection—that is, they join the elevated corps of the Lord's eternal associates. The mystic *yogī's* eightfold mystic perfection is not the same as the devotee's *para-siddhi,* or "highest perfection." While mystic *yoga* brings perfections that are material and temporary, devotional service to the Supreme Lord brings absolute perfection, which is transcendental and eternal. The Supreme Lord incessantly manifests His ever-fresh transcendental pastimes within this unlimited material universe, which He has created. These pastimes, known as *bhauma-līlā,* have been going on since time immemorial. The sun remains in one place, yet somewhere on the earth people see it rising, while elsewhere people see it setting. This rising and setting has been going on since the dawn of creation. Similarly, although Lord Kṛṣṇa eternally resides in Goloka, His eternal abode, He manifests His transcendental pastimes at every moment in the countless universes of this cosmic creation. As it is a mistake to think the sun rises and sets, it is a gross misconception to think that Lord Kṛṣṇa was born on such-and-such a day and was slain by someone on such-and-such a day. The Lord's birth and activities are all transcendental and miraculous. And those who can comprehend this esoteric truth attain the highest perfection. As the Lord states in the *Bhagavad-gītā* (4.9):

janma karma ca me divyam
evaṁ yo vetti tattvataḥ
tyaktvā dehaṁ punar janma
naiti mām eti so 'rjuna

> One who knows the transcendental nature of My appearance and activities does not, upon leaving the body, take his birth again in this material world, but attains My eternal abode, O Arjuna.

When Lord Kṛṣṇa desires to manifest His earthly pastimes, He appears through His eternal parents, Śrīmatī Devakī and Śrī Vasudeva, and is later brought up by His foster parents, mother Yaśodā and Nanda Mahārāja. Saintly souls who perfect their devotional service by following in the footsteps of the Lord's eternal parents are elevated to the highest position as eternal associates of the Supreme Lord. Once having entered into the Lord's eternal transcendental pastimes, these great souls relish superexcellent devotional mellows in ecstatic love of Godhead.

In the innumerable universes, Lord Kṛṣṇa reveals His earthly pastimes with His intimate friend and eternal associate Arjuna. The Lord makes this clear in two *Bhagavad-gītā* verses (4.5–6):

bahūni me vyatītāni
janmāni tava cārjuna
tāny ahaṁ veda sarvāṇi
na tvaṁ vettha parantapa

ajo 'pi sann avyayātmā
bhūtānām īśvaro 'pi san
prakṛtiṁ svām adhiṣṭhāya
sambhavāmy ātma-māyayā

> Many, many births both you and I have passed. I can remember all of them, but you cannot, O subduer of the enemy! Although I am unborn and My transcendental body never deteriorates, and although I am the Lord of all living entities, I still appear in every millennium in My original transcendental form.

As for those unfortunate souls who do not strive for the supreme goal of entering the eternal pastimes of the Supreme Lord and instead become attracted to the mundane practices of *karma, jñāna,* and *yoga,* which ultimately elevate one to the heavenly planets—such souls must once again take birth in this material world. Although they may reach a high status in this cosmic system, they must come down as if on a ferris wheel. Kṛṣṇa describes this phenomenon in the *Bhagavad-gītā* (8.16):

ā-brahma-bhuvanāl lokāḥ
punar āvartino 'rjuna
mām upetya tu kaunteya
punar janma na vidyate

> From the highest planet in the material world down to the lowest, all are places of misery wherein repeated birth and death take place. But one who attains to My abode, O son of Kuntī, never takes birth again.

The higher planetary systems in this material world are Bhūrloka, Bhuvarloka, Svargaloka, Maharloka, Janaloka, Tapoloka, and up to Satyaloka, or Brahmaloka. Whichever of these planets one rises to in his next life, one must finally return to earth. What to speak of the next life, even in *this* life the high position one attains after considerable hard work—such as king, emperor, minister, governor, or president—is lost after some time, and one is thrown back to a mean and humble status. Only leaders who have experienced this kind of humiliation can know the trepidation that accompanies it. But if at any stage of life the grossly foolish miscreants described in the *Gītā* decide to render devotional service to Lord Kṛṣṇa, they can escape the ferris wheel of *karma.* On this wheel, sometimes one goes to heaven and sometimes to hell, sometimes one is born a king and sometimes a slave, sometimes one becomes a *brāhmaṇa* and sometimes a *śūdra,* and so it goes on. But once a person enters the spiritual abode of the Supreme

Lord, he begins his eternal life in his original, constitutional position.

By the influence of *karma,* one who is attached to the material body and mind has to change bodies life after life. In this way the soul roams the fourteen planetary systems within this material universe, sometimes going up and sometimes coming down. These planets are transitory—merely theatrical stages upon which the soul enacts his mundane existence. But when the living entity is elevated to spiritual perfection and is situated in his pure, eternal identity, devoid of all mundane designations, he attains the natural habitat of the spirit soul, the supramundane realm transcending this material creation and the intermediary zone of the unmanifested Brahman effulgence.

The material body, made up of material ingredients such as earth, water, fire, and air, is mortal. Similarly, because this material universe is an amalgam of earth, water, fire, air, etc., it is also transitory. But the spirit soul (which, incidently, has never been duplicated in the laboratory despite repeated efforts) is imperishable, as is its natural, eternal home—the kingdom of God. The process that takes the eternal soul to his eternal home is called *sanātana-dharma* or the "eternal religion."

Empirical, atheistic philosophers like Kapila spent innumerable tedious hours researching the material phenomena of this cosmic creation. Yet it remained beyond the grasp of their limited intelligence to understand that there exists a realm transcendental and far superior to this manifested material world. Finally, when their probing minds failed to sight land in an ocean of speculation, they concluded that the absolute truth is unmanifest.

Compared to other species, human beings are certainly endowed with good intelligence, yet unless they are devotees of the Lord, all their thinking is limited within mundane boundaries. Therefore it is impossible for the mundane mind to approach the transcendence. But instead of surrendering to the Supreme Lord or His representative, the empirical philosophers try to explain away as "unmanifest" that which is beyond their mundane minds. This is known as the logic of the frog in the well.

No matter how big a thinker a tiny living entity may be, all his activities are limited by mundane boundaries, just as a frog in the well can never comprehend that such a thing as an ocean exists outside his little domain. He refuses to acknowledge that a mass of water infinitely bigger than his tiny puddle can at all be possible. Similarly, we are trapped in the dark well of our body and mind. And although we may try hard through *yoga* or empirical speculation to overcome our limitations, no matter how erudite we are it is impossible to reach beyond the limitations of our self-made well.

So, who can bring us news of the great ocean? Is there any record of how long we have been struggling in the water to stay afloat in the well of this material world, sometimes going up to the higher planets, sometimes coming down? Only the Supreme Lord Himself or His empowered representative can possibly free us from confinement in this dark well. Under their guidance we can come to know of the limitless ocean of the spiritual sky. This process—hearing from higher authorities—is called the deductive, or descending, process of knowledge. It is the only authorized way to learn transcendental knowledge. By this method alone is eternal truth transmitted.

And what can we learn by this process? Lord Kṛṣṇa describes the spiritual and material worlds as follows in the *Bhagavad-gītā* (8.17–20):

> By human calculation, a thousand ages taken together form the duration of Brahmā's one day. And such also is the duration of his night. At the beginning of Brahmā's day, all living entities become manifest from the unmanifest state, and thereafter, when the night falls, they are merged into the unmanifest again. Again and again, when Brahmā's day arrives, all living entities come into being, and with the arrival of Brahmā's night they are helplessly annihilated. Yet there is another unmanifest nature, which is eternal and is transcendental to this manifested and unmanifested matter. It is supreme and is never annihilated. When all in this world is annihilated, that part remains as it is.

People become awestruck when they learn that the life span on Brahmaloka is many millions of years. One has to undergo severe austerities and renunciation, accepting the *sannyāsa* order of life, in order to reach Brahmaloka. However, we must consider one essential fact: even Lord Brahmā, the presiding deity of that planet, is not immortal. Those who have researched the Vedic scriptures in depth can calculate the lifetime of Brahmā. Human beings count 365 days in their year, and the cycle of four *yugas* comprises approximately 4,320,000 such years. A thousand cycles of four *yugas* make up one day (twelve hours) of Lord Brahmā's life. In this way his month and year can be calculated, and Brahmā lives for a hundred years of his time. But despite this vast life span—311 trillion 40 billion human years—Lord Brahmā is a mortal being, and this universe created by him is also perishable. Thus it is not strange that human beings, who are also his creation, should perish. As human beings seem immortal to a tiny insect, so Lord Brahmā and the demigods seem immortal to us. In fact, however, no material body of any form is ever eternal.

At the end of Lord Brahmā's day, when night approaches, a partial dissolution inundates the universe up to Svargaloka, the abode of the demigods. All the living entities of this world are created at the dawn of Lord Brahmā's day and annihilated at dusk, and this creation and annihilation go on in a continuous cycle.

The Supreme Lord Always Resides in the Eternal Vaikuṇṭha Planets

This material creation is manifested and subsequently destroyed during Lord Brahmā's day and night. But beyond this material world is an eternal existence—the spiritual sky—which is untouched by creation and annihilation. That spiritual abode is known as the Vaikuṇṭha planets. Even when this material creation is destroyed, the Vaikuṇṭha planets remain unscathed and intact. Once anyone enters these planets, he never again suffers the repetition of birth and death, which is inevitable for earthly beings. While the material world is covered and pervaded by the material sky, the spiritual planets are suspended in the spiritual sky, known as *paravyoma.* All the planetary systems within the *paravyoma* are transcendental abodes where the Supreme Lord performs His pastimes eternally.

Earlier we discussed that the Supreme Lord possesses two main energies, the material energy and the spiritual energy. The Vaikuṇṭha planets are a product of the spiritual energy of the Lord. The living entities belong to this spiritual energy, but because they can reside in either the spiritual world or the material world, even though they are originally spiritual they are designated as *taṭastha-śakti*, or "marginal potency."

The Vaikuṇṭha planets are a manifestation of the Lord's internal potency, while the material world is a manifestation of His external potency. Since the Supreme Lord is the master of all energies, it is an irrefutable fact that He is in full control of both the spiritual and material worlds. The perfect analogy is an earthen pot: what is needed to manufacture an earthen pot are clay, a potter's wheel, and a potter. The clay is the material, or ingredient cause of the pot, the wheel is the instrumental or efficient cause, and the potter is the prime cause. Similarly, while the material energy is both the ingredient and efficient cause of this cosmic creation, the Supreme Lord, Kṛṣṇa, is the prime cause. Like a shadow, the material energy works strictly in accordance with the Supreme Lord's dictates. As Lord Kṛṣṇa explains in the *Bhagavad-gītā* (9.10):

> *mayādhyakṣeṇa prakṛtiḥ*
> *sūyate sa-carācaram*
> *hetunānena kaunteya*
> *jagad viparivartate*

> This material nature, which is one of My energies, is working under My direction, O son of Kuntī, producing all moving and nonmoving beings. Under its rule this manifestation is created and annihilated again and again.

The sad fact is that although Kṛṣṇa reveals the truth about Himself throughout the *Bhagavad-gītā* and other Vedic literatures, the luckless populace cannot regard Him as the Supreme Lord. In particular, the impersonalistic philosophers, who make tall claims of being bastions of religiosity, reduce the Supreme Lord to the level of a mediocre mortal and thereby accrue heavy sins. Such atheistic offenders can never approach the subject of God on their own merit. The Supreme Lord and His surrendered servitors have in various ways clarified and transmitted the knowledge of the Supreme Absolute, but those who offend the Supreme Lord and His devotees can never comprehend such topics. As Śrī Prahlāda Mahārāja says in the *Śrīmad-Bhāgavatam* (7.5.30–31):

matir na kṛṣṇe parataḥ svato vā
mitho 'bhipadyeta gṛha-vratānām
adānta-gobhir viśatāṁ tamisraṁ
punaḥ punaś carvita-carvaṇānām

na te viduḥ svārtha-gatiṁ hi viṣṇuṁ
durāśayā ye bahir-artha-māninaḥ
andhā yathāndhair upanīyamānās
te 'pīśa-tantryām uru-dāmni baddhāḥ

Because of their uncontrolled senses, persons too addicted to materialistic life make progress toward hellish conditions and repeatedly chew that which has already been chewed. Their inclinations toward Kṛṣṇa are never aroused, either by the instructions of others, by their own efforts, or by a combination of both. Persons who are strongly entrapped by the consciousness of enjoying material life, and who have therefore accepted as their leader or *guru* a similar blind man attached to external sense objects, cannot understand that the goal of life is to return home, back to Godhead, and engage in the service of Lord Viṣṇu. As blind men guided by another blind man miss the right path and fall into a ditch, materially attached men led by another materially attached man are bound by the ropes of fruitive labor, which are made of very strong cords, and they continue again and again in materialistic life, suffering the threefold miseries.

Lord Kṛṣṇa also describes this kind of person in the *Bhagavad-gītā* (9.11):

avajānanti māṁ mūḍhā
mānuṣīṁ tanum āśritam
paraṁ bhāvam ajānanto
mama bhūta-maheśvaram

Fools deride Me when I descend in the human form. They do not know My transcendental nature as the Supreme Lord of all that be.

Puny human beings can manufacture only insignificant items like pots, pans, and factories. Therefore, when a personality who was born not so long ago in Mathurā and who looks like a human being is introduced as the supreme controller of the entire cosmic manifestation, the Lord of all lords and possessor of all absolute qualities, then, no matter how clearly one explains these truths, ordinary people cannot absorb them, due to their tiny dog's-bent-tail intelligence. Thus they embrace monistic, impersonal philosophy. Denying that Lord Kṛṣṇa alone is God, they insist that they are also "Gods." In this manner they embrace grossly foolish ideas about themselves and God and try to compete with Him, completely disregarding all etiquette and sound philosophical conclusions.

Spiritualists from the West often conclude that such atheistic people are possessed by Satan. In bygone ages many such satanic persons—Rāvaṇa, Hiraṇyakaśipu, Jarāsandha, Kaṁsa—challenged the Supreme Lord's authority. In modern times they have steadily multiplied. These demons have dismissed even Lord Caitanya Mahāprabhu, insulting Him with derogatory name-calling as "son of aunt Śacī."

The point to consider is that no one can really compete with God. The Supreme Lord is unparalleled, second to none. As it is said in the *Caitanya-caritāmṛta, ekale īśvara kṛṣṇa, āra saba bhṛtya:* "Lord Kṛṣṇa alone is the Supreme Godhead, and all others are His servants." Only those who go through life being kicked about by fate, slaving hard to fill their bellies and maintain a roof overhead, can harbor so preposterous a wish as to compete with the omnipotent Supreme Controller. It is ludicrous. They dare harbor such desires because they are totally ignorant of the supreme, transcendental position of the Lord. Yet the Supreme Lord is so compassionate that by various tricks He tries to teach even these fools the facts of His transcendental and supreme position. And the Lord's confidential servitors, accepting many hazards and pains, also try every possible means to exorcise Satan from these people, who are possessed by the demon of atheism.

Then there are those so-called scholars who claim that they alone know the scriptures and that all others are illiterate fools. Such "scholars" say that research of the holy texts clearly reveals that Kāraṇodakaśāyī Viṣṇu is the cause of this material creation and that Lord Kṛṣṇa, the son of Vasudeva and Devakī, is at best Viṣṇu's partial expansion. Thus we see that even intelligent men are sometimes bewildered by the illusory potency, *māyā,* and subscribe to demoniac ideas. How is it possible for such bewildered souls to accept that Lord Kṛṣṇa is the Supreme Personality of Godhead, the cause of all causes?

If we consult the *śruti* and *smṛti* scriptures on this topic, we will find many references proving that Lord Govinda, Kṛṣṇa, is the origin of Kāraṇodakaśāyī Viṣṇu, and not vice-versa. For example, the *Brahma-saṁhitā* (5.47) states:

yaḥ kāraṇārṇava-jale bhajati sma yoga-
nidrām ananta-jagad-aṇḍa-sa-roma-kūpaḥ
ādhāra-śaktim avalambya parāṁ sva-mūrtiṁ
govindam ādi-puruṣaṁ tam ahaṁ bhajāmi

I adore the primeval Lord Govinda who assuming His own great subjective form, who bears the name Śeṣa, replete with the all-accommodating potency, and reposing in the Causal Ocean with the infinity of the worlds in the pores of His hair, enjoys creative sleep [*yoganidrā*].

The Bible says, "God created man after His own image." According to this statement, man possesses two hands because he has a form similar to God's. But this does not mean that God is a human being because He has two hands. It is a heinous offense to try to diminish the position of Lord Kṛṣṇa because He appeared in a human form. The truth about His divine potency and supreme position should be learned from the self-realized spiritual master, the saintly souls, and the revealed scriptures.

Demonic persons fail to understand the real purpose of human life. Instead, they are always quick to try to diminish the supreme position of Lord Kṛṣṇa. Such atheists may have very high ambitions and may perform great, noble deeds, but because their ambitions and deeds are cut off from a loving relationship to Lord Kṛṣṇa, the Supreme Godhead, they are all useless. The demon Rāvaṇa wanted to reach heaven by constructing a stairway, but he failed. And all atheists' ambitions are like that. A zero placed next to the number one gives ten, a second zero makes one hundred, and so on. As long as the number one is there, the value keeps rising as the zeroes increase. But without the number one, any number of zeroes are valueless. Similarly, if a person spends his whole life simply increasing the "zeroes" of material wealth, fame, and learning, without any relationship to the "one"—Lord Kṛṣṇa—then his whole life is valueless. As Lord Kṛṣṇa says in the *Bhagavad-gītā* (9.12):

moghāśā mogha-karmāṇo
mogha-jñānā vicetasaḥ
rākṣasīm āsurīṁ caiva
prakṛtiṁ mohinīṁ śritāḥ

Those who are thus bewildered are attracted by demoniac and atheistic views. In that deluded condition, their hopes for liberation, their fruitive activities, and their culture of knowledge are all defeated.

Although a person may call himself a devotee of Lord Kṛṣṇa, if he considers Kṛṣṇa a human being or thinks that He started off as a human being and then evolved into God (as is now in vogue, with so many "incarnations" mushrooming), then such a person is not a devotee but an imposter. One often comes across monists and pseudo-devotees posing as Lord Kṛṣṇa's devotees, but eventually they try to usurp Kṛṣṇa's position. They want to be Lord Kṛṣṇa themselves. Persons with such insidious desires are totally bewildered. If a fruitive worker thinks that Lord Kṛṣṇa is an ordinary mortal, he does not attain the goal of his fruitive work—elevation to the heavenly planets. And if an anthropomorphist happens to be a *jñānī,* an empirical philosopher, then he also fails to achieve the goal of his pursuit of knowledge—liberation from the material modes.

Following in the Footsteps of Self-Realized Saints

Atheists gradually develop a demoniac nature and live in the world like beggars chasing after name, fame, wealth, and so on. Constantly deluded by *māyā,* they live useless lives. On the other hand, those who are truly dedicated to serving the Supreme Lord are never attacked by such a demoniac mentality. These great souls do not carry the title "Mahātmā" as an appendage. Someone who follows the satanic path and always challenges the Supreme Lord may try to fool the people into thinking he is a *mahātmā*, but the characteristics of an actual *mahātmā* are found in the *Bhagavad-gītā* (9.13):

mahātmānas tu māṁ pārtha
daivīṁ prakṛtim āśritāḥ
bhajanty ananya-manaso
jñātvā bhūtādim avyayam

> O son of Pṛthā, those who are not deluded, the great souls, are under the protection of the divine nature. They are fully engaged in devotional service because they know Me as the Supreme Personality of Godhead, original and inexhaustible.

Real *mahātmās* do not distract their minds with sense gratification and material desires, but with single-minded resolve they engage in the devotional service of the Supreme Lord. Because they are under the protection of His divine energy, they understand that Lord Kṛṣṇa is the supreme cause of all causes. Such persons alone possess all saintly qualities. Lord Kṛṣṇa's devotees are exceptional personalities, for at all times they are embellished with extraordinary characteristics rarely attained even by the demigods. To usher in the age of peace in this world, the presence of such *mahātmās* is imperative.

Recently, at a medical convention held in New Delhi, our honorable prime minister made the following observation in his speech:

> We go in for public health, sanitation, and all kinds of preventive measures rather than wait for people to fall ill and then treat them. Why not apply that principle in the larger sphere and prevent social diseases that, left untreated, we will have to deal with later in a much more difficult form? So when wise men like you gather together, perhaps you might think of the ills and diseases of humanity as a whole that create so many conflicts and troubles and impede human progress.

Factually, whatever problems crop up in the world are caused by the mind. *Paṇḍitas* have researched the scriptures thoroughly and held many discussions on this topic. If we can follow the example set by the subjects of King Ambarīṣa, who under his guidance concentrated their minds on the lotus feet of Lord Kṛṣṇa, then the mind can be cured of all ills. Any other process will bring upon us the fate described by Prahlāda Mahārāja in the *Śrīmad-Bhāgavatam* (5.18.12): *harāv abhaktasya kuto mahad-guṇāḥ mano-rathenāsati dhāvato bahiḥ.*

> ... a person devoid of devotional service and engaged in material activities has no good qualities. Even if he is adept at the practice of mystic *yoga* or the honest endevor of maintaining his family and relatives, he must be driven by his own material speculations and must engage in the service of the Lord's external energy. How can there be any good qualities in such a man?

The only way to cure this mental disease is to wholeheartedly follow Lord Caitanya's instruction to chant the holy names of Kṛṣṇa. This will cleanse the heart of all impurities. Until this esoteric truth is propagated widely, the world will remain deprived of the panacea that cures all mental diseases. Our honorable prime minister should seriously considered this. If the number of Lord Kṛṣṇa's devotees even slightly increases, there will immediately be a resurgence of peace and prosperity in the world. For man to rise to the glorious heights of a demigod, he needs only to revive his latent Kṛṣṇa consciousness. Thus Kṛṣṇa consciousness is the greatest boon to humanity.

The *mahātmās* possess other wonderful qualities, some of which Lord Kṛṣṇa describes in the *Bhagavad-gītā* (9.14):

satataṁ kīrtayanto māṁ
yatantaś ca dṛḍha-vratāḥ
namasyantaś ca māṁ bhaktyā
nitya-yuktā upāsate

> Always chanting My glories, endeavoring with great determination, bowing down before Me, these great souls perpetually worship Me with devotion.

This text gives some hints of how to become a devotee of Lord Kṛṣṇa. The word *satatam* ("always") has been used to indicate that the process of purifying one's consciousness does not depend on fruitive activity, empiric knowledge, *yoga,* or on time, place, or circumstance.

A living entity becomes free from all suffering as soon as he admits that he is an eternal servant of Lord Kṛṣṇa. Such a servant of the Lord need not perform fruitive activity or cultivate empiric knowledge, nor does he have to undergo any other process of purification. The only essential factor is his intense greed for devotional service to the Lord.

An extreme longing for Lord Kṛṣṇa is the only means for attaining Him. Thus intense, unflinching devotional service is another symptom of a *mahātmā*. These *mahātmās* execute all nine limbs of devotional service, beginning with hearing, chanting, and remembering the name, form, qualities, pastimes, and paraphernalia of Lord Kṛṣṇa. Such devotional service is transcendental to any mundane consideration of time, place, or circumstance. *Mahātmās* are always eager to render loving devotional service to the Lord. They tirelessly dedicate their lives, energy, words, intelligence, body, society—everything—in the service of the Lord.

The great endeavor the *mahātmā* undertakes to execute devotional service is more intense than the ordinary man's voluntary acceptance of excessive pains and troubles to maintain his family and home. The struggle for maintaining family and relatives is illusion, or *māyā*. Hence it is truly distressing. By contrast, the difficulties one accepts in serving the Supreme Lord are transcendental, and therefore they are a source of sublime bliss. Moreover, a person who serves the Supreme Lord automatically serves his family. But the opposite is not true: serving the family is not equivalent to serving the Lord. All *mahātmās* agree on this point. Not only does the person who serves the Supreme Lord serve his relatives, but he also serves the entire world of moving and nonmoving living beings. Thus service to Lord Kṛṣṇa is the prime cause of world peace and harmony.

The *mahātmās* are always ready to render such service to the Lord with great determination. In this regard His Divine Grace Śrīla Bhaktisiddhānta Sarasvatī Ṭhākura once made this comment in a lecture:

> The neophyte Vaiṣṇava devotees' ringing the bell even once during worship of the Deity of the Supreme Lord is a million times more valuable, spiritually and otherwise, than the charitable fruitive workers building many hospitals, feeding thousands of the poor, or building homes, or even

the empirical philosophers' Vedic studies, meditation, austerities, and penances.

The *mahātmās* have shown the perfect path of charity: devotional service to the Lord. If anyone ignores this path and instead builds hospitals, his effort to help humanity is a mere pretense. Humanity can never reap any permanent advantage from such activities. Indeed, the number of patients only increases along with the number of hospitals. And as for feeding the poor, this will never eradicate poverty, but encourage it. Frankly speaking, we are not against opening hospitals or feeding the poor, or any other such humanitarian service. But what we have learned from our beloved spiritual master is that when devotional service to the Lord is neglected, every other activity is illusory and futile. Without genuine devotional service, even opening hospitals and feeding the poor in the name of Lord Kṛṣṇa is futile. Spiritual groups that do not strictly follow in Lord Caitanya's line cannot comprehend this because they do not wish to abide by the instructions of the *mahātmās*. They do not follow Lord Caitanya's injunction to be "more humble than a blade of grass." If they were that humble, they would give up their pride in being the doer of good deeds, the wisest person, the most devoted, and so on.

Those who strive to emulate the *mahātmās* never fall prey to passivity and regression. Their eagerness and determination to serve the Lord steadily increase. Such followers observe spiritual occasions like Janmāṣṭamī* and Ekādaśī§ for the pleasure of the Lord, in the way that the previous *ācāryas* and *mahātmās* have recommended. This is devotional service proper. Because the *mahātmās* are more humble than a blade of grass, they worship Lord Kṛṣṇa and everything in relation to Him. Atheists, however, exhibit a different mentality altogether: they want to flaunt their abilities and charitable disposition. They may pretend to serve Lord Kṛṣṇa, but their aim is "to sit on the Lord's head" once they attain perfection. In other words, they want to usurp His position. Therefore they do not

---

* Janmāṣṭamī is the appearance festival of Lord Kṛṣṇa.

§ Ekādaśī—literally the eleventh day. In the lunar month it is the eleventh day of the waxing and waning moon. Vaiṣṇavas abstain from grains on this day.

really serve Lord Kṛṣṇa, nor is He their real object of worship. The *mahātmās* never associate with these demoniac people. They are fixed in their resolve to serve the Lord, and thus they always remain connected to Him through devotional service.

The Supreme Lord: Lover of His Devotees

Members of the so-called educated class ask, "If one is busy all the time rendering devotional service to Lord Kṛṣṇa, how is one to maintain himself and his family?" The so-called educated men think only a fool would be blind to his immediate physical needs and uselessly waste his time in devotional service so he could rise to the platform of a *mahātmā*. In fact, they think that a real *mahātmā* is he who strives to improve his material facilities from good to better. They say that it is because of the economists' poor planning that the world is facing a major crisis in food production. Both the economists and their critics should turn to the *Bhagavad-gītā* (9.22) and hear what Lord Kṛṣṇa has to say on this subject:

ananyāś cintayanto māṁ
ye janāḥ paryupāsate
teṣāṁ nityābhiyuktānāṁ
yoga-kṣemaṁ vahāmy aham

> But those who always worship Me with exclusive devotion, meditating on My transcendental form—to them I carry what they lack, and I preserve what they have.

It is relevant to mention here how in the Western world one atheistic government tried to induce the innocent citizens to embrace atheistic views. The government sent their propagandists to proselytize the people in the villages. They asked the innocent villagers, "Why do you all go to church? What do you pray to God for?" The villagers simply answered, "God gives us food." The atheists then led the villagers to the church and asked them to pray to God for food. The villagers, of simple faith, began to pray to God. At the end of their prayers, the officials asked them if they had received food or not. Bewildered, the people shook their heads. The atheists then asked the villagers to pray to them for food, which they did. Immediately, with a look of triumph, the atheists brought out baskets of bread. The villagers became happy and thought that the government representatives were more responsive and productive than God.

Alas! If only a devotee of the Lord had been present there, the villagers' devotion would not have been molested. The neophyte devotees' tender devotion is always susceptible to damage. But bread, after all, *does* come from God, and not from the atheists. If those villagers had been more conversant with the scriptures, the atheists would never have been successful in their evil plan. The simple villagers were illiterate, and hence they had no idea that the Supreme Lord alone can give them food. If the earth did not produce grain, then the atheists, despite their advanced material science, could never make bread or other foods.

Many may claim that in the modern age material scientists have helped increase agricultural yield. But we fearlessly proclaim that it is precisely such atheistic views that have brought the world to the present acute food crisis. If we are not careful, the day will soon come when fruits will be reduced to just skin and seed, cows' udders will dry up, and paddy fields will grow only grass. The scriptures predict that these things will come to pass in the Kali-yuga.

In reality, the Supreme Lord is always protecting us. The inmates of a prison are being punished by the government, yet the same government feeds them and looks after them. Similarly, sinful, atheistic people, though punished by the Lord's illusory energy (*māyā* personified as Durgā-devī), are still fed and cared-for by the Lord Himself. And if the Supreme Lord feeds and maintains even the worst sinners, reprobates, and helpless souls, then what to speak of those who are eternally surrendered to His lotus feet? He is like a king who takes proper care of his subjects, but who especially looks after the needs of his near and dear relatives. Therefore it is not true that a comfortable life can be enjoyed only by those who perform ordinary pious activities, but not by the devotees, who are free from fruitive action and empirical knowledge. The devotees do not always suffer, for the Supreme Lord personally takes care of them. The devotees are the Lord's relatives and family members. Just as ordinary people feel joy and satisfaction when they look after the needs and comforts of their family, the Lord also feels pleasure when he tends to the well-being of His devotees. Thus the Supreme Lord is known as Bhakta-vatsala, "the maintainer of the devotees." But He is never referred to as Karmī-vatsala, "the maintainer of fruitive workers," or Jñānī-vatsala, "the maintainer of empiric philosophers."

The devotees of the Lord fully depend on Him for everything, and so whatever they do to maintain themselves and their families is favorable to devotional surrender. Such pure souls are always fixed in devotion, never wasting a moment in activities outside the Lord's service. They are not assailed by materialistic desires, because everything they do is for the Lord's pleasure. Hence they alone are truly peaceful.

The devotee himself arranges for all expenditures incurred in executing devotional service. To an ordinary eye, earning and spending money in this way may look like sense enjoyment. But when the devotee is devoid of all material desires, the Supreme Lord feels great satisfaction in fulfilling all his needs. Though the obedient son may never express his wants to his father, the loving father spontaneously tries to make his son happy and derives joy from doing so. Therefore the Lord's devotees never lack anything, even materially, and at the end of this life, after leaving the body, they are situated in eternal bliss. This is the transcendental wealth a devotee inherits. Others—the fruitive workers, empiric philosophers, demigod-worshippers, and mystic *yogīs*—cannot attain eternal bliss.

Although Lord Kṛṣṇa is equally disposed toward all, He is nonetheless especially concerned about His devotees' well-being. However, one should not conclude that the Lord is nepotistic. As He declares in the *Bhagavad-gītā* (4.11), *ye yathā māṁ prapadyante tāṁs tathaiva bhajāmy aham:* "As all surrender unto Me, I reward them accordingly." Though the devotees are desireless and undemanding, the Lord always sees to their requirements. The devotees are ever-joyful upon receiving such grace from the Lord, and there is no offense or sin in accepting His benedictions.

Here one may pose a question: "Why do only the devotees of Lord Kṛṣṇa attain to His transcendental abode? After all, the demigods are simply energies of Lord Kṛṣṇa, and the scriptural conclusion is that the energy and the energetic are nondifferent. Therefore, why can't those who worship the demigods, Kṛṣṇa's energies, attain to the transcendental abode of the Lord?"

In reply, let us first refer to what Lord Kṛṣṇa Himself says on this subject in the *Bhagavad-gītā* (9.23):

ye 'py anya-devatā-bhaktā
yajante śraddhayānvitāḥ
te 'pi mām eva kaunteya
yajanty avidhi-pūrvakam

Those who are devotees of other gods and who worship them with faith actually worship only Me, O son of Kuntī, but they do so in a wrong way.

People worship demigods to fulfill temporary material desires, and the results they achieve from such worship are equally temporary and material. But if one worships the demigods with the knowledge that they are the Supreme Lord's energies, then this worship is accepted as authorized, and gradually such a worshipper becomes a devotee of Lord Kṛṣṇa, the Supreme Godhead. But if one worships the demigods with the idea that they are on an equal level with Lord Kṛṣṇa, then such worship is unauthorized, because Lord Kṛṣṇa is the Supreme Personality of Godhead, unequalled and unsurpassed. Therefore no demigod can exist independent of Lord Kṛṣṇa. Lord Kṛṣṇa is just like a king, and the demigods are like his ministers. The minister may sit on a throne and manage state affairs, but he is not independent: his powers come from the king.

By virtue of being the Supreme Absolute Truth, Lord Kṛṣṇa is eternally full of knowledge and bliss, beyond this material world. In the material world we often compare one person with another in terms of their position and power, and so we can rightly say that in comparison with human beings, the demigods are very highly placed. But there is no comparison between the Supreme Lord and the demigods, who are simply living entities belonging to the same category as humans. Living entities, or *jīvas,* belong to the Lord's marginal potency, which emanates from His transcendental, internal potency. Therefore anyone who considers the demigods to be independent Supreme Gods is speculating and is totally wrong, because as *jīvas* they are invested only with temporary powers and position.

If a highly placed servant in the king's court is mistakenly honored as the king, that does not mean the king becomes the servant and vice versa. Similarly, Lord Kṛṣṇa is the only Supreme Person, and everyone else is His servant. The *Brahma-saṁhitā* clearly explains the relationship between Lord Kṛṣṇa and the demigods. There are numerous proofs that beings who are in the category of *viṣṇu-tattva*—supreme personalities on the level of Lord Viṣṇu—are the highest absolute beings. The *Śrīmad-Bhāgavatam* confirms this truth by proclaiming that of all kinds of worship, worship of Lord Viṣṇu, or Kṛṣṇa, is the most elevated.

In India, the Hindus worship many gods—the sun-god, the moon-god, and so on. But the rituals of worship always begin with the worship of Lord Viṣṇu, and in the end everything is offered to Lord Viṣṇu's lotus feet because He is the Supreme Personality of Godhead. A *brāhmaṇa*, a member of the priestly class, must start every ritual of worship by invoking Lord Viṣṇu as the Supreme Being; otherwise all his worship and rituals will be rendered useless. This same Lord Viṣṇu is, in fact, a partial expansion of Lord Kṛṣṇa, who is the ultimate cause of all causes and the original Supreme Lord. Therefore Lord Kṛṣṇa is the receiver of all oblations and sacrifices and is the ultimate benefactor of all worship. As He says in the *Bhagavad-gītā* (9.24):

ahaṁ hi sarva-yajñānāṁ
bhoktā ca prabhur eva ca
na tu mām abhijānanti
tattvenātaś cyavanti te

> I am the only enjoyer and master of all sacrifices. Therefore, those who do not recognize My true transcendental nature fall down.

At the time of worshipping the demigods, the reason for placing Lord Nārāyaṇa, or Kṛṣṇa, on the throne as the supreme enjoyer of the ritual or sacrifice is that the various demigods also worship Him and offer Him sacrifices. Therefore He is the Lord and master of all sacrifices. The Supreme Lord fulfills the desires of the demigod worshippers through the agency of the demigods, but because the demigod worshippers are ignorant of the Supreme Lord's transcendental position, their unauthorized demigod-worship leads them to confusion and illusion.

Demigod worshippers often try to rationalize their worship of the demigods by thinking, "I am a devotee of this demigod, so he will certainly shower his grace upon me and fulfill all my heart's desires. Hence he is indeed the Supreme Lord." But the authorized scriptures condemn such demigod worshippers and their worship as unethical and philosophically wrong. Such worshippers cannot understand that Kṛṣṇa is the Supreme Lord, the ultimate source of all energies. The demigods are in fact manifestations of the Lord's energies, though to the illusioned demigod worshippers they appear to be the ultimate object of their worship and devotion. Those who persist in this misunderstanding will never attain the Absolute Truth. On the other hand, those who worship the demigods strictly according to scriptural injunctions quickly realize that their object of worship is subordinate to the Supreme Lord, Kṛṣṇa. With this realization, their illusion is destroyed and they take shelter of Lord Kṛṣṇa's lotus feet.

Offering a Leaf, a Flower, a Fruit, or a Little Water

One should always keep in mind that it is unnecessary to worship anyone but Lord Kṛṣṇa. Especially in this Age of Kali it is impossible to perform opulent sacrifices and worship. Of late, it has become a popular practice to publicly worship demigods with great pomp. Such worship is conducted whimsically, without following the scriptural rules. It is an excuse for people in the mode of ignorance to engage in base sense enjoyment and fiendish revelry. No ethics are maintained, no arrangements made for sumptuous public feasting, no authorized *mantras* chanted, no proper offerings made to the deities. These occasions are simply an excuse for wild singing, dancing, and misbehaving. All such worship is unauthorized.

Therefore intelligent people will follow the process of the congregational chanting of the holy names of God and in this way worship Lord Gaurāṅga, who is Kṛṣṇa Himself with a golden complexion. Worshipping Lord Kṛṣṇa is not an expensive affair, and worshipping Lord Caitanya is even easier and less expensive than worshipping Lord Kṛṣṇa. The reason is that the little effort taken to collect a leaf, a flower, a fruit, or some water for the worship of Lord Kṛṣṇa is not even required in Lord Caitanya's worship. But in any case, both the Supreme Lords can be worshipped easily in any country, in any condition, by anyone—be he foolish or wise, sinful or pious, highborn or low-born, rich or poor. Thus we find Lord Kṛṣṇa saying in the *Bhagavad-gītā* (9.26):

patraṁ puṣpaṁ phalaṁ toyaṁ
yo me bhaktyā prayacchati
tad ahaṁ bhakty-upahṛtam
aśnāmi prayatātmanaḥ

> If one offers Me with love and devotion a leaf, a flower, a fruit, or water, I will accept it.

Once the Supreme Lord is satisfied, the entire world is automatically satisfied, for by worshipping Him, one worships everyone else. Just as an entire tree—branches, leaves, and so on—receives water once the root of the tree is watered, so when Lord Kṛṣṇa is worshipped and satisfied, then all the demigods and human beings are worshipped and satisfied.

There is no mention anywhere that worship of Lord Kṛṣṇa has to be conducted with large expenditures and pomp. Nor is there any restriction of time, place, or circumstance. Just as everyone has the right to bathe in the Ganges, so everyone has the right to serve Lord Kṛṣṇa. Flowers, fruit, leaves, and water are available everywhere. Even a pauper can arrange to find these four things with very little effort and at no cost. Thus the process of worshipping Lord Kṛṣṇa is so simple that anyone from anywhere can participate.

Lord Kṛṣṇa is unborn, yet He can accept any form imaginable. And because He is the supreme father of every living being, anyone—whether a high-born *brāhmaṇa* or a social outcaste—can offer Him a flower, a fruit, a leaf, and water with love and devotion. Then Lord Kṛṣṇa, the cause of all causes, will accept this offering, and by such spiritual activity the worshipper becomes eligible to enter His eternal abode. Who could be more foolish than the person who rejects this easy and joyful process and, becoming captivated by the mirage of material existence and craving for temporary mundane facilities, takes shelter of demigods? Recent times have witnessed a concerted and noble effort on all fronts to bring about unity, peace, and harmony in the world, but these are possible only when people worship Lord Kṛṣṇa and render Him devotional service.

Such a proposal is neither preposterous nor comic. In fact, if someone is a sincere seeker of the Absolute Truth, then whatever his present situation may be, by regularly offering the Supreme Lord flowers, fruit, leaves, and water with love and devotion, he will readily experience that the Supreme Absolute Truth, Lord Kṛṣṇa, is gradually coming nearer to him. We humbly request all our readers to kindly try this excellent method of approaching Lord Kṛṣṇa's lotus feet. This method requires no monetary expenditure, physical exertion, philosophical knowledge, or noble birth.

The differences between a demigod worshipper and a devotee of Lord Kṛṣṇa are wide and numerous. In general, persons approach demigods only out of temporary material desires, whereas the devotees aim to re-establish their eternal loving relationship with the Supreme Lord. To that end the devotees offer Him worship, gifts, and anything they can collect, together with love and devotion, and the Lord accepts all these with relish. Such devotional offerings are free of any cravings for material benefit.

By contrast, the polytheists' offerings, which are laden with selfish motivations for material gain, are never accepted by the Supreme Lord, even if these offerings are opulent and elaborate. The demigod worshippers have no real love or devotion for the particular demigod they worship, yet Lord Kṛṣṇa is so merciful that He fulfills the material desires of the foolish demigod worshippers.

Lord Kṛṣṇa never accepts any offering bereft of love and devotion. A person who is not hungry cannot suddenly develop an appetite, even if he is given delectable food. Similarly, the Lord has no attraction for opulent offerings made without love and devotion. We have already discussed that unauthorized worship of the Supreme Lord stems from the absence of devotion and the presence of material desire. One who is full of devotion aims to satisfy the Supreme Lord's senses, while one who is full of material desire aims to gratify his own senses. Those who carry in their hearts the desire to gratify themselves but make a show of serving the Supreme Lord will never experience the joys of being a real devotee. The scriptures have aptly described them as mercenaries. Devotion's prime objective is the attainment of God. Therefore, one must offer the Lord everything in one's possession, including the results of *karma-yoga, jñāna-yoga, mystic yoga,* austerity, meditation, and so on. This perfect process of surrender will lead to the attainment of God. Thus Lord Kṛṣṇa openly proclaims in the *Bhagavad-gītā* (9.27):

yat karoṣi yad aśnāsi
yaj juhoṣi dadāsi yat
yat tapasyasi kaunteya
tat kuruṣva mad-arpaṇam

> Whatever you do, whatever you eat, whatever you offer or give away, and whatever austerities you perform—do that, O son of Kuntī, as an offering to Me.

If a person follows this injunction and with love offers the Lord everything he has—wife, house, family, intelligence, learning, business, religiosity, labor, food, water, whatever is required to maintain the body, and even lust, greed, and anger—then the Lord accepts these offerings and completely satisfies the offerer. And at the time of death the Lord takes such a surrendered soul to His Supreme abode.

The demigods are empowered to accept only certain types of offerings, whereas Lord Kṛṣṇa can accept the *karma-phala,* or fruitive results, of everyone. The Supreme Lord alone is powerful enough to accept conflicting fruitive results and moods of worship. This indicates Kṛṣṇa's supreme lordship and absolute position. It is unlikely that all of humanity will be able to understand the science of pure devotional service, yet everyone always has the ability to attain the Lord's lotus feet, even in the face of striking odds. Therefore the best course is to offer everything to the Supreme Lord.

All the points we have discussed regarding *niṣkāma-karma* are mentioned in detail in the scriptures. *Paṇḍitas* define *niṣkāma-karma* as "activities free from the desire for fruitive gain or empirical knowledge." Only such transcendental activities can be offered to Lord Kṛṣṇa. But all activities—whether verbal, physical, or mental—are transcendental if offered to the Lord with love and devotion. And He duly receives these offerings by His causeless mercy.

However, at this juncture we must avoid committing a mistake. Our present discussion does not include the materialistic caste *brāhmaṇas'* offering of oblations or fruitive work to Lord Nārāyaṇa. Because such offerings are not devoid of lust, there is no love or devotion in them. We have earlier established that the main criterion for a proper offering to the Lord is that it be done with love and devotion, for the satisfaction of His senses. Hence we must understand that only those things or services offered solely for the pleasure of the Supreme Lord are actually accepted by Him.

Exerting oneself to satisfy one's own hunger is *kāma-karma,* fruitive activity, but tireless effort to feed the Supreme Lord with delicacies is *niṣkāma-karma,* transcendental work aimed at pleasing Him. Pleasing the Lord should be the sole purpose of commerce and trade, and also of research, science, charity, austerity, and all other activities. Such a practice will inspire one to hear and chant transcendental topics related to Lord Kṛṣṇa, and this hearing and chanting are the foremost of the ninefold devotional activities. In Vedic times, all human activities were strongly affiliated with devotional service to the Supreme Lord. Today the same eternal principle applies: everything must be utilized in the Lord's service.

Lord Kṛṣṇa is the supreme enjoyer of all sacrifices. Thus He accepts the fruits of everyone's labor, and by so doing He crowns all His devotees' endeavors with glowing success. Such is the transcendental potency possessed by the omnipotent Lord. We must pay careful heed, however, never to allow the desire for self-aggrandizement or sense gratification to surreptitiously slip into our consciousness while we are performing devotional service. We should simply follow in the footsteps of the previous spiritual masters. In the Lord's presence, everyone is equal. Therefore, whoever serves the Lord with unwavering single-mindedness is listed among His close associates. They are truly "*hari-janas,*" Lord Hari's own men. To rubber-stamp as a *hari-jana* a person who does not possess the prerequisite—devotional service—is a farce and an onerous hindrance on the path of devotional surrender.

Lord Kṛṣṇa says in the *Bhagavad-gītā* (9.29):

samo 'haṁ sarva-bhūteṣu
na me dveṣyo 'sti na priyaḥ
ye bhajanti tu māṁ bhaktyā
mayi te teṣu cāpy aham

I envy no one, nor am I partial to anyone. I am equal to all. But whoever renders service unto Me in devotion is a friend, is in Me and I am also a friend to him.

One must not misunderstand the meaning of the word *samaḥ*, "equal." It does not mean that the Lord is impersonal and that He will bless any whimsical act, even unruly behavior. The Lord is absolutely personal, the reservoir of divine sentiments, the supreme performer of transcendental pastimes. And He is the well-wishing friend of all living beings. But friendship has different degrees of intimacy. Thus the Lord's equal disposition is not without varieties of personalism. In other words, the Lord reciprocates with us according to our intensity of love for Him. In the *Gītā* (4.11) He says, *ye yathā māṁ prapadyante tāṁs tathaiva bhajāmy aham*: "As all surrender unto Me, I reward them accordingly." He responds to all the different devotional mellows—servitorship, fraternity, parental affection, and conjugal love. Similarly, he ignores those who disrespect Him by regarding Him as an ordinary mortal. Conversely, He always shelters and protects those who accept Him as the Supreme Lord and serve Him with loving devotion, following in the footsteps of past saintly masters.

"Give Up all Kinds of Religion and Surrender unto Me"

The so-called progressive modern civilization has produced reprobate human beings, whose sins have been accumulating over many lifetimes. Yet if they surrender to Lord Kṛṣṇa, even they will have all their sins eradicated forever. The process of devotional service and remembrance of Lord Kṛṣṇa will gradually dissipate unwanted, base desires from within their hearts.

And those hearts, which previously sheltered immoral yearnings, will become fully cleansed and auspicious.

The sinful and the destitute can understand their mistakes and misfortune only by Lord Kṛṣṇa's mercy. Once they begin to repent for their sins and surrender to the Lord, they are saved; they become purified and start manifesting saintly characteristics. And if even after a person takes to the devotional process some vestige of immorality remains in his character, that also will soon be eradicated by the Lord's grace. The single-minded devotee who never offends the Supreme Lord or His devotees is to be considered a saintly soul. Even if it seems that such a saint is not yet rid of all sinful propensities, he will never be destroyed, as are the *yogīs* and *karmīs* in a similar situation. This the Supreme Lord Himself has declared.

The *Śrīmad-Bhāgavatam's* account of the deliverance of Ajāmila conclusively proves this fact. Once undeviating faith in devotional service to Lord Kṛṣṇa penetrates a person's heart, the process of purification is firmly underway, even though his external activities may show residues of sin. Lord Kṛṣṇa has boldly broadcast in the *Bhagavad-gītā* (9.31) His promise that His surrendered devotees can never be vanquished: *kaunteya pratijānīhi na me bhaktaḥ praṇaśyati*. That Lord Kṛṣṇa will always protect His devotees is proved in this verse, especially since the Lord, instead of declaring the promise Himself, asks the valiant prince Arjuna to do so on His behalf. The Lord may break His own promise, but because He is favorable to His devotees, He will always try to uphold their promises. By breaking His own promise and keeping Bhīṣmadeva's on the Battlefield of Kurukṣetra, the Lord has proved beyond a doubt that He favors His surrendered devotees.

A *brāhmaṇa* or someone of noble birth endowed with beauty, wealth, and learning may fallaciously conclude that elimination of degraded habits still visible in a devotee can occur only in the case of a *brāhmaṇa* like Ajāmila. Ajāmila was a *brāhmaṇa* by birth, but on account of sinful activities caused by bad reactions from his past life, he began performing abominable activities. At the end of his life, however, his remembrance of the Supreme Lord absolved him of all sins. But deliverance is possible for everyone, not just those of high birth. Even the lowest people, who are naturally given to base activities, can reach the spiritual abode of Lord Kṛṣṇa if they simply surrender at His lotus feet. As He says in the *Bhagavad-gītā* (9.32):

māṁ hi pārtha vyapāśritya
ye 'pi syuḥ pāpa-yonayaḥ
striyo vaiśyās tathā śūdrās
te 'pi yānti parāṁ gatim

> O son of Pṛthā, those who take shelter in Me, though they be of lower birth—women, *vaiśyas* [merchants], and *śūdras* [workers]—will attain the supreme destination.

When the lowest of human beings can attain the supreme destination by surrendering to Lord Kṛṣṇa, then what to speak of high-born *brāhmaṇas*? Those who follow the path of devotional service to the Supreme Lord are not hounded by caste and color discrimination. Monotheism—one religion and one creed—is possible only under the shelter of Lord Kṛṣṇa's lotus feet, and not in any other way.

The illusory potency, *māyā,* constantly terrorizes and shackles the people in the present Age of Quarrel, Kali-yuga. Due to forgetting their real identity as spirit souls, they bring disaster to the world. Under such a siege, modern-day thinkers and philosophers are desperately trying to bring purity and unity into society. They are conducting in-depth research into this problem. But Lord Kṛṣṇa long ago gave the solution to our modern problems in the *Bhagavad-gītā* (9.34):

man-manā bhava mad-bhakto
mad-yājī māṁ namaskuru
mām evaiṣyasi yuktvaivam
ātmānaṁ mat-parāyaṇaḥ

> Engage your mind always in thinking of Me, become My devotee, offer obeisances to Me and worship Me. Being completely absorbed in Me, surely you will come to Me.

O people of the world! Please try to translate the *Gītā's* message into action and channel your thoughts toward Lord Kṛṣṇa's lotus feet. Serve Him with your mind and body. If you dovetail all your energy in the Lord's service, then not only will you feel intense exhilaration in this lifetime, but you will be immersed in eternal bliss in the spiritual world, perpetually serving Him. The most munificent incarnation of Godhead, Lord Caitanya Mahāprabhu, recently advented in the Age of Kali to propagate this message. By the great fortune of all Bengalis, He appeared in Bengal and blessed the Bengali race. Thus Bengalis can preach His mission and instructions to the entire human race and deliver the people of the planet and themselves. The presentation of this knowledge in a systematic and scientific manner will bring about universal sublime peace. Yet the shocking fact is that thirteen unauthorized cults have mushroomed into prominence and are fast expanding their illegitimate fold with naive disciples. What one fails to comprehend is how the leaders of these cults, who have never accepted discipleship and tutelage from any bona fide spiritual master, can suddenly rise to the position of spiritual master themselves. The subject matter that needs to be promulgated among the people is not some cheap, sentimental concoction meant to deceive them; it is in fact a deeply profound and esoteric theology. The words of Lord Caitanya can never be disseminated by unscrupulous self-styled *"gurus"* who fake spiritual sentiments to impress the ignorant mass of people. All saintly persons beware!

Our general experience is that impersonalists, given as they are to speculation and sophistry, hesitate to accept Lord Kṛṣṇa as the Supreme Godhead. Thus they will always be frustrated in their endeavors to know the Supreme Absolute Truth by dint of their own intelligence. They cannot perceive this shortcoming in themselves, and even if it is pointed out to them by persons who know the science of Kṛṣṇa consciousness, they cannot grasp it. Such polluted consciousness is a result of not surrendering to Lord Kṛṣṇa. The Lord's name, form, qualities, pastimes, and paraphernalia are all transcendental and extraordinary; hence blunt material senses cannot perceive them. The sun becomes visible only by the help of sunlight; similarly, the Supreme Lord reveals Himself only to those engaged in His devotional service.

The facilities available to us in our material condition are many. One facility in the mode of goodness is intelligence, which gives us the ability to distinguish subtle elements and to discriminate between matter and spirit, and in this way to avoid coming under illusion. Also in the mode of goodness are tolerance, truthfulness, control of the senses, equanimity, and other such qualities. Added to the list are qualities in the mode of passion, such as strong desire, fearlessness, and unwavering determination, as well as qualities in the mode of ignorance, such as fear, madness, and distress over birth, death, old age, and disease. All these facilities are products of the Lord's external, material energy. Since *māyā* is under the Supreme Lord's control, all the above-mentioned qualities also emanate from Kṛṣṇa Himself. But Lord Kṛṣṇa is beyond the periphery of our sensual experience, and therefore simply cultivating the nobler qualities—those in the mode of goodness—is not sufficient spiritual practice to elevate us to the Lord's lotus feet. The only way to overcome *māyā* is to take complete shelter at the Lord's lotus feet. Kṛṣṇa states in the *Gītā* (7.14) that those who surrender to Him can easily cross beyond *māyā*. Once *māyā* is surmounted, one's endeavor is crowned with the realization that Lord Kṛṣṇa is the Supreme Personality of Godhead. As Lord Brahmā says in the *Brahma-saṁhitā* (5.1):

īśvaraḥ paramaḥ kṛṣṇaḥ
sac-cid-ānanda-vigrahaḥ
anādir ādir govindaḥ
sarva-kāraṇa-kāraṇam

> Kṛṣṇa who is known as Govinda is the Supreme Godhead. He has an eternal blissful spiritual body. He is the origin of all. He has no other origin and He is the prime cause of all causes.

Only when one is free from the influences of *māyā* can one perceive the transcendental opulence, power, fame, beauty, knowledge, and renunciation of the Supreme Lord. With this transcendental realization one can fathom the Supreme Lord's own words in the *Bhagavad-gītā* (10. 8–10):

> I am the source of all spiritual and material worlds. Everything emanates from Me. The wise who perfectly know this engage in My devotional service and worship Me with all their hearts. The thoughts of My pure devotees dwell in Me, their lives are fully devoted to My service, and they derive great satisfaction and bliss from always enlightening one another and conversing about Me. To those who are constantly devoted to serving Me with love, I give the understanding by which they can come to Me.

All Perfections Come from Bhakti-yoga

Whatever exists—manifest or unmanifest, material or spiritual—has one primary source: the Supreme Lord, Kṛṣṇa. He is the primeval, supreme controller, the cause of all causes, the Lord of all lords. As the Supersoul within the heart, He inspires all the activities of a transcendentally situated devotee. Those who possess true knowledge of the Absolute can render service to Lord Kṛṣṇa in the mood of a servitor, a friend, and so on. Their hearts are always absorbed in thoughts of Lord Kṛṣṇa, and they yearn to perceive and relish His eternal, transcendental pastimes.

By the grace of the Supreme Lord, these unalloyed devotees can unravel the mysteries of His intimate worship. Then, due to their love for the Lord, they find it difficult to maintain their lives without hearing and chanting the glories of the Lord's name, form, qualities, pastimes, associates, and paraphernalia. They seek the association of like-minded devotees, and with them they dive into the ocean of the nectar of devotion. Situated in their spiritual identity, they relish spiritual exchanges and hear, discuss, and remember the all-auspicious topics of Lord Kṛṣṇa's transcendental pastimes, thus practicing the ninefold devotional process.

They execute this ninefold devotional service in the stage of *sādhana,* or practice, and feel deep satisfaction in the perfected, or *siddha,* stage. They become saturated with the transcendental spiritual mellows of servitorship, friendship, and so on, from which they derive divine ecstasy. Lord Kṛṣṇa grants genuine transcendental understanding, *buddhi-yoga,* to those devotees who experience spiritual satisfaction and divine bliss through constant devotional service; gradually their specific devotional attitude increases to the point where they can relish pure love of God.

In the stage of *bhāva,* or spontaneous devotional service in ecstasy, there is a direct transcendental exchange of mellows between Lord Kṛṣṇa and His pure devotee. The Supreme Lord Himself gives His devotee *buddhi-yoga,* or spiritual intelligence, and the devotee, acting with that intelligence, serves the Lord until he gradually approaches the Lord's supreme abode. Such a devotee can never be affected by ignorance.

The impersonalists and empiric philosophers consider the unalloyed devotees of the Lord sentimental fools, and thus they deride them. This is a big offense. Such offenses cause the impersonalists and pseudo-devotees to slowly become demoniac. Having lost good sense and a stable mind, they gradually develop animosity toward the Supreme Lord and find all their life's endeavors reduced to suffering and futility. If one of these deluded demoniac impersonalists comes in contact with a pure devotee and by his mercy regains his lost insight, then he can begin to understand that the pure devotees he offended are exchanging spiritual mellows with Lord Kṛṣṇa and are thus forever free from ignorance and illusion. The impersonalists must understand that the Supreme Lord, acting from within as the Supersoul, removes all ignorance from the devotee's heart. As Lord Kṛṣṇa states in the *Bhagavad-gītā* (10.11):

teṣām evānukampārtham
aham ajñāna-jaṁ tamaḥ
nāśayāmy ātma-bhāva-stho
jñāna-dīpena bhāsvatā

To show them special mercy, I, dwelling in their hearts, destroy with the shining lamp of knowledge the darkness born of ignorance.

The dry speculative philosophers may kindly note one point: by using the word *teṣām,* Lord Kṛṣṇa openly declares that He is always merciful to His surrendered devotees. The reason that the Lord expands Himself as the Supersoul and enters everyone's heart is not to bless the empiric philosophers and *yogīs* but to bless the devotees from within. If the Supreme Lord Himself wishes to enlighten the devotees with spiritual knowledge and gradually draw them closer to Him, then what question is there of such devotees ever coming under the spell of nescience? Rather, it is out of nescience only that the empiric philosophers try to approach the Supreme Truth on the strength of their own intellect. We know that the Supreme Lord can dissipate the darkness of ignorance with the spiritual effulgence emanating from His body. Can the empiricists do the same? One can never lift the gloom of nescience by one's own efforts. Empiricists such as the atheist Kapila, unable to reach enlightenment by their own efforts, feel great relief in trying to explain away the Absolute Truth as unknowable and unmanifest. But great suffering befalls these dry speculators attached to the theory of the unmanifest Absolute, as Lord Kṛṣṇa confirms in the *Bhagavad-gītā* (12.5):

kleśo 'dhikataras teṣām
avyaktāsakta-cetasām
avyaktā hi gatir duḥkhaṁ
dehavadbhir avāpyate

> For those whose minds are attached to the unmanifested, impersonal feature of the Supreme, advancement is very troublesome. To make progress in that discipline is always difficult for those who are embodied.

The austerities a monist performs are painful both during the initial stage of practice (*sādhana*) and when he has supposedly reached perfection. The impersonalists suffer excruciating pains trying to establish the oneness of matter and spirit through speculative theories. Thinking that Brahman is impotent, through sophistry they try to equate the Lord's inferior, material energy with His superior, spiritual energy, thus reaping ridicule from truly learned circles. In attempting to prove that the Absolute Truth cannot be the Supreme Personality of Godhead with unlimited energies, they argue that this would mean immutable Brahman is actually mutable. Thus their logic loses all cohesion and they become a laughingstock. In trying to refute the established theory of *pariṇāma-vāda,* or the "transformation of energy," they accuse Śrīla Vyāsadeva of being mistaken when he says that the material universe and the living entities are all transformations of the Lord's energy and are therefore real, not false. Thus in their philosophical discussions the monists reject the main purport and essence of all Vedic scriptures and their corollaries and hang on to nonessential injunctions, such as *tat tvam asi,* "You are that." They like to deliberate on these subpoints, but when confronted with the arguments of a learned Vaiṣṇava, they turn and run from the battlefront.

Without understanding that the Supreme Lord is a transcendental personality, the monists make futile and grossly mundane attempts at restraining their senses, meditating on the Lord's impersonal aspect as the ultimate and original Absolute Truth. As it is impossible to dam a flooding river, so it is impossible to control the senses by meditating on the impersonal Brahman. As the great sage Sanat Kumāra says in the *Śrīmad-Bhāgavatam* (4.22.39):

yat-pāda-paṅkaja-palāśa-vilāsa-bhaktyā
karmāśayaṁ grathitam udgrathayanti santaḥ
tadvan na rikta-matayo yatayo 'pi ruddha-
sroto-gaṇās tam araṇaṁ bhaja vāsudevam

The devotees, who are always engaged in the service of the toes of the lotus feet of the Lord, can easily overcome hard-knotted desires for fruitive activities. Because this is very difficult, the nondevotees—the *jñānīs* and *yogīs*—although trying to stop the waves of sense gratification, cannot do so. Therefore you are advised to engage in the devotional service of Kṛṣṇa, the son of Vasudeva.

Lord Viṣṇu's impersonal aspect is known as Brahman. So when the *jīva* soul, a product of Lord Viṣṇu's superior, spiritual energy, attains *sāyujya-mukti,* or liberation by merging with Brahman, it is not at all surprising. The energetic principle always enjoys the prerogative of enfolding within itself His own energy, but that does not destroy the energy's eternal individuality. The impersonalists, desiring to merge with Brahman and knowing that it is feasible, still experience intense suffering in their effort to reach *brahmānanda,* "the bliss of Brahman." The Lord's devotees consider the pleasures of such liberation worse than hell. The impersonalists, in trying to destroy the illusion inherent in material forms, do away with even the eternal spiritual forms. That is indeed very foolish. Treating a patient to cure his disease is one thing, but ending the patient along with the disease is the work of an idiot. Thus we have this instruction from the great authority Brahmā in the *Śrīmad-Bhāgavatam* (10.14.4):

śreyaḥ-sṛtiṁ bhaktim udasya te vibho
kliśyanti ye kevala-bodha-labdhaye
teṣām asau kleśala eva śiṣyate
nānyad yathā sthūla-tuṣāvaghātinām

> My dear Lord, devotional service unto You is the best path for self-realization. If one gives up that path and engages in the cultivation of speculative knowledge, he will simply undergo a troublesome process and will not achieve his desired result. As a person who beats an empty husk of wheat cannot get grain, one who simply speculates cannot achieve self-realization. His only gain is trouble.

Instead of becoming an impersonalist and inviting misfortune and misery, the devotee surrenders to Lord Kṛṣṇa and never suffers in this world. When he leaves his present body, he transcends the material platform and becomes eligible to participate in the Lord's eternal pastimes. As the Supersoul, Lord Kṛṣṇa enlightens the devotee from within the heart and disperses the gloom of ignorance. The Lord gives the devotee the spiritual intelligence to attain Him. The ocean of nescience is very difficult to cross, but when the devotee attempts to cross it, the Lord Himself intervenes to help. Alone the devotee would surely drown, but with the Lord's help he easily crosses over. Thus taking shelter of the Lord is the surest way to surmount the ocean of material existence. As Lord Kṛṣṇa says in the *Bhagavad-gītā* (12.6–7):

ye tu sarvāṇi karmāṇi
mayi sannyasya mat-parāḥ
ananyenaiva yogena
māṁ dhyāyanta upāsate

teṣām ahaṁ samuddhartā
mṛtyu-saṁsāra-sāgarāt
bhavāmi na cirāt pārtha
mayy āveśita-cetasām

> But those who worship Me, giving up all their activities unto Me and being devoted to Me without deviation, engaged in devotional service and always meditating upon Me, having fixed their minds upon Me, O son of Pṛthā—for them I am the swift deliverer from the ocean of birth and death.

Those who surrender to Lord Kṛṣṇa, who repose their unflinching faith in the personal form of the Supreme Lord, offer Him their mental and physical activities, along with everything else. With unalloyed, single-minded devotion unencumbered by desires for empirical knowledge, fruitive activity, or severe austerities, they worship and meditate on the eternal, beautiful, two-handed form of Lord Kṛṣṇa playing a flute. Such pure devotees, their hearts saturated with love for Kṛṣṇa, quickly and easily transcend the cycle of material existence, for Lord Kṛṣṇa personally helps them. The merciful Lord promises to reciprocate with each one according to his degree of devotion.

The impersonalists are obsessed with the idea that the Supreme Being is impersonal and that the final goal is to merge into that Brahman existence. Naturally the Lord does not object. If a patient wants to end his disease by ending his life, then who will suffer but he? The more intelligent person will surely want to cure his disease without ending his life, and to that end he will strive to regain his original health. Similarly, the soul infected with the material disease should want to return to his pure, original state without annihilating his individual identity. Lord Kṛṣṇa saves such persons from the jaws of the demoniac conception of trying to become one with God. It is suicidal for the spirit soul to attempt to lose his inherent individuality. The happiness the impersonalist experiences by disentangling himself from the knots of material existence is automatically available to the Lord's devotee as a by-product of devotional service. As the *Nāradīya Purāṇa* says:

> One should not engage in fruitive activity or cultivate knowledge by mental speculation. One who is devoted to the Supreme Lord, Nārāyaṇa, can attain all the benefits derived from other processes, such as *yoga,* mental speculation, rituals, sacrifices, and charity. That is the specific benediction of devotional service.

And in the *Kṛṣṇa-karṇāmṛta* (107), Bilvamaṅgala Ṭhākura states:

bhaktis tvayi sthiratarā bhagavān yadi syād
daivena naḥ phalati divya-kiśora-mūrtiḥ
muktiḥ svayaṁ mukulitāñjali sevate 'smān
dharmārtha-kāma-gatayaḥ samaya-pratīkṣāḥ

O Lord! If our devotion to You is undeviating, then Your ever-youthful form will spontaneously manifest within our heart. At that time liberation personified will serve us like a maidservant, and religiosity, economic development, and sense gratification [the other three goals of the *Vedas*] will humbly await our bidding.

yā vai sādhana-sam pattiḥ
puruṣārtha-catuṣṭaye
tayā vinā tad āpnoti
naro nārāyaṇāśrayaḥ

Even without the usual requirements for achieving the perfection of life, a person will gain that perfection if he is simply a surrendered devotee of Nārāyaṇa. (*Nāradiya Purāṇa*)

<u>*Jñāna Katha*</u>

Topics of Spiritual Science

Extinguishing the Flames of Material Existence

koṭi-janme brahma-jñāne yei 'mukti' naya
ei kahe—"nāmābhāse sei 'mukti' haya"

After many millions upon millions of births, when one is complete in absolute knowledge, one still may not attain liberation, yet this man says that one may attain it simply by the awakening of a glimpse of the holy name.

(*Caitanya-caritāmṛta, Antya-līlā* 3.194)

Śrīla Raghunātha dāsa Gosvāmī's father and uncle—Hiraṇya Majumdara and Govardhana Majumdara, respectively—were big landowners of the ancient village of Cāndapura at Saptagrāma. One of their employees, a *brāhmaṇa* by birth named Gopāla Cakravartī, locked the great Vaiṣṇava saint Śrīla Haridāsa Ṭhākura in a debate on the scriptures. The *brāhmaṇa* was a sheer empiricist, and the Vaiṣṇava saint was an absolute authority on the chanting of the holy names of God, Kṛṣṇa. The *brāhmaṇa* asked Śrīla Haridāsa at what stage of realization liberation is attained. Citing many appropriate verses from the scriptures, Śrīla Haridāsa explained that just as fear of nocturnal creatures like thieves, ghosts, and hobgoblins evaporates at dawn's first light, so all sins and offenses are erased and liberation is attained in the clearing stage of chanting the holy name, called *nāma-ābhāsa,* which comes long before pure chanting. Only a liberated, highly evolved soul can utter the Lord's name purely and thus achieve the highest realization, untainted love of Godhead. The speculative philosopher *brāhmaṇa,* who was very much addicted to sophism, could not fathom the saint's instructions and so ended up offending him. The foolish *brāhmaṇa* tried to impose his own interpretations on the excellences of the holy name and concluded that Śrīla Haridāsa Ṭhākura was a mere sentimentalist. He insolently rebuked the saint in public and tried to ridicule his explanations and character.

Argumentative impersonalists fail to grasp that without first properly understanding the science of the Absolute Truth, one cannot possibly develop firm devotion to the Supreme Lord. Hence when a person is seen to be situated on the platform of pure devotional service, it is to be understood that his ignorance has been destroyed. We have discussed this point in some detail in the previous essay, "*The Science of Devotion.*" The empirical philosophers generally put forward the idea that human life is meant for achieving perfect knowledge. To them, knowledge means the ability to discern reality from illusion. By eradicating illusion and establishing that truth and reality are nondifferent from Brahman, they want to merge into the existence of Brahman. This, then, is their definition of perfect knowledge, which they aspire to attain birth after birth. They declare that the highest stage of knowledge is reached when the knower, the knowledge, and the object of knowledge become one entity, which then finally merges into Brahman, attaining liberation. Lord Caitanya has described this state of liberation as *bhava-mahādāvāgni-nirvāpanam,* "extinguishing the flames of material existence." He cited many verses from the revealed scriptures proving that a pure devotee easily attains this state of liberation by chanting the holy names of God.

Unfortunately, the stubborn impersonalists cannot comprehend that the final spiritual destination, beyond even the four Vedic goals (religiosity, economic development, sense gratification, and liberation) is absolutely pure and transcendental love of Godhead. They mistake the devotees of the Lord for sentimentalists and consider them their philosophical opponents. Besides these out-and-out impersonalists, there is a certain group of devotees that has deviated from the path of pure devotion and fallen prey to pretension. These cheaters actually end up following the impersonalists' path of trying to merge with the Supreme Lord. Such materialistic sentimentalists are not counted among the devotees of the Lord. Like their impersonalist counterparts, they cannot understand the true position of the Supreme Lord's name, form, qualities, pastimes, associates, or paraphernalia, for they wrongly consider these transcendental subjects illusory. They act capriciously and confuse the mass of people.

These materialistic sentimentalists reject the spiritual conclusions of Śrīla Rūpa Gosvāmī and try to take shelter of impersonalism. Yet they miserably lack the scholarship and discipline of the impersonalists. They divorce themselves from the impersonalists' scriptural studies and philosophical discussions, regarding discussions on the scripture as dry speculation and their ignorant, sentimental outbursts as spontaneous devotional fervor.

Some of these pretenders very closely follow in the impersonalists' footsteps and so may be accepted as a deranged offshoot of the impersonalist line. But they are certainly not part of the Vaiṣṇava discipline followed by those in the line of Śrīla Rūpa Gosvāmī. These pretenders diligently cultivate and exhibit certain mannerisms of devotees, and so the impersonalists reject them from their fold. Thus ostracized by both impersonalists and Vaiṣṇavas, they form a cult of demented sentimentalists. Śrīla Rūpa Gosvāmī declares that such pretenders create an outrage in spiritual society. As the *Brāhma-yamāla* says:

śruti-smṛti-purāṇādi-
pañcarātra-vidhim vinā
aikāntikī harer bhaktir
utpātāyaiva kalpate

> Devotional service of the Lord that ignores the authorized Vedic literatures like the *Upaniṣads, Purāṇas,* and the *Nārada-pañcarātra* is simply an unnecessary disturbance in society.

To show mercy to such pretenders, impersonalists, empiricists, and fruitive workers, the Supreme Lord, Kṛṣṇa, has in the *Bhagavad-gītā* discussed *jñāna-yoga,* or *yoga* through knowledge. I therefore embark upon the same subject in this essay.

Real knowledge means to discriminate between truth and illusion. *Jñāna-yoga* is the process by which one becomes eternally fixed on the path of transcendental devotional service to the Supreme Lord, who is the source of the Supersoul and Brahman. *Jñāna-yoga* should never be interpreted to mean the ascending process of enquiry, the inductive method, through which one aims only at separating reality from illusion by gradually rejecting the unreal. It is impossible to attain perfect knowledge without serving the Supreme Lord, who is full with all opulences and potencies, whose bodily luster is the Brahman effulgence, and whose partial expansion is the Supersoul. The *brāhmaṇa* Gopāla Cakravartī believed that *jñāna,* perfect knowledge, is far superior to devotional service of the Lord. But as recorded in the *Caitanya-caritāmṛta* (*Antya* 3.201):

balāi-purohita tāre karilā bhartsana
"ghaṭa-paṭiyā mūrkha tumi bhakti kāṅhā jāna?"

> The priest named Balarāma Ācārya chastised Gopāla Cakravartī. "You are a foolish logician," he said. "What do you know about the devotional service of the Lord?"

If one pretends to be a devotee of the Lord but does not understand the difference between dry speculative knowledge and knowledge of the Supreme Absolute Truth, then such a person's devotion borders on impersonalism and is rank with cheap sentimentalism, which is totally against the spiritual teachings of Śrīla Rūpa Gosvāmī. Therefore *jñāna-yoga* is not speculation or empirical research; nor is it the sudden emotional outbursts of upstarts pretending to be devotees. By practicing genuine *jñāna-yoga,* even an empirical philosopher will develop a taste for hearing purely spiritual topics from the scriptures. Eventually he will come to understand the Supreme Lord's transcendental position and potency, and ultimately he will relish the Lord's form, which is eternal and full of knowledge and bliss. He will perceive the Lord as the embodiment of all transcendental mellows. And if the pretentious nondevotee sentimentalists, who like to imitate the empiricists, practice genuine *jñāna-yoga,* then they too will gain an accurate perspective on the Absolute Truth. They will become firmly established in the understanding that the Supreme Lord's form is spiritual and transcendental, and then they will begin to render unflinching devotional service.

In the *Caitanya-caritāmṛta* (*Ādi* 2.117), Śrīla Kṛṣṇadāsa Kavirāja advises:

siddhānta baliyā citte nā kara alasa
ihā ha-ite kṛṣṇe lāge sudṛḍha mānasa

> A sincere student should not neglect the discussion of such [scriptural] conclusions, considering them controversial, for such discussions strengthen the mind. Thus one's mind becomes attached to Śrī Kṛṣṇa.

Through such discussion and inquiry, we become aware that we are *jīvas,* individual souls, upon which our bodies and minds are temporary and illusory impositions. The scriptures refer to the *jīva,* a product of the Lord's superior, spiritual energy, as the *kṣetra-jña,* or "knower of the field," while they refer to the temporary, material body and mind as the *kṣetra,* or "field." Just as the *jīva* is the *kṣetra-jña* in relation to his individual body and mind, so the Lord is the *kṣetra-jña* in relation to His vast universal form. As Lord Kṛṣṇa informs us in the *Bhagavad-gītā* (13.3), *kṣetra-jñaṁ cāpi māṁ viddhi sarva-kṣetreṣu bhārata:* "O scion of Bharata, you should understand that I am also the knower in all bodies."

Therefore the *jīva* and the Supreme Lord are nondifferent in the sense that both are *kṣetra-jña,* "knowers of the field." But when we look at which *kṣetra* each of them is knowing, the difference between the *jīva* and the Supreme Lord is seen to be incalculably wide. The Supreme Lord is infinite, while the *jīva* is infinitesimal. As consciousness, the *jīva* pervades his body and mind, which he has acquired due to his *karma,* or fruitive activities. Similarly, the Supreme Lord pervades the entire creation—His universal body—with His consciousness. Though the *jīva* permeates his body as impersonal consciousness, he is always a person. Similarly, although in His impersonal, all-pervasive feature the Supreme Lord saturates the cosmic manifestation with His consciousness, in His personal feature He remains eternally in Goloka Vṛndāvana performing pastimes. This point is substantiated by the *Brahma-saṁhitā* (5.37): *goloka eva nivasaty akhilātma-bhūto.* "Although residing always in His abode called Goloka, the Lord is the all-pervading Brahman and the localized Paramātmā as well." And in the *Bhagavad-gītā* the Lord Himself explains the functions of the field and the knower of the field, and He says that He is present throughout the creation as the knower.

The dry speculators describe the field and its knower according to their own lopsided logic. They say that the body is like a container and that Brahman enters this container like the all-pervasive sky. Once this container is broken—that is, at the time of liberation—the *jīva* merges back into Brahman, symbolized by the sky. There are many loopholes in this argument. First of all, the *jīva* is spiritual energy, while the sky is matter. It is wrong to compare a spiritual subject to a material object. This is a typical example of how the impersonal speculators waste their time trying to equate spiritual substance with mundane things. Such empirical exercises can never be termed *jñāna-yoga,* the path of perfect knowledge. According to the impersonalists, the infinitesimal *jīva* merges into the infinite Brahman at the time of liberation. But such merging does not affect the infinite in any way. Unfortunately, the impersonalists are oblivious of the tremendous damage such liberation causes to the infinitesimal living entity.

Devotion Resides in Perfect Knowledge of the Supreme

If the infinitesimal soul merges his individuality, or inherent personality, with the infinite being, then that individuality is rendered worthless. Those who want to commit spiritual suicide by sacrificing their individuality are a breed by themselves. Such self-destroyers are known as pure monists. On the other hand, those who desire to maintain their individuality are dualists, or personalists.

Once the *jīva* manifests his original transcendental nature, he is easily liberated from material conditioning, yet even in such an elevated state he does not lose his individual identity as a spirit soul. In fact, in that pure state he engages in the eternal service of the Supreme Lord and relishes the immortal nectar of sublime bliss.

For eons, all over the world, research on the subject of *kṣetra* and *kṣetra-jña* has been going on. In India the six philosophical schools* have extensively discussed this topic, but this discussion has merely been an exercise in logic and sophistry that has

---

*The six philosophicals schools and their proponants are: Sā khya—Kapila (atheistic); Patanjali yoga—Patanjali; Nyāya—Gautama; Vaiśesika—Kanāda; Mimaṁsa—Jaimini; Vedānta—Vyasadeva.

led to many differing opinions among the sages. Hence none of these schools has truly practiced *jñāna-yoga,* the path of perfect knowledge. Only when discussion of *kṣetra* and *kṣetra-jña* is applied in the Lord's service does the exercise become *jñāna-yoga.*

The process of *jñāna-yoga* has been delineated in the *Vedānta-sūtra,* the philosophical essence of the *Vedas.* The Supreme Lord, Kṛṣṇa, accepts the authority of the *Vedānta-sūtra* and considers the philosophical presentation proper. Up till the present day, every spiritual line, even in the impersonalist school, has based its philosophical authority on the *Vedānta-sūtra.* And the *Śrīmad-Bhāgavatam* is the natural and faultless commentary on the *Vedānta-sūtra.* This is Lord Caitanya's opinion.

Learned circles consider a disciplic line bereft of a commentary on the *Vedānta-sūtra* to be unauthorized and useless. Śrīpāda Śaṅkarācārya's *Vedānta* commentary, entitled *Śārīraka-bhāṣya,* is the main commentary of the impersonal, monistic school. Among the Vaiṣṇavas, besides Śrīpāda Rāmānujācārya's commentary, Śrīla Baladeva Vidyābhūṣaṇa's *Govinda-bhāṣya* is the main commentary in the line of Lord Caitanya, known as the Mādhva-Gauḍīya-sampradāya.

Those who are keen to engage in deep discussions on the esoteric conclusions of the scriptures should certainly delve into the philosophy of the *Vedānta-sūtra.* The point to be emphasized is that a well-versed *Vedānta* philosopher is not a philosopher in the line of Śaṅkarācārya but is actually a Vaiṣṇava spiritual preceptor, a liberated soul.

According to the *Vedas* and the sages, the five gross elements are earth, water, fire, air, and ether. Material nature is produced from a combination of false ego (*ahaṅkāra*), the ingredients of the material energy (*mahat-tattva*), and the cause of the *mahat-tattva* (*prakṛti*). There are five knowledge-gathering senses and five working senses. The mind is the internal sense, the sixth knowledge-gathering sense. Form, taste, smell, touch, and sound are the five sense objects.

We have already enumerated these material ingredients in our description of the Sāṅkhya philosophy of the atheist Kapila. The *kṣetra,* or "field," is the combination of the twenty-four ingredients mentioned above. When these twenty-four ingredients interact the result is the transformation of material nature, which gives rise to the gross material body composed of five gross elements (*pañca-mahābhūta*), as a result of material desires, hate, enjoyment, lamentation, and so on. The shadow of consciousness in the form of mind and will are transformations of that field.

What will soon be discussed is that the *kṣetra-jña* is completely different from the *kṣetra* and its transformations. But to properly understand the knowledge concerning the *kṣetra* and the *kṣetra-jña,* one must first cultivate at least twenty good qualities listed in the *Bhagavad-gītā* (13.8–12):

> Humility; pridelessness; nonviolence; tolerance; simplicity; approaching a bona fide spiritual master; cleanliness; steadiness; self-control; renunciation of the objects of sense gratification; absence of false ego; the perception of the evil of birth, death, old age, and disease; detachment; freedom from entanglement with children, wife, home, and the rest; even-mindedness amid pleasant and unpleasant events; constant and unalloyed devotion to Me; aspiring to live in a solitary place; detachment from the general mass of people; accepting the importance of self-realization; and philosophical search for the Absolute Truth—all these I declare to be knowledge, and besides this whatever there may be is ignorance.

Persons bereft of these qualities are not eligible to discuss spiritual topics. The false logicians mistake the above-mentioned qualities, which are meant to lead the conditioned soul to liberation, for mundane qualities acquired as a result of transformations of the mind, such as lust, anger, and hate. But factually, the above-mentioned qualities represent spiritual knowledge. Even if one accepts the false logicians' argument that the qualities Lord Kṛṣṇa enumerates in the *Gītā* as prerequisites for absolute knowledge are mental transformations, still we cannot agree that these transformations are equivalent to such qualities as lust, greed, anger, and illusion, which result from gross ignorance. One kind of mental transformation drags the soul down to depravity, whereas the other redeems the soul from doom. Both disease and medicine are products of material nature, yet one pushes a man toward the jaws of death, while the other saves him from destruction. So one must avoid becoming the laughing-stock of society by accepting the foolish theory of *yata mata, tata path*—"All ways lead to the Truth"—and on this basis professing that the medicine and the disease are one and the same.

There is one quality among the twenty qualities Kṛṣṇa lists that is especially noteworthy, and that is *mayi cānanya-yogena bhaktir avyabhicāriṇī:* "Constant and unalloyed devotion to Me [Kṛṣṇa]." The other qualities are required to cleanse the consciousness. Once the mirror of the mind is purified and the blazing fire of material existence extinguished, constant and unalloyed devotion to Lord Kṛṣṇa begins to appear on the horizon of the heart. The great saintly spiritual master Śrīla Narottama dāsa Ṭhākura has sung, "When will my mind become purified and detached from matter? Oh, when in that purified state will I be able to see the transcendental realm of Vṛndāvana?"

It is interesting to note that once constant and unalloyed devotion to Lord Kṛṣṇa blossoms in the heart of a person, the other nineteen qualities automatically manifest in him. As mentioned in the *Śrīmad-Bhāgavatam* (5.18.12), *yasyāsti bhaktir bhagavaty akiñcanā sarvair guṇais tatra samāsate surāḥ:*

> All the demigods and their exalted qualities, such as religion, knowledge and renunciation, become manifest in the body of one who has developed unalloyed devotion for the Supreme Personality of Godhead, Vāsudev.

By patiently collecting ten, twenty, thirty rupees daily, one will someday have a million rupees. But if one comes upon a million rupees all at once, one does not have to endeavor separately to collect ten, twenty, or thirty rupees and waste valuable time. Similarly, when one develops unalloyed devotion to Lord Kṛṣṇa, all the other above-mentioned qualities automatically adorn that person without extra effort. On the other hand, one who leaves aside unalloyed devotion to Lord Kṛṣṇa and tries to cultivate the other nineteen qualities separately may temporarily receive wealth and honor, but he will become unqualified for achieving the highest goal. In the same verse of *Śrīmad-Bhāgavatam* mentioned above (5.8.12), Prahlāda Mahārāja says, *harāv abhaktasya kuto mahad-guṇā mano-rathenāsati dhāvato bahiḥ:*

> On the other hand, a person devoid of devotional service and engaged in material activities has no good qualities. Even if he is adept at the practice of mystic *yoga* or the

> honest endeavor of maintaining his family and relatives, he must be driven by his own mental speculations and must engage in the service of the lord's external energy. How can there be any good qualities in such a man?

It is futile to make an external show of good qualities like humility and nonviolence while disrespecting the Lord's lotus feet and denouncing the process of devotional service. Such so-called good qualities may be of some material value, but ultimately they are useless and temporary. In fact, the nineteen other qualities combine to make a throne from which unalloyed devotion may rule. These qualities are various limbs of the Absolute Truth, and everything outside this absolute knowledge is nescience.

By cultivating these limbs of knowledge, one attains self-realization. In other words, one is elevated from mundane knowledge of the *kṣetra* to spiritual knowledge of the *kṣetra-jña*. We have previously established that the word *kṣetra-jña* implies both the living entity and the Supreme Brahman. Sometimes material nature, or *prakṛti*, is referred to as Brahman, the reason being that Brahman is the cause of the material nature. In one sense a cause and its effect are identical. But Lord Kṛṣṇa is the ultimate source of Brahman. The Lord impregnates Brahman in the form of the material nature with the seed of Brahman known as the *jīva*. As Kṛṣṇa says in the *Bhagavad-gītā* (14.3):

> *mama yonir mahad brahma*
> *tasmin garbhaṁ dadhāmy aham*
> *sambhavaḥ sarva-bhūtānāṁ*
> *tato bhavati bhārata*

> The total material substance, called Brahman, is the source of birth, and it is that Brahman that I impregnate, making possible the births of all living beings, O scion of Bharata.

This verse explains the famous saying *sarvaṁ khalv idaṁ brahma* from the *Upaniṣads*, meaning "Everything is Brahman." In other words, the Supreme Brahman, Lord Kṛṣṇa, is identical with both the *jīva* and *prakṛti* in that they are all Brahman. Thus in one sense the Vaiṣṇavas are pure monists. Previously we deliberated upon another verse from the *Bhagavad-gītā* (9.10):

mayādhyakṣeṇa prakṛtiḥ
sūyate sa-carācaram
hetunānena kaunteya
jagad viparivartate

This material nature, which is one of My energies, is working under My direction, O son of Kuntī, producing all moving and nonmoving beings. Under its rule this manifestation is created and annihilated again and again.

The *Gītā* verse under discussion (14.3) gives a clearer understanding of the other verse (9.10).

The Mind Is Purified of Its Attachment to Matter

To shed more light on the meaning of the Upaniṣadic aphorism *sarvaṁ khalv idaṁ brahma*, we cite a verse from the *Viṣṇu Purāṇa* (1.22.56):

eka deśa-sthitasyāgner
jyotsnā vistāriṇī yathā
parasya brahmaṇaḥ śaktis
tathedam akhilaṁ jagat

A fire radiates light all around although remaining in one spot. Similarly, the Supreme Brahman radiates energy everywhere, which is manifested as this material world.

In their philosophical discussions the Māyāvādīs deny the existence of the Supreme Lord's multifarious energies. Such sub-standard debates are indeed on the kindergarten level. According to Śrīla Bhaktisiddhānta Sarasvatī Ṭhākura, the Māyāvādīs have a poor fund of knowledge and are thus prevented from understanding that the Supreme Brahman is full with six opulences. To save these poor Māyāvādī impersonalists from philosophical impoverishment, Lord Kṛṣṇa has mercifully instructed them in the *Bhagavad-gītā* (7.19):

bahūnāṁ janmanām ante
jñānavān māṁ prapadyate
vāsudevaḥ sarvam iti
sa mahātmā su-durlabhaḥ

After many births and deaths, he who is actually in knowledge surrenders unto Me, knowing Me to be the cause of all causes and all that is. Such a great soul is very rare.

As the saying goes, "A tethered cow goes as far as the rope." Similarly, one who uses the inductive method to search for ultimate knowledge will fail. His attempt is futile because one cannot know the supramundane with a mundane mind. Complete comprehension of the Absolute Truth is impossible with an unholy, demoniac mind. When one is possessed of a demoniac mentality that tries to reduce the supremely omnipotent Personality of Godhead to impersonal Brahman, all so-called philosophical debates will fail to discover the realm of absolute knowledge or the truth about the nondual substance. Vaiṣṇavas alone are eligible to cultivate such knowledge.

Of course, not all impersonalists are demoniac. As soon as an impersonalist realizes that the Absolute Truth is a person endowed with all transcendental qualities, he immediately begins to serve Him. This is confirmed in the *Śrīmad-Bhāgavatam* (1.7.10), which states:

ātmārāmāś ca munayo
nirgranthā apy urukrame
kurvanty ahaitukīṁ bhaktim
ittham-bhūta-guṇo hariḥ

All different varieties of *ātmārāmas* [those who take pleasure in the ātmā, or spirit self], especially those established on the path of self-realization, though freed from all kinds of material bondage, desire to render unalloyed devotional service unto the Personality of Godhead. This means that the Lord possesses transcendental qualities and therefore can attract everyone, including liberated souls.

It is rare to find that great soul who is attracted by the Lord's transcendental qualities and thus surrenders to Him. The only person who can surrender to the Supreme Lord is one who does not attempt to rob Him of His personality but who views the material nature as a transformation of His multifarious energies. Thus the Māyāvādīs can never be called *mahātmās,* or "great souls." Only when they realize that the nondual Absolute Truth is none other than the Supreme Personality of Godhead, full with six opulences, can they be called *mahātmās.*

Vaiṣṇava *mahātmās* have explained the aphorism *sarvaṁ khalv idaṁ brahma* in this manner: the philosophical school known as Viśiṣṭādvaita propounds the idea that the Supreme Lord eternally exists with His two principal potencies: the *cit-śakti,* or spiritual potency, and the *acit-śakti,* or material potency. Though the Lord is one nondual entity, He exists dynamically, manifesting His multifarious energies under the main headings of the *cit* and *acit* potencies, which He absolutely controls. Although He is the source of unlimited potencies, He eternally exists in His transcendental, personal form. This form manifests in three aspects, namely, as He sees Himself, as a loving devotee sees Him, and as He is seen by His competitors and enemies. The Śrī Vaiṣṇava disciplic succession, headed by Śrī Rāmānujācārya, cites the same text we have cited above to explain the situation of the Lord and His energies:

> A fire radiates light all around although remaining in one spot. Similarly, the Supreme Brahman radiates energy everywhere, which is manifested as this material world.

Thus the entire creation is proof of the existence of the Lord. One who is in complete knowledge understands that the Absolute Truth is the Supreme Personality of Godhead, who exists eternally as the source and controller of all energies. The *mahātmās* fully realize this knowledge, and having taken shelter of the Lord's transcendental energy (*cit-śakti*), they eternally render loving devotional service to Him. Lord Kṛṣṇa confirms this in the *Bhagavad-gītā* (9.13–14):

mahātmānas tu māṁ pārtha
daivīṁ prakṛtim āśritāḥ
bhajanty ananya-manaso
jñātvā bhūtādim avyayam

satataṁ kīrtayanto māṁ
yatantaś ca dṛḍha-vratāḥ

namasyantaś ca māṁ bhaktyā
nitya-yuktā upāsate

O son of Pṛthā, those who are not deluded, the great souls, are under the protection of the divine nature. They are fully engaged in devotional service because they know Me as the Supreme Personality of Godhead, original and inexhaustible. Always chanting My glories, endeavoring with great determination, bowing down before Me, these great souls perpetually worship Me with devotion.

The mental speculators and logicians, as well as the Māyāvādīs—who are neophytes depending on the empirical, inductive process—should properly understand the position of the pure devotees of the Lord, who have realized the Absolute Truth. In the *Bhagavad-gītā* (4.23) Lord Kṛṣṇa gives this explanation of the activities of the devotees:

gata-saṅgasya muktasya
jñānāvasthita-cetasaḥ
yajñāyācarataḥ karma
samagraṁ pravilīyate

The work of a man who is unattached to the modes of material nature and who is fully situated in transcendental knowledge merges entirely into transcendence.

The activities performed as sacrifices are all devotional service. The Sanskrit word *yajña* means "sacrifice," but it can also mean Lord Viṣṇu Himself. To perform one's activities as transcendental devotional service is possible only for those advanced souls who are fully situated in the Absolute Truth. Again, Kṛṣṇa describes His devotees in the *Bhagavad-gītā* (7.17):

teṣāṁ jñānī nitya-yukta
eka-bhaktir viśiṣyate
priyo hi jñānino 'tyartham
ahaṁ sa ca mama priyaḥ

Of these, the one who is in full knowledge and is always engaged in pure devotional service is the best. For I am very dear to him, and he is dear to Me.

If an impersonalist philosopher, due to some piety, engages in devotional service to the Supreme Lord, then only does he becomes dear to the Lord. But as long as the impersonalists try to rob the Supreme Lord of His divine potencies, they can never be dear to Him, nor can they be called *mahātmās*. They will continue to be counted among the demoniac atheists deluded by the Lord's illusory potency. These atheists are not wise men: they are simply ordinary mortals who are offenders against the Lord.

Wherever the word *jñāna* appears in the Vedic literature, it should be understood to mean *sambandha-jñāna,* knowledge of the relationship between the Lord and His energies. It does not refer to the impersonalist concept of the Supreme. After a person understands *sambandha-jñāna,* he comes to the stage of *abhidheya-jñāna,* knowledge of how to act in his relationship with the Supreme Lord. This is devotional service, practiced by liberated souls. The mature stage of *abhidheya-jñāna* leads one to love of Godhead, the ultimate goal of all living entities.

It is the general opinion that among modern-day spiritualists who have tried to know the Supreme through their own puny efforts, Śrī Aurobindo has attained some degree of realization. The reason for his success, it is claimed, is that the object of his search was not material knowledge. The Māyāvādīs attempt to know the oneness of everything, but their search takes them only up to realization of the impersonal, nondual Brahman. They do not know that becoming free from disease is not perfection, that after the diseased material condition comes the healthy state of spiritual existence, wherein a liberated soul is still an individual with personality. This fact is incomprehensible to them.

Śrī Aurobindo rose beyond this limited sphere of thinking and talked about "supramental consciousness" in such books as *Life Divine.* We consider this book a hazy attempt to present the Supreme Lord's transcendental potencies. He accepted that the Supreme Lord is endowed with transcendental potency, and therefore we have some appreciation for him, but we feel that many persons cannot understand Śrī Aurobindo's explanation of transcendence in his books. Although he uses fairly simple English, the reader remains puzzled. Those who are unacquainted with such Vaiṣṇava philosophies as Viśiṣṭādvaita, Śuddhādvaita, Dvaitādvaita, and finally Lord

Caitanya's *acintya-bhedābheda-tattva,* cannot understand Śrī Aurobindo. And those who are learned only in impersonal philosophy, who are searching for the nondual Brahman, have even less access to Śrī Aurobindo's works.

Much of Śrī Aurobindo's stream of thinking has been borrowed from Vaiṣṇava philosophy. In *Light on Yoga* and in an essay entitled "*The Goal,*" we find the following passages:

> In order to get dynamic realization, it is not enough to rescue the Puruṣa from the subjugation of Prakṛti. One must transfer the allegiance of the Puruṣa from the lower Prakṛti, with its play of ignorant forces, to the supreme Divine Śakti—the Mother.

> It is a mistake to identify the Mother with the lower Prakṛti and its mechanism of forces. Prakṛti here is a mechanism only, which has been formed for the evolution of ignorance. As the ignorant mental, vital, or physical being is not itself the Divine, although it comes from the Divine, so the mechanism of Prakṛti is not the Divine Mother. No doubt something of her is there in and behind this mechanism, maintaining it for the evolutionary purpose, but she in herself is not the Śakti of Avidya but the Divine consciousness, the Power, Light, and Para-prakṛti, to whom we turn for release and divine fulfillment...

> If the supermind could not give us a greater and more complete truth than any of the lower planes, it would not be worthwhile trying to reach it. Each plane has its own truth. Some of these truths are no longer needed as we rise to higher planes. For example, desire and ego are truths of the mental, vital, and physical plane, as a man on that plane without ego or desire would be a mere automaton. As we rise higher, ego and desire appear no longer as truths: they are falsehoods disfiguring the true person and the true will. The struggle between the powers of light and the powers of darkness is a truth here, but it becomes less and less of a truth as one rises higher, and in the supermind it has no truth at all. Other truths remain, but change their character, importance, and place in the whole. The contrast between the Personal and the Impersonal is a truth of the overmind; there is no separate truth of them in the supermind: they are inseparably one. But one who has not mastered the lower planes cannot reach the supramental

> truth. The incompetent pride of man's mind makes a sharp distinction and wants to call all else untruth and leap at once to the highest truth, whatever it may be. But that is an ambitious and arrogant error. One has to climb the stairs and rest one's feet firmly on each step in order to reach the summit.

If one is serious about the real meaning of life, then simple endeavoring to escape the crippling clutches of *māyā* is not the only undertaking. The ultimate goal is to liberate ourselves from the enthrallment of the illusory energy and become wholly subservient to the transcendental, spiritual energy.

In the *Caitanya-caritāmṛta* (*Madhya* 20.108-09, 111, 117-18, 120, and 122), Lord Caitanya gives some illuminating advice to Sanātana Gosvāmī:

> It is the living entity's constitutional position to be an eternal servant of Kṛṣṇa because he is the marginal energy of Kṛṣṇa and a manifestation simultaneously one with and different from the Lord, like a molecular particle of sunshine or fire.
>
> Lord Kṛṣṇa naturally has three energetic transformations, and these are known as the spiritual potency, the living entity potency and the illusory potency... Forgetting Kṛṣṇa, the living entity has been attracted by the external feature from time immemorial. Therefore the illusory energy (māyā) gives him all kinds of misery in his material existence. In the material condition, the living entity is sometimes raised to higher planetary systems and material prosperity and sometimes drowned in a hellish situation. His state is exactly like that of a criminal whom a king punishes by submerging him in water and then raising him again from the water. ... If the conditioned soul becomes Kṛṣṇa conscious by the mercy of saintly persons who voluntarily preach scriptural injunctions and help him to become Kṛṣṇa conscious, the conditioned soul is liberated from the clutches of *māyā*, who gives him up. The conditioned soul cannot revive his Kṛṣṇa consciousness by his own effort. But out of causeless mercy, Lord Kṛṣṇa compiled the Vedic literature and its supplements, the *Purāṇas*.

Constitutionally, the Jīva Is an Eternal Servant of Kṛṣṇa

The profound esoteric conclusions Lord Caitanya revealed in a few aphorisms of instruction to Śrī Sanātana Gosvāmī are only partially discussed in all the works of Śrī Aurobindo. In language full of complex syntax and obscure terms, Śrī Aurobindo tries to express the knowledge that is easily available through the practice of *vaidhi-bhakti*, devotional service rendered according to regulations given by the authorized spiritual master and the scriptures. Because of his high-flown literary style, and for other technical reasons, Śrī Aurobindo's writings are not easily understood by the ordinary reading public, and so his literature is, in a sense, ineffectual.

Lord Caitanya discusses in detail the *jīva*'s eternal constitutional position as Lord Kṛṣṇa's servant and how the *jīva* is put into illusion, or *māyā,* when he tries to be the supreme enjoyer. Lord Caitanya further explains that when the *jīva* forgets his eternal position as a servant of Lord Kṛṣṇa, he becomes eternally conditioned and illusioned. Thus *māyā* inflicts the miseries of material life upon the *jīva.* If a person artificially tries to be something he is not, then he can expect only misery. In this regard we recall a short story we read as a child in school that tells of a crow who tried to become a peacock. The creator and master of this universe is its rightful owner as well. Thus He is the sole enjoyer of everything. But if one among the creator's many servants tries to usurp His position and play the role of the Lord and enjoyer, how can he expect anything but suffering?

In the *Śrīmad-Bhāgavatam* (10.87.30), one of the four Kumāras, Sanandana, recites to an assembly of sages in Janaloka the prayers the personified *Vedas* previously recited to the Supreme Lord. One of the prayers is as follows:

aparimitā dhruvās tanu-bhṛto yadi sarva-gatās
tarhi na śāsyateti niyamo dhruva netarathā
ajani ca yan-mayaṁ tad avimucya niyantṛ bhavet
samam anujānatāṁ yad amatam mata-duṣṭatayā

> If the countless living entities were all-pervading and possessed forms that never changed, You could not possibly be their absolute ruler, O immutable one. But since they are Your localized expansions and their forms are subject to change, You do control them. Indeed, that which supplies the ingredients for the generation of something is necessarily its controller because a product never exists apart from its ingredient cause. It is simply illusion for someone to think that he knows the Supreme Lord, who is equally present in each of His expansions, since whatever knowledge one gains by material means must be imperfect.

The last word in knowledge is certainly not self-realization or Brahman realization. There is more to realize—namely, that the *jīva* is the eternal servant of Lord Kṛṣṇa. This realization is the awakening of supramental consciousness, and the activities a *jīva* performs in such consciousness are the beginning of his eternal life. When the *jīva* performs all his activities under the direction of the Lord's internal, spiritual energy, he enjoys eternal transcendental bliss, which is a billion times greater than the happiness of Brahman realization. The difference in transcendental joy between the two is like the difference between the vast ocean and the water collected in a calf's hoofprint. When Śrī Aurobindo wrote of "the Divine Mother," he was likely referring to this internal, spiritual energy, the predominating Deity of eternal transcendental bliss. He also pointed out that the activities of the inferior, material energy should not be mistaken for those of this spiritual potency. Once the famous impersonalist and monist *sannyāsī* Ramana Maharshi of Madras was asked by a foreign disciple, "What is the difference between God and man?" His cryptic reply was "God plus desire equals man, and man minus desire equals God." We say that man can never be free of desire. In his eternal conditioned existence the *jīva* is full of the desire to enjoy matter, while in his eternal liberated state he is full of the desire to render devotional service to the Lord. Thus the *jīva* can never become God. It is sheer insanity to equate man with God, or vice versa. The Māyāvādī's unnatural desire to deny the inherent characteristics of his conscious self is the very same desire that keeps him from attaining liberation. Hence the Māyāvādīs' false and arrogant claim of liberation is merely a demonstration of their perverted intelligence.

According to the *Śrīmad-Bhāgavatam,* desire can never be nullified. While conditioned, the *jīva* is a repository of unlimited material desires, summarized as the *catur-varga,* the four goals of human life enunciated in the Vedic literature (religiosity, economic development, sense gratification, and liberation). However, in the liberated state produced by acting under the direction of the Lord's internal, spiritual energy, the *jīva's* true, spiritual desires become manifest. Śrī Aurobindo has discussed this subject (though not in detail), and for this we appreciate him more than Ramana Maharshi. Ramana Maharshi has more or less tried to completely choke the life out of desire. This forcible elimination of desire is spiritual suicide. There is no credit in finishing off the patient without curing his disease; the doctor is qualified when he can cure the disease and save the patient. Those who pursue the four Vedic goals mentioned above, even up to impersonal liberation, find themselves imprisoned by their senses and enslaved by their desires. On the other hand, one who can teach people how to engage their daily activities in the service of the Supreme Lord is the real benefactor of humanity.

In the *Bhagavad-gītā* (9.4) Lord Kṛṣṇa says:

mayā tatam idaṁ sarvaṁ
jagad avyakta-mūrtinā
mat-sthāni sarva-bhūtāni
na cāhaṁ teṣv avasthitaḥ

> By Me, in My unmanifested form, this entire universe is pervaded. All beings are in Me, but I am not in them.

In His unmanifested impersonal form Lord Kṛṣṇa pervades this entire universe, which is a transformation of His external energy. Therefore all living entities in the material creation rest on His energies. Energy cannot exist by itself, without an energetic source. Thus the material energy and the Supreme Energetic, Lord Kṛṣṇa, are in principle one, though the Energetic is far removed from the workings of His energy. The *jīva,* being marginal, is moved by desire to serve either the manifestation of the Lord's external energy—this physical world—or the Lord Himself in the spiritual world, which is an expansion of His superior, internal potency. In other words, in every situation the *jīva* maintains his constitutional position as a servant. Thus he cannot relieve the suffering he undergoes as a servant of this material nature by artificially giving up his desire to serve. Inherently a servant, the *jīva* can never forsake his desire to serve. But if he so desires, he can quit his bad service for a good one. He should abandon his service of the four Vedic goals, including impersonal liberation—which will altogether throttle the life out of his desire to serve—and carefully try to manifest his original spiritual desire to serve the Lord. Śrī Aurobindo has mentioned this same point in the passage quoted above:

> If the supermind could not give us a greater and more complete truth than any of the lower planes, it would not be worthwhile trying to reach it.

If a human being tries to exist without ego, desire, feelings, dislikes, and so on, he will be converted into inert matter. This is not spiritual elevation. When a person gradually progresses from materialistic perception to spiritual perception, he can clearly understand how trivial are his mundane desires, feelings, dislikes, and so on which were so long contaminated by ignorance. As this ignorance dissipates, mundane desires become insignificant. Desires remain, but they are no longer mundane. They become transcendental. In that state, one perceives Brahman, the Supersoul, and the Supreme Lord as one. Such higher perceptions are possible only when one's mind and senses are transcendental, a stage impossible to reach in one leap. Those who try the impossible are irrational and overambitious. Everyone has to proceed gradually, placing each step securely before taking the next one. In this way one will ultimately reach the goal.

In his essay entitled "*Yoga,*" Śrī Aurobindo does not recommend destroying desire but rather changing its character. It is a perennial truth that the *jīva* is by nature an eternal servant of Lord Kṛṣṇa. The *jīva* has no other identity, whether he is conditioned or liberated. His position is similar to that of a citizen of a country: he is always subject to the government laws, whether he is in or out of jail. When he is inside the jail, all his activities are painful, but as a free citizen he feels content in everything he does. It is merely a matter of changing his character.

Similarly, even when the *jīva* refuses to serve the Supreme Energetic, Śrī Kṛṣṇa, and instead serves His illusory energy, *māyā,* he remains a servant of the Lord. But in that condition he is ignorant of the bliss of devotional service to the Lord. Only when the *jīva* casts away his mundane characteristics can he experience transcendental joy in devotional service. Still, in no situation does the *jīva* ever give up his inherent nature as Kṛṣṇa's eternal servant, for he emanates from the Lord's marginal potency.

The Means to Liberation

Nowhere do the Vedic scriptures say that one has to annihilate desire in order to comprehend the Upaniṣadic statement *sarvaṁ khalv idaṁ brahma.* But there are many statements recommending that the character of desire should be transformed. It is because of the force of desire that all activities in the world are carried out, and in the *Bhagavad-gītā* (10.4–11) Lord Kṛṣṇa discusses the multifarious ways in which desire influences these activities:

> Intelligence, knowledge, freedom from doubt and delusion, forgiveness, truthfulness, control of the senses, control of the mind, happiness and distress, birth, death, fear, fearlessness, nonviolence, equanimity, satisfaction, austerity, charity, fame and infamy—all these various qualities of living beings are created by Me alone.
>
> The seven great sages and before them the four other great sages and the Manus (progenitors of mankind) come from Me, born from My mind, and all the living beings populating the various planets descend from them.
>
> One who is factually convinced of this opulence and mystic power of Mine engages in unalloyed devotional service; of this there is no doubt.
>
> I am the source of all spiritual and material worlds. Everything emanates from Me. The wise who perfectly know this engage in My devotional service and worship Me with all their hearts. The thoughts of My pure devotees dwell in Me,

> their lives are fully devoted to My service, and they derive great satisfaction and bliss from always enlightening one another and conversing about Me. To those who are constantly devoted to serving Me with love, I give the understanding by which they can come to Me. To show them special mercy, I, dwelling in their hearts, destroy with the shining lamp of knowledge the darkness born of ignorance.

Those who understand that the multifarious human desires are a reflection of the Supreme Brahman's desires are careful not to discard them but to use them in the Lord's service. Long ago, the seven great sages and the Manus all used their God-given desires in the Lord's service, and anyone today who emulates the example of these illustrious ancestors will never see desire as mundane or as an impediment to spiritual progress. If Ramana Mahārṣi advises us to negate desire, then we must conclude that he misunderstands the Vedic statement *sarvaṁ khalv idaṁ brahma.* Those who have realized that all desires and feelings are Brahman by nature, and who thus engage them in the Supreme Lord's service, should be considered perfected souls. They are totally free from nescience. The desires of these self-realized, elevated, blissful devotees become purified to such an extent that not an iota of ignorance can influence their consciousness, for the Lord Himself destroys the nescience in their hearts.

The Māyāvādīs are hard pressed to understand that there is a wide gulf of difference between their individual efforts to nullify nescience and the Supreme Lord's mercifully enlightening His devotees. The Māyāvādīs are always eager to deny the Supreme Energetic His potencies. They are no better than demons like Rāvaṇa, who tried to usurp the Lord's potency, and Kaṁsa, who tried to kill Him outright. This sort of behavior is expected of demons. Aspiring for evil powers, they abandon devotional service to the Lord and take to sinful activities. In this way they forfeit all knowledge. Lord Kṛṣṇa aptly describes them in the *Gītā* (7.15) as *māyāpahṛta-jñānāḥ,* "those whose knowledge is stolen by illusion." Many, many philosophers, scholars, and so-called invincible heroes have tried to make the Supreme Lord impotent, formless, and impersonal, but in the end they always suffered terribly.

Thus in the *Śrīmad-Bhāgavatam* (10.14.4) we find this statement by Lord Brahmā:

śreyaḥ-sṛtiṁ bhaktim udasya te vibho
kliśyanti ye kevala-bodha-labdhaye
teṣām asau kleśala eva śiṣyate
nānyad yathā sthūla-tuṣāvaghātinām

> My dear Lord, devotional service unto You is the best path for self-realization. If someone gives up that path and engages in the cultivation of speculative knowledge, he will simply undergo a troublesome process and will not achieve his desired result. As a person who beats an empty husk of wheat cannot get grain, one who simply speculates cannot achieve self-realization. His only gain is trouble.

Where can one see qualities such as intelligence, knowledge, freedom from doubt, joy, sorrow, fear, fearlessness, nonviolence, equanimity, contentment, austerity, charity, fame, and infamy? These qualities are indicative of consciousness, so they are present wherever consciousness is present. The Supreme Lord has declared that these qualities are His, that they have sprung from Him. And the *Kaṭha Upaniṣad* states, *nityo nityānāṁ cetanaś cetanānām eko bahūnāṁ yo vidadhāti kāmān:* "Among all the eternal, conscious living entities, there is one supreme conscious being who supplies all others with their necessities." Therefore, to deny that these qualities are inherent in all conscious beings, and in this way to equate both the minute living entities and the Supreme Soul with dead matter, results in complete confusion and certainly demonstrates a severe lack of insight. The Māyāvādīs are confused as to whether refuting the existence of consciousness or accepting it will give them contentment. The conscious beings always control inert matter. A simple example proves this point: we see how a puny conscious being like a crow defecates fearlessly on the head of a stone statue of some hero, thus demonstrating the conquest of dynamic spirit over dead matter. Only those with stonelike intelligence will try to make the supreme conscious being into an unfeeling, formless object. Such an attempt is utter foolishness.

Śrī Aurobindo has accomplished something commendable by presenting today's learned circles with a "new" concept:

instead of trying to deny the inherent qualities of consciousness, one should transform one's mundane consciousness into supramental consciousness by engaging in service of the Supreme Lord under the direction of His divine potency. Of course, those who prefer to emulate the modern philosophers rather than the realized souls of bygone ages will find Śrī Aurobindo's presentation novel. But those who follow in the footsteps of pure, loving devotees of the Lord linked to an authorized disciplic succession know that Śrī Aurobindo's words echo the annals of age-old wisdom. Indeed, they sound close to the essence of the *Vedas*.

The six Gosvāmīs of Vṛndāvana excavated this extraordinary esoteric essence of the *Vedas* and described the workings of the internal potency of the Lord. Before the advent of Lord Caitanya, subjects of this nature had never been discussed in such detail by any spiritual authority. Śrīla Rūpa Gosvāmī, in his play *Vidagdha-mādhava*, glorifies Lord Caitanya's unique contribution to mankind:

> *anarpita-carīṁ cirāt karuṇayāvatīrṇaḥ kalau*
> *samarpayitum unnatojjvala-rasāṁ sva-bhakti-śriyam*
> *hariḥ puraṭa-sundara-dyuti-kadamba-sandīpitaḥ*
> *sadā hṛdaya-kandare sphuratu vaḥ śacī-nandanaḥ*

> May that Lord, who is known as the son of Śrīmatī Śacīdevī, be transcendentally situated in the innermost core of your heart. Resplendent with the radiance of molten gold, He has descended in the Age of Kali by His causeless mercy to bestow what no incarnation has ever offered before: the most elevated mellow of devotional service, the mellow of conjugal love.

In an essay entitled "*Surrender and Opening,*" Śrī Aurobindo writes:

> The whole principle of this *yoga* is to give oneself entirely to the Divine alone and to nobody and nothing else, and to bring down to ourselves, by union with the Divine Mother, all transcendent light, power, breadth, place, purity, truth, consciousness, and Ananda of the Supramental Divine.
>
> Rādhā is the personification of absolute love for the Divine, total and integral in all parts of Her being, from the highest

> spiritual to the physical, bringing the absolute self-going and total consecration of all being and calling down into the body and the most material nature the supreme Ananda.

Although there are disparities in conclusions in the above statements, still on his own Śrī Aurobindo has pointed in the right direction. It is impossible to comprehend the conjugal mellow, which is the most elevated and brilliant of spiritual mellows, without the mood of surrender. The Māyāvādīs are totally bereft of this attitude of surrender; hence when they try to understand the nondual concept on their own, they end up becoming impersonalists. Let us read what Śrī Aurobindo has to say about these Māyāvādīs:

> To seek after the impersonal is the way of those who want to withdraw from life. Usually such impersonalists try by their own effort and not by opening themselves to the superior power, or by the way of surrender, for the impersonal is not something that guides or helps but something to be attained, and it leaves each man to attain it according to the way and capacity of his nature. On the other hand, by opening and surrendering to the Mother, one can realize the Impersonal and every other aspect of truth also.

The Māyāvādīs are never successful in their efforts to attain liberation by dint of their own effort. The only way to conquer illusion and achieve liberation is to surrender to the Supreme Lord, who is complete with six absolute opulences. As Lord Kṛṣṇa clearly states in the *Gītā* (7.14), *mām eva ye prapadyante māyām etān taranti te:* "Those who surrender unto Me can easily cross beyond it [the modes of material nature]."

The first step in learning the process of surrendering to the Lord is to surrender to the pure devotee of the Lord. In the *Caitanya-caritāmṛta* (*Madhya* 20.120 and 122), we find this statement:

sādhu-śāstra-kṛpāya yadi kṛṣṇonmukha haya
sei jīva nistare, māyā tāhāre chāḍaya
māyā-mugdha jīvera nāhi svataḥ kṛṣṇa-jñāna
jīvere kṛpāya kailā kṛṣṇa veda-purāṇa

> If the conditioned soul becomes Kṛṣṇa conscious by the mercy of saintly persons who voluntarily preach scriptural injunctions, he is liberated from the clutches of Māyā, who gives him up.
>
> The conditioned soul cannot revive his Kṛṣṇa consciousness by his own effort. But out of causeless mercy, Lord Kṛṣṇa compiled the Vedic literature and its supplements, the *Purāṇas.*

All the *Vedas* and *Purāṇas* deal with the subject of Lord Kṛṣṇa. In the Lord's own words in the *Bhagavad-gītā* (15.15), *vedaiś ca sarvair aham eva vedyo:* "By all the *Vedas,* I am to be known."

Muni-gaṇera Matibram

The Deluded Thinkers

The Fundamental Question Evades the Erudite Scholar

In the First Canto of *Śrīmad-Bhāgavatam*, in the very first verse of the first chapter, the highest truth has been propounded in these words:

janmādy asya yato 'nvayād itaratas cārtheṣv abhijñaḥ svarāṭ
tene brahma hṛdā ya ādi-kavaye muhyanti yat sūrayaḥ
tejo-vāri-mṛdāṁ yathā vinimayo yatra tri-sargo 'mṛṣā
dhāmnā svena sadā nirasta-kuhakaṁ satyaṁ paraṁ dhīmahi

I meditate upon Lord Śrī Kṛṣṇa because He is the Absolute Truth and the primeval cause of all causes of the creation, sustenance and destruction of the manifested universes. He is directly and indirectly conscious of all manifestations, and He is independent because there is no other cause beyond Him. It is He only who first imparted the Vedic knowledge unto the heart of Brahmājī, the original living being. By Him even the great sages and demigods are placed into illusion, as one is bewildered by the illusory representations of water seen in fire, or land seen on water. Only because of Him do the material universes, temporarily manifested by the reactions of the three modes of nature, appear factual, although they are unreal. I therefore meditate upon Him, Lord Śrī Kṛṣṇa, who is eternally existent in the transcendental abode, which is forever free from the illusory representations of the material world. I meditate upon Him, for He is the Absolute Truth.

After defining the Absolute Truth and expanding upon it in the *Vedas, Purāṇas,* and vast corollary literatures, Śrīla Vyāsadeva still felt discontented. His spiritual master, Devarṣi Nārada, finding his disciple so dejected, inspired him to go inwards, into deep meditation. In that state he perceived the highest Absolute Truth, who is free from the slightest illusion. The verse quoted above reflects Śrīla Vyāsadeva's spiritual perception. Nārada instructed his disciple to reveal the nature of the Supreme Lord's transcendental name, form, qualities, pastimes, paraphernalia, and associates. The result of Śrīla Vyāsadeva's efforts is the spotless *Purāṇa, Śrīmad-Bhāgavatam.*

Śrīla Vyāsadeva went to Badarikāśrama and, in the nearby place called Śamyāprāsa, went into *samādhi* and saw the Supreme Personality of Godhead. He also saw *māyā,* the divine potency of the Lord that deludes the conditioned souls. In this realized consciousness Śrīla Vyāsadeva described the Absolute Truth, the Supreme Personality of Godhead, as fully independent and transcendental. This implies that there is no one superior to Him or equal to Him. In the material world Lord Brahmā is accepted as the highest personality among the living entities. But even Lord Brahmā, who is described here as the *ādi-kavi,* the original intelligent being, is subservient to the fully independent Supreme Lord. Indeed, it was the Supreme Lord who first imparted the Vedic knowledge unto Lord Brahmā.

What to speak of the ordinary mortals, even great sages and powerful demigods become totally bewildered in their efforts to know the Supreme Lord. The purport of the word *dhīmahi*—"I meditate upon"—is that only those who have perfected the chanting of the Gāyatrī *mantra* can understand the supremely independent Lord. Who is eligible to chant the Gāyatrī *mantra?* Those who are controlled by the modes of ignorance and passion can never chant the Gāyatrī *mantra,* what to speak of attaining perfection in chanting it. Only those who possess the qualities of a *brāhmaṇa* and are situated in the mode of goodness are eligible to chant the Gāyatrī *mantra.* Gradually, by constant chanting, they come to realize Parabrahman (the Supreme Brahman), or the Absolute Truth. Only then can they perceive the Supreme Personality of Godhead, along with His transcendental name, form, qualities, pastimes, and paraphernalia, as well as the Vaikuṇṭha planets and the Lord of the Vaikuṇṭha planets, Nārāyaṇa. And when one develops a taste for engaging properly in the Lord's transcendental service and realizes the sublime mellows of devotion, one can see Lord Vāsudeva, Kṛṣṇa.

Mundane philosophers who try to attain the Supreme through the ascending process of knowledge can never achieve their goal. The only result of such an attempt, which naturally confuses them, is that they become rooted in the misunderstanding that man is God and vice versa, thus clearing their way to hell. A few among them may have a moment's glimpse of transcendence, but end up concluding everything backwards. They fall prey to the erroneous impersonal principle.

To refute this impersonal conception of the Absolute, the previously quoted verse from *Śrīmad-Bhāgavatam* unequivocally states that the Absolute Truth is a person. This transcendental personality is so powerful that He could impart the knowledge of the *Vedas* even to Lord Brahmā, who then went on to create the material universe. Lord Brahmā did not receive this extraordinary Vedic knowledge after creation but before he began the work of creation. The knowledge that existed before the mundane nature came into being is transcendental and is known as *saṁvit*. The *Viṣṇu Purāṇa* delves into the subjects of *sandhinī, saṁvit,* and *hlādinī,* the Lord's potencies of existence, knowledge, and pleasure. All together, these are known as the Lord's internal potency, or spiritual potency. The *Śrīmad-Bhāgavatam* also discusses the subject of the Lord's internal potency. This superior potency is quite different from the Lord's inferior, external potency, which is qualified by the three material modes. An example of the Lord's superior, spiritual potency is the *jīvas*. One who can understand that the *jīvas* are a product of the Lord's internal potency, not His external potency, can immediately grasp the difference between these two potencies.

Delusion is the perverted image of reality and is the hallmark of *māyā,* the Lord's external energy. This delusion is totally absent in His internal, spiritual potency. The *jīva* is a product of the Lord's superior, transcendental energy, but he becomes deluded into identifying his body as his self. Once this ignorance is dissipated, he can immediately understand the actual nature of the body. Illusion is possible on the mundane plane but never in the spiritual energy.

The variety visible in material nature is due to the influence of the Lord's spiritual energy. In other words, material nature is but a perverted reflection of spiritual energy. For example, sunlight is ever existing, but when sunlight is reflected on water, there comes into being a new source of light that must accept the cycle of creation, maintenance, and annihilation. The original sun, of course, is not bound by such changes. This practical analogy helps us understand that the spiritual nature is transcendental to creation, maintenance, and annihilation, whereas the perverted reflection of the spiritual energy—the material nature—is bound by these three conditions. The material nature is illusory: sometimes it is there, and at other times it is not. When this illusory, temporary existence of "there and not there" is totally removed and in its place are manifested the name, form, qualities, associates, paraphernalia, and abode of the Lord, one is on the platform of *satyaṁ param,* the Absolute Truth, who is described here has *nirasta-kuhakam,* "forever free from the illusory representation of the material world".

The *jīva* has been referred to as the Lord's marginal potency. The *jīva* is unpredictable: sometimes he is under the material energy's control, and at other times under the spiritual energy's shelter. But the supreme, infallible Lord never comes under the sway of any of His energies: He forever remains the absolute autocrat, the master of all energies, the Supreme Personality of Godhead, Vāsudeva. All energies emanate from Him, and thus He is the supreme energetic principle. When the two words *sva-rāṭ* ("independent") and *param* ("supreme") are used to describe an entity, then He must be the Supreme Personality of Godhead, the eternal cause of all causes. That the Supreme Lord never comes under the influence of *māyā* is confirmed elsewhere in the *Śrīmad-Bhāgavatam* (1.11.38):

etad īśanam īśasya
prakṛti-stho 'pi tad-guṇaiḥ
na yujyate sadātma-sthair
yathā buddhis tad-āśrayā

> This is the divinity of the Personality of Godhead: He is not affected by the qualities of material nature, even though He is in contact with them. Similarly, the devotees who have taken shelter of the Lord do not become influenced by the material qualities.

It is the Supreme Lord's special prerogative to descend to this material world and remain unaffected by it and detached from it. And like Him, His pure devotees also remain unattracted by the glare of the phenomenal world. As the Supreme Lord is eternal, liberated, and pure, so are His devotees, whatever situation they may be in. This can easily be understood through a simple example: technological advancement has added things like cinemas to the material attractions nature already has to offer, and yet, strangely, these illusory enticements have failed to attract genuine saints and hermits even to this day. And although we do see that some so-called modern saints and mendicants are addicted to cannabis and tobacco, even they are repulsed by many other modern sensual distractions. If the illusory material world holds little or no attraction for the Lord's devotees, how much less must the Lord Himself be attracted to it! Therefore, although out of ignorance one might claim that mere mortals are God, that does not change the reality—that man is always man and God is always God, and never otherwise.

Once one of the *brahmacārīs* of our *āśrama* met Dr. Sarvapalli Radhakrishnan, who is a spiritualist of sorts and an erudite scholar. Dr. Radhakrishnan is the vice-president of India as I write this essay. On meeting him, our *brahmacārī* received from him a copy of his *Bhagavad-gītā* as a gift. Dr. Radhakrishnan had translated this *Gītā* into English and written a commentary on it, and it sold well in the market for ten rupees in those days [1954].

The *brahmacārī* read the book and came to us a little dissatisfied, though the book itself was deeply esoteric. The reason for his dissatisfaction was that Dr. Radhakrishnan's writing lacked spiritual insight: in many places he had mishandled and misinterpreted the text, and thus he had made his book unacceptable to spiritualists in the line of pure devotion. This is a perfect example of the *Śrīmad-Bhāgavatam's* statement (1.1.1) that "by Him even the great sages and demigods are placed into illusion" (*muhyanti yat sūrayaḥ*). When the Lord so easily bewilders Lord Brahmā, Lord Śiva, Lord Indra, and other great universal controllers, it is not at all surprising that Dr. Radhakrishnan is placed into illusion.

The *brahmacārī* was especially shocked and hurt by Dr. Radhakrishnan's misinterpretation of Text 34 of Chapter 9, which appears in his book on page 254. He came to us very depressed, wanting to discuss this passage. The following words were found in the book:

> It is not the personal Kṛṣṇa to whom we have to give ourselves up utterly but the Unborn, Beginningless, Eternal who speaks through Kṛṣṇa.

We have not the slightest intention of confronting a world-famous philosopher like Dr. Radhakrishnan with arguments, yet on the *brahmacārī's* repeated request we have to scrutinize the text and point out the discrepancies. We have great respect for Dr. Radhakrishnan, not only because he is the vice-president of our country but also because of his scholarship and his position as an erudite master of Hindu philosophy. Furthermore, he is faithful to the brahminical tradition he hails from and is a follower of the Māyāvāda school. Going by the oft-quoted dictum that it is better to have a learned enemy than a foolish friend, I feel encouraged in this matter. An intelligent opponent will present reasonable rebuttals, but an ignorant friend may bring about disaster with his floundering. Therefore we feel no compunction about strongly arguing against the points Dr. Radhakrishnan makes in his *Bhagavad-gītā* commentary.

A well-known Bengali saying goes, "After reading the whole *Rāmāyaṇa,* you want to know whose father Sītā is?" This question is ludicrous, since Sītā is Lord Rāma's wife, and thus such a query will naturally invite quips and laughter. We find the same absurdity in Dr. Radhakrishnan's English commentary on the *Gītā.* He writes that we do not have to surrender to the person Kṛṣṇa but to "the Unborn, Beginningless, Eternal" within Kṛṣṇa. This implies that Lord Kṛṣṇa and His "inner self" are two separate identities. According to Dr. Radhakrishnan, since there is a difference between Kṛṣṇa's body and His soul, we must surrender to Kṛṣṇa's soul and not His body. This new discovery in the field of religious philosophy reminds us of the "*paṇḍita*" of the Rāmāyaṇa referred to above. Lord Śrī Kṛṣṇa's sole purpose in speaking the *Bhagavad-gītā* is to convince us to surrender to His lotus feet. Yet right at the outset Dr. Radhakrishnan is unwilling to accept this point. Lord Kṛṣṇa gives the central instruction in the *Bhagavad-gītā* (18.66):

sarva-dharmān parityajya
māṁ ekaṁ śaraṇaṁ vraja
ahaṁ tvāṁ sarva—pāpebhyo
mokṣayiṣyāmi mā śucaḥ

Abandon all varieties of religion and just surrender unto Me. I shall deliver you from all sinful reactions. Do not fear.

Lord Kṛṣṇa spoke these words to Arjuna so that he would surrender to Him. The Sanskrit word *śaraṇam* in this *Gītā* text means "surrender." On page 62 of his "*Introductory Essay*", Dr. Radhakrishnan has also discussed the idea of surrender in some detail. He writes,

> *Prapatti* [surrender] has the following accessories—good will to all (*ānukūlyasya saṅkalpaḥ*); (ii) absence of ill will (*prātikūlyasya varjanam*); (iii) faith that the Lord will protect (*rakṣiṣyatīti viśvāsaḥ*); (iv) resort to Him as savior (*goptṛtve varanam*); (v) a sense of utter helplessness (*kārpaṇyam*); (vi) complete surrender (*ātma-nikṣepaḥ*).

These six limbs of surrender should be followed in relation to Kṛṣṇa, or Viṣṇu, because this instruction on the process of surrender appears in a Vaiṣṇava scripture. Dr. Radhakrishnan has translated the first limb (*ānukūlyasya saṅkalpaḥ*) as "good will to all." Question: is it possible to surrender to everyone? Surrender should be directed toward the Supreme Lord alone. Dr. Radhakrishnan's proposal is impractical, and indeed impossible. Long before Dr. Radhakrishnan wrote his commentary, many realized spiritual preceptors, including the famous Gosvāmīs of Vṛndāvana, explained that the words *ānukūlyasya saṅkalpaḥ* mean that one should render transcendental loving service to the Supreme Lord, Kṛṣṇa, favorably. No genuine scholar would be willing to disregard all other spiritual authorities and accept Dr. Radhakrishnan's version.

When Dr. Radhakrishnan uses the words "faith in the Lord," he definitely refers to the Supreme Personality of Godhead. By what logic does he say "Lord" but mean the impersonal Brahman? Arjuna certainly means the person Kṛṣṇa when he says (*Bhagavad-gītā*. 2.7), *śiṣyas te 'haṁ śādhi māṁ tvāṁ prapannam:* "Now I am Your disciple, and a soul surrendered unto You. Please instruct me." With these words he addresses Kṛṣṇa at the beginning of the *Bhagavad-gītā*. At this stage of the *Gītā* the impersonal Brahman is still to be discussed. When the subject of the impersonal Brahman is finally raised, Lord Kṛṣṇa unequivocally declares that He is the source of the impersonal Brahman. Sound logic says that one cannot surrender to something impersonal and formless. Those who are overly attached to the impersonal Brahman will find surrendering to this formless concept very painful and, indeed, impossible, and if they persist along this path they will end up surrendering to their wife, family, and relatives.

Transcendental Devotional Service Reveals the Real Form of the Lord

We learn from the *Śrīmad-Bhāgavatam* that, due to *māyā*, which makes the living entity fall down from spiritual practice, certain obnoxious atheists try hard to create a smokescreen of philosophical jargon around the Supreme Lord to keep Him hidden from the general populace. The result of this effort is also described in the *Bhāgavatam* (12.3.43):

kalau na rājan jagatāṁ paraṁ guruṁ
tri-loka-nāthānata-pāda-paṅkajam
prāyeṇa martyā bhagavantam acyutaṁ
yakṣyanti pāṣaṇḍa-vibhinna-cetasaḥ

> O King! in the Age of Kali people's intelligence will be diverted by atheism, and they will almost never offer sacrifice to the Supreme Personality of Godhead, who is the supreme spiritual master of the universe. Although the great personalities who control the three worlds all bow down to the lotus feet of the Supreme Lord, the petty and miserable human beings of this age will not do so.

A good example of such philosophical jargon meant to bewilder the public is Dr. Radhakrishnan's translating *ānukūlyasya saṅkalpaḥ* as "good will to all" instead of "surrendering to the Supreme Lord," its proper meaning. Such an interpretation is what we can expect from a mundane scholar.

The first word in devotional service is surrender. The only meaning of surrender is to accept that one is a servant of God.

Even great scholars and philosophers like Dr. Radhakrishnan will have to perform heaps of austerities and penances before they will yield to the process of surrender. This is the conclusion of *Bhagavad-gītā*. Dr. Radhakrishnan's explanation of the six limbs of surrender is superficial. Originally defined in a Vaiṣṇava text, these six limbs of surrender pertain to Lord Viṣṇu, or Kṛṣṇa. *Ānukūlya* means "loving devotion to Lord Kṛṣṇa." The *Bhakti-rasāmṛta-sindhu* states, *ānukūlyena kṛṣṇānu-śīlanaṁ bhaktir uttamā:* "One should render transcendental loving service to Lord Kṛṣṇa favorably. That is called pure devotional service."

Everyone in the world is rendering service to Lord Kṛṣṇa in one way or another. Some are doing it favorably, and others antagonistically. Those who are serving unfavorably are inimical atheists, the foolish nondevotees, while those who do it with pleasure are truly intelligent. In other words, the devotees of Kṛṣṇa are very intelligent, while the mundane scholars are in the same category as the nondevotee atheists led by the demons Kaṁsa and Jarāsandha.

The main instruction in the *Bhagavad-gītā* is to take complete shelter of Lord Kṛṣṇa. Yet this cardinal conclusion, which emanated from Lord Kṛṣṇa's own lotus lips, is reversed by Dr. Radhakrishnan when he writes that one should surrender not to the person Kṛṣṇa but to the "Unborn, Beginningless, Eternal who speaks through Kṛṣṇa." It is an exercise in futility to take up the *Gītā* for discussion only in order to ostentatiously display one's erudition, and thus to foolishly misinterpret the text so much that one concludes that the speaker of the *Bhagavad-gītā,* Lord Kṛṣṇa, is a mere mortal. This use of Vedic knowledge to pronounce that God does not exist is a clear example of serving Kṛṣṇa unfavorably.

How does Lord Kṛṣṇa describe scholars like Dr. Radhakrishnan, who propagate atheism in the name of the *Vedas*? In the *Bhagavad-gītā* (7.15) we find this statement:

na māṁ duṣkṛtino mūḍhāḥ
prapadyante narādhamāḥ
māyayāpahṛta-jñānā
āsuraṁ bhāvam āśritāḥ

Those miscreants who are grossly foolish, who are lowest among mankind, whose knowledge is stolen by illusion,

> and who partake of the atheistic nature of demons do not surrender unto Me.

Enemies of the Lord like Kaṁsa and Jarāsandha always meditated on Kṛṣṇa, but unfavorably. Similar to these demons are the atheistic scholars who always challenge and misrepresent the real teachings of the *Bhagavad-gītā*. Though they think about the Lord, they do so with enmity because their intelligence has been covered by *māyā*. Kaṁsa and Jarāsandha were also erudite scholars, but because they were obsessed with Kṛṣṇa in enmity, they were demons.

We understand from Lord Caitanya's teachings and exemplary actions that it is our duty to follow the instructions of the *Bhagavad-gītā* favorably. During Lord Caitanya's tour of South India, when He entered the premises of the Śrī Raṅganātha temple, He came upon a simple *brāhmaṇa* engrossed in reading the *Bhagavad-gītā*. The Lord was overjoyed to see how attentively the *brāhmaṇa* was reading, and how tears were streaming down his cheeks. Other *brāhmaṇas* sitting nearby knew that he was illiterate, and so they wondered how he could possibly read the *Gītā*.

Lord Caitanya easily solved this problem. He said that even an uneducated person can understand transcendental words if he is a fully surrendered soul. But without that mood of surrender, *Bhagavad-gītā* remains incomprehensible.

When Lord Caitanya saw the *brāhmaṇa* in tears, He asked him what part of the *Gītā* moved him to cry. With proper Vaiṣṇava humility, the *brāhmaṇa* answered,

> I am merely pretending to read the *Gītā;* in truth I am illiterate. But my *guru* instructed me to regularly read the entire *Bhagavad-gītā*, though I am unlettered. Not wanting to disobey my *guru,* I try to execute my duty, and so I make a show of reading the *Gītā*.

The Lord then asked him why he was crying. The *brāhmaṇa* replied,

> Whenever I sit down to read the *Gītā,* the form of Lord Kṛṣṇa as Pārtha-sārathi [Arjuna's chariot driver] appears in my heart. And as soon as I see this form I immediately remember how the Lord is *bhakta-vatsala* [especially kind to His devotees]. This thought makes me cry.

The Māyāvādīs are always eager to merge with the nondual Supreme Brahman and become God. But their small brains cannot understand how the Supreme Personality of Godhead can become the charioteer of His devotee and carry out his orders. In truth the Supreme Lord and the *jīvas* are eternally related, and because of this relationship many wonderful things are possible. But the Māyāvādīs cannot understand this truth, and many who have tried to make them understand have failed miserably. In the *śruti* (*Śvetāśvatara Upaniṣad* 6.23) we find this statement:

yasya deve parā bhaktir
yathā deve tathā gurau
tasyaite kathitā hy arthāḥ
prakāśante mahātmanaḥ

Only unto those great souls who have implicit faith in both the Lord and the spiritual master, all the imports of Vedic knowledge are automatically revealed.

Upon seeing the devotion of the South Indian *brāhmaṇa* as he read the *Gītā,* Lord Caitanya embraced him and then told him that he had perfected the reading of the *Gītā.* What fool would deny that Lord Caitanya's approval is far superior to millions of university doctorates? This accolade from the Lord proves that the *Bhagavad-gītā* cannot be studied with material intelligence. The knowledge of the *Gītā* must be received through the chain of *ācāryas,* or spiritual masters, coming down in disciplic succession. That is the only method; otherwise studying the *Gītā* is an exercise in futility. The scriptural conclusion is that since the Supreme Lord is transcendental, His words are also transcendental, and hence the esoteric subject matter of the *Bhagavad-gītā* can be received only through a disciplic succession that is equally transcendental. As the *Padma Purāṇa* states,

atah śrī-kṛṣṇa-nāmādi
na bhaved grāhyam indriyaiḥ
sevonmukhe hi jihvādau
svayam eva sphuraty adaḥ

No one can understand the transcendental nature of the name, form, quality, and pastimes of Śrī Kṛṣṇa through his materially contaminated senses. Only when one becomes spiritually situated by transcendental service to the Lord are the transcendental name, form, quality, and pastimes of the Lord revealed to him.

This is confirmed in the *Brahma-saṁhitā* (5.38):

premāñjana-cchurita-bhakti-vilocanena
santaḥ sadaiva hṛdayeṣu vilokayanti
yaṁ śyāmasundaram acintya-guṇa-svarūpaṁ
govindam ādi-puruṣaṁ tam ahaṁ bhajāmi

I worship Govinda, the primeval Lord, who is Śyāmasundara, Kṛṣṇa Himself with inconceivable innumerable attributes, whom the pure devotees see in their heart of hearts with the eye of devotion tinged with the salve of love.

Therefore, the scriptural conclusion is that mundane philosophers like Dr. Radhakrishnan are not qualified to delve into spiritual subjects. The devotees of the Lord alone are eligible to understand Lord Kṛṣṇa; no one else is qualified. As Kṛṣṇa Himself states in the *Bhagavad-gītā* (18.55), *bhaktyā mām abhijānāti yāvān yaś cāsmi tattvataḥ:* "One can understand Me as I am, as the Supreme Personality of Godhead, only by devotional service."

Scholars like Dr. Radhakrishnan should understand that within Lord Kṛṣṇa there is only Lord Kṛṣṇa and nothing else. Lord Kṛṣṇa's body and soul are the same. The *Gītā's* conclusion is that the nondual truth is Kṛṣṇa, the Absolute Supreme Being. But Dr. Radhakrishnan has somehow discovered another, second being within Kṛṣṇa. This discovery then converts Dr. Radhakrishnan into a believer in dualism! The manifestation of the Absolute Truth who resides in every *jīva*'s heart is lucidly described by Lord Kṛṣṇa in *Bhagavad-gītā*. In the *Bhagavad-gītā* (10.8), Lord Kṛṣṇa explains who the being residing in every *jīva's* heart is:

ahaṁ sarvasya prabhavo
mattaḥ sarvaṁ pravartate
iti matvā bhajante māṁ
budhā bhāva-samanvitāḥ

I am the source of all spiritual and material worlds. Everything emanates from Me. The wise who perfectly know this engage in My devotional service and worship Me with all their hearts.

And later in the *Gītā* (15.15) He says,

sarvasya cāhaṁ hṛdi sanniviṣṭo
mattaḥ smṛtir jñānam apohanaṁ ca
vedaiś ca sarvair ahaṁ eva vedyo
vedānta-kṛd veda-vid eva cāham

I am seated in everyone's heart, and from Me come remembrance, knowledge, and forgetfulness. By all the *Vedas,* I am to be known. Indeed, I am the compiler of Vedānta, and I am the knower of the *Vedas.*

The wise men with perfect knowledge—i.e. those who have purified their materialistic intelligence and are thus situated in spiritual knowledge—can understand Lord Kṛṣṇa as the source of everything. Unless the intellect is purified and spiritualized, even the most erudite philosopher and the greatest mystic *yogī* will become perplexed in trying to understand Lord Kṛṣṇa. As the Lord says in the *Bhagavad-gītā* (7.3), *yatatām api siddhānāṁ kaścin māṁ vetti tattvataḥ:* "Of those who have achieved perfection, hardly one knows Me in truth."

The Supreme Lord's name, form, qualities, pastimes, associates, and paraphernalia are all of the same spiritual nature. In fact, anything in relation to Lord Kṛṣṇa is nondifferent from Him. As the *Padma Purāṇa* states,

nāma cintāmaṇiḥ kṛṣṇaś
caitanya-rasa-vigrahaḥ
pūrṇaḥ śuddho nitya-mukto
'bhinnatvān nāma-nāminoḥ

The holy name of Kṛṣṇa is transcendentally blissful. It bestows all spiritual benediction, for it is Kṛṣṇa Himself, the reservoir of all pleasure. Kṛṣṇa's name is complete, and it is the form of all transcendental mellows. It is not a material name under any condition, and it is no less powerful than Kṛṣṇa Himself. Since Kṛṣṇa's name is not contaminated by the material qualities, there is no question of its being

> involved with *māyā*. Kṛṣṇa's name is always liberated and spiritual; it is never conditioned by the laws of material nature. This is because the name of Kṛṣṇa and Kṛṣṇa Himself are identical.

Only saintly souls can perceive the truth of these statements; those whose intelligence has been corrupted by Māyāvāda philosophy cannot understand.

In general, the monists cannot grasp the intricate philosophy of nondualism. So Dr. Radhakrishnan has spun out of his imagination a theory by which he tries to establish dualism in nondualism. When Dr. Radhakrishnan writes that we must surrender to "the Unborn, Beginningless, Eternal who speaks through Kṛṣṇa," he implies that it is the impersonal Brahman within Kṛṣṇa who is speaking about surrender. Once it is established that the impersonal Brahman can speak, then He must also possess the instrument of speech, namely the tongue. Thus we see that Dr. Radhakrishnan's whole concept of impersonalism is immediately undermined. There is sufficient evidence in the scriptures to conclude that one who talks can also walk. And a being capable of speaking and walking must indeed be endowed with all the senses. Then He must also be able to perform other activities, such as eating and sleeping. So how can Dr. Radhakrishnan claim that his beginningless, eternal object is impersonal?

In his "*Introductory Essay*", on page 62, Dr. Radhakrishnan writes,

> When we are emptied of our self [?], God takes possession of us. The obstacles to this God-possession are our own virtues, pride, knowledge, our subtle demands, and our unconscious assumptions and prejudices.

From his own arguments we can safely surmise that Dr. Radhakrishnan, due to his carelessness and previous upbringing, is seeing a difference between Lord Kṛṣṇa's body and His soul. He is still not free from false ego, that is, "emptied of self." Therefore his "virtues, pride, knowledge, subtle demands, and unconscious assumptions and prejudices" are all preventing him from understanding the transcendental truth. He must have been brought up in an atmosphere of Māyāvāda thought; for this reason he was unable to grasp the truth.

Śrīpāda Śaṅkarācārya, the founder and propagator of Māyāvāda philosophy, proved that the material world was an illusion—*mithyā*—and so he diligently pursued the path of austerity and renunciation, and he stressed it in his teachings. He did not waste valuable time trying to lord it over this illusory material world. But if he were to see the present condition of the philosophy he propounded, perhaps he would be ashamed. We have no doubt that Dr. Radhakrishnan was influenced by him; this is evident from his writings. Yet in his "*Introductory Essay*", page 25, he writes, "The emphasis of the *Gītā* is on the Supreme as the personal God who creates the perceptible world by His Nature (*prakṛti*). He resides within the heart of every being; He is the enjoyer and Lord of sacrifices. He stirs our heart to devotion and grants our prayers. He is the source and retainer of values. He enters into personal relations with us in worship and prayer."

After writing this and thus accepting the real purport of the *Gītā,* how can Dr. Radhakrishnan later state that Lord Kṛṣṇa's body and soul are different? Such an idea must be a result of his materialistic education. What a strange monism he propounds, in which the Absolute Truth, the nondual Supreme Being, is supposedly separate from His inner existence! Can Dr. Radhakrishnan explain these obvious flaws in his philosophy? When the Supreme Lord Himself is present in everyone's heart as the omniscient Supersoul, then who else can sit in *His* heart? In the *Gītā,* Lord Kṛṣṇa Himself speaks about His transcendental qualities, making statements that Dr. Radhakrishnan, armed with his material erudition, has made but a feeble attempt to contradict. Through such foolishness Dr. Radhakrishnan has made a show of spreading education, but in fact he has preached untruth.

Brahman, Paramātmā (the Supersoul), and Bhagavān (the Supreme Personality of Godhead)—all three are the same nondual Supreme Absolute. It would be ridiculous to say that Dr. Radhakrishnan is ignorant of this subject, yet we fail to see the logic in his claim that when the Supreme Lord incarnates He comes under the sway of *māyā.* The Lord unequivocally states in the *Gītā* that when He appears, He does so in His original transcendental form. Hence there can be no difference between Him and His body. The Lord further states that His appearance, activities, and so on are all transcendental, beyond the realm of matter. He is eternal, supremely pure, the original Supreme Personality and Supreme Brahman. We all agree that the *jīva* is covered by *māyā,* but if the Supreme Brahman, or Parabrahman, is also covered by *māyā,* then is *māyā* superior to Parabrahman?

Lord Kṛṣṇa Is the Supreme Controller Godhead

Since Dr. Radhakrishnan implies that the impersonal Brahman alone possesses such transcendental qualities as being inexhaustible, imperishable, and unborn, we must turn to the *Gītā* for a proper reply. In truth, all the divine expansions of the nondual Supreme Being are endowed with these same superexcellent qualities. As Arjuna declares in the *Bhagavad-gītā* (11.18):

tvam akṣaraṁ paramaṁ veditavyaṁ
tvam asya viśvasya paraṁ nidhānam
tvam avyayaḥ śāśvata-dharma-goptā
sanātanas tvaṁ puruṣo mato me

> You are the supreme primeval objective. You are the ultimate resting place of all this universe. You are inexhaustible, and You are the oldest. You are the maintainer of the eternal religion, the Personality of Godhead. This is my opinion.

We should understand that those passages in the *Gītā* which describe Parabrahman as *akṣara* ("indestructible") are references to Lord Kṛṣṇa, the Supreme Controller Godhead. Not once is Lord Kṛṣṇa equated with the *kṣara,* the conditioned *jīvas.* Not only big philosophers like Dr. Radhakrishnan, but even mighty demigods like Lord Brahmā and Lord Indra are in the category of *kṣara.* The Lord maintains the entire cosmic manifestation merely by His separated energy. Just as fire, though situated in one place, spreads its light and heat in all directions, so the unborn Supreme Lord, Kṛṣṇa, while maintaining His full personality, eternality, and imperishability, expands Himself into countless Viṣṇu forms, *jīvas,* and internal and external potencies. Expanding Himself in this way never diminishes or in any way affects His status as the Absolute Whole. As the *Īśopaniṣad* (Invocation) declares, *pūrṇasya pūrṇam ādāya pūrṇam evāvaśiṣyate:*

> Whatever is produced of the complete whole is also complete in itself. Because He is the complete whole, even though so many complete units emanate from Him, He remains the complete balance."

The Lord is the eternal Supreme Person, and therefore His name, form, qualities, pastimes, and so on are all eternal. The Sanskrit word *puruṣa* means "enjoyer." An enjoyer can never be a formless, impersonal, impotent being. Certainly Lord Kṛṣṇa is without material qualities, yet He is the enjoyer and possessor of all spiritual qualities.

In the *Bhagavad-gītā,* Arjuna glorifies Lord Kṛṣṇa as a *kṣara,* Parabrahman, and *ādi-deva* (the original Personality of Godhead), Dr. Radhakrishnan writes that the term *akṣara,* "inexhaustible," is synonymous with the word *avyaya,* "without deterioration." Therefore why does he conclude that Lord Kṛṣṇa and His body are different? This we fail to understand. On page 275, Dr. Radhakrishnan admits that Arjuna says Lord Kṛṣṇa is Parabrahman, Bhagavān, the Absolute Truth. In the same book and on the same page he writes something quite incoherent and fictitious and attributes it to Arjuna: "Arjuna states that the Supreme [Śrī Kṛṣṇa] is both Brahman and Īśvara, Absolute and God." If Dr. Radhakrishnan possesses such a sketchy and incorrect perception of the *Gītā* that he thinks Bhagavān is different from Brahman then how can he claim to have read the *Gītā?* He argues that Bhagavān and Supersoul Kṛṣṇa are products of *māyā,* while Brahman is not! Śrīla Kṛṣṇadāsa Kavirāja Gosvāmī has severely criticized such speculative philosophy. In the *Caitanya-caritāmṛta* he writes, "Not knowing that Brahman, Paramātmā, and Bhagavān are all features of Kṛṣṇa, foolish scholars speculate in various ways."

We accept both Arjuna and Śrīla Kṛṣṇadāsa Kavirāja Gosvāmī as greater authorities than Dr. Radhakrishnan. Arjuna directly heard the *Bhagavad-gītā,* and the President of India, Dr. Rajendraprasad, has accepted *Śrī Caitanya-caritāmṛta* as an authentic and authoritative scripture. Those who try to understand the *Bhagavad-gītā* by receiving it from one in the disciplic succession coming down from Arjuna can actually understand its esoteric knowledge; others fail miserably. It is imperative that one attentively hear what the *Bhagavad-gītā* and other authorized scriptures have to say about the impersonal Brahman. The scriptures amply prove that the impersonal Brahman is the Supreme Lord's bodily effulgence, just as sunshine is the brilliant emanation from the sun. Furthermore, as the sun's rays are dependent on and subservient to the sun, so the impersonal *brahmajyoti* effulgence, Lord Kṛṣṇa's bodily luster, is dependent on and subservient to the Lord. In the *Gītā* (14.27) He says:

brahmaṇo hi pratiṣṭhāham
amṛtasyāvyayasya ca
śāśvatasya ca dharmasya
sukhasyaikāntikasya ca

> And I am the basis of the impersonal Brahman, which is immortal, imperishable, and eternal and is the constitutional position of ultimate happiness.

The Lord's statements in the *Gītā* concerning the impersonal Brahman are unequivocal, yet Dr. Radhakrishnan seems unsatisfied with them. He grudgingly translates Text 27 of the Fourteenth Chapter, "For I am the abode of Brahman, the immortal and the Imperishable, of eternal law and of absolute bliss." Since Lord Kṛṣṇa is the basis of the impersonal, formless Brahman, He is certainly far superior to it. The mosquito net is inside the house, not the other way around; the ink-pot is on the table, not vice versa. Even a small boy can grasp this. Then why does Dr. Radhakrishnan hesitate to accept this truth? There are countless proofs in the scripture of Lord Kṛṣṇa's supreme absolute personality, but Dr. Radhakrishnan is like an owl in the daylight of truths. He tries to cover the sun of truth by creating a dark cloud of word jugglery. Thus instead of truth and knowledge, confusion is paraded before the world. We strongly condemn this sort of activity. Whether directly or indirectly, Dr. Radhakrishnan has tried to circumvent the truth—that Lord Kṛṣṇa is the basis of Brahman—and in the process he has been defeated. If Dr. Radhakrishnan really accepts Lord Kṛṣṇa as the absolute God, then what inspired him to see another being within Kṛṣṇa and to write, "It is not the personal Kṛṣṇa to whom we have to give ourselves up…"?

The truth is that only those who have been blessed by the Lord can fathom the spiritual science dealing with God. Dr. Radhakrishnan's book irrefutably proves this. The Māyāvādī philosophers are big offenders to the Supreme Lord, and therefore He never manifests Himself to them. As the Lord Himself declares in the *Gītā* (7.25), *nāhaṁ prakāśaḥ sarvasya yoga-māyā samāvṛtah muḍhaḥ:* "I am never manifest to the foolish and unintelligent. For them I am covered by My internal potency…" All previous spiritual authorities have condemned the Māyāvādīs, but Lord Śrī Kṛṣṇa Caitanya Mahāprabhu has directly censured them, calling them the greatest offenders against the Supreme Lord. He said that if a person simply hears philosophy from a Māyāvādī, his spiritual life is in jeopardy. As quoted in the *Śrī Caitanya-caritāmṛta* (*Madhya* 17.129–132 and 134–135), the Lord speaks about the Māyāvādīs in this way:

> Śrī Caitanya Mahāprabhu replied, "Māyāvādī impersonalists are great offenders unto Lord Kṛṣṇa; therefore they simply utter the words *brahman, ātmā* and *caitanya.* The holy name of Kṛṣṇa is not manifest in their mouths because they are offenders unto Kṛṣṇa, the Supreme Personality of Godhead, who is identical with His holy name. The Lord's holy name, His form and His personality are all one and the same. There is no difference between them. Since all of them are absolute, they are transcendentally blissful. There is no difference between Kṛṣṇa's body and Himself or between His name and Himself. As far as the conditioned soul is concerned, everything is different. One's name is different from the body, from one's original form and so on. The holy name of Kṛṣṇa, His body, and His pastimes cannot be understood by blunt material senses. They are manifest independently. The holy name of Kṛṣṇa, His transcendental qualities and pastimes as well as Lord Kṛṣṇa Himself are all equal. They are all spiritual and full of bliss."

The Māyāvādīs try to imitate Śrīpāda Śaṅkarācārya. Pretending to be orthodox, they reject the truth that the *jīva* is part and parcel of Parabrahman, the Supreme Lord. They also deny the fact that it is only the part and parcel aspect of Parabrahman (the *jīva*) and not Parabrahman Himself who falls under the spell of *māyā*. And worst of all, they deny that Parabrahman is none other than the Supreme Personality of Godhead. According to their lop-sided argument, when the *jīva* attains *mukti* (liberation) he merges into the impersonal Brahman and loses his individual identity. By this logic, when the Supreme Lord, the Parabrahman, incarnates in this material world or appears in the Deity form, He becomes an ordinary *jīva*. Thus the foolish Māyāvādīs draw a distinction between the Lord and His form, and in this way they commit great offenses against Him.

So, by knocking a wedge between Lord Kṛṣṇa and His form, Dr. Radhakrishnan has demonstrated his lack of intelligence; indeed, *māyā* has robbed him of intelligence, and according to Lord Caitanya Mahāprabhu he is the worst offender. In the *Bhagavad-gītā* the Lord describes such offenders as *mūḍhās* because they ascribe human frailties and faults to the Supreme Lord. Today the world has become a hell because of an excess of atheists, and this is due only to the preaching of Māyāvāda philosophy by enemies of the Supreme Lord. Lord Caitanya's mission is to save the *jīvas* from the clutches of these offenders. Those who are unconcerned about this mission commit offenses against Lord Caitanya.

The Māyāvādīs try hard to look like spiritualists, but in fact they are gross materialists. They may be able to confuse and mesmerize the public with word jugglery, but in truth their so-called renunciation is as false as the monkeys', for they have become mere beggars looking for distinction, adoration, position, and wealth. They are busy only with worldly progress; forgotten are the spiritual message and spiritual goals and ideals. The *Śrīmad-Bhāgavatam* (1.1.2) has defined such showbottle religion as *kaitava-dharma*, "cheating religion." Those who are attracted to such cheating religious groups are themselves deceitful. Their show of spirituality is abominable; they have no desire for either liberation or devotion and surrender. They are addicted to speculation and can never understand Kṛṣṇa.

When the Māyāvādīs pretend to perform *kīrtana* or hold discourses on the *Bhāgavatam* for personal name and fame, they may sing and talk about Brahman, Caitanya, and Paramātmā, but they cannot utter Lord Kṛṣṇa's name. Although the words *śrī-bhagavān uvāca* ("the Supreme Personality of Godhead said") appear throughout the *Bhagavad-gītā,* the Māyāvādīs are prepared to say everything else except the name of Kṛṣṇa. It is a well known scriptural truth that the words Brahman and Paramātmā refer ultimately to Lord Kṛṣṇa and that Kṛṣṇa is the principal name of the Supreme Absolute Person. But even when the Māyāvādīs chant such names of God as Kṛṣṇa, Govinda, or Hari, they do so not with the understanding and faith that these names are God's principal names and that they are nondifferent from the Supreme Lord, but rather with the idea that chanting them is a temporary means of *sādhana,* or spiritual practice. They also do not admit that such chanting of the holy name is an offense. Of course, their biggest offense is to distinguish between Lord Kṛṣṇa and His form. Thus in the *Gītā* (9.11), Lord Kṛṣṇa Himself condemns these offenders:

avajānanti māṁ mūḍhā
mānuṣīṁ tanum āśritam
paraṁ bhāvam ajānanto
mama bhūta-maheśvaram

Fools deride Me when I descend in the human form. They do not know My transcendental nature as the Supreme Lord of all that be.

Let us study how Dr. Radhakrishnan has translated this verse, which appears on page 242 of his book: "The deluded despise Me clad in human body, not knowing My higher nature as Lord of all existences." In other words, when the person who is "Lord of all existences" is "clad in human body," those who see from a materialistic perspective take Him for an ordinary mortal, while those who see from a spiritual perspective understand that He is the Supreme Being, the cause of all causes. So if it is the deluded who despise Lord Kṛṣṇa, then is it not time for Dr. Radhakrishnan himself to admit that he is guilty of this crime? Let him realize how he has abused the "Lord of all existences," equating Him with a mere mortal. When we see such big scholars are inimical toward Lord Kṛṣṇa, we can conclude, following the *Gītā,* that their intelligence has been stolen by *māyā.*

All the previous spiritual authorities have accepted Lord Kṛṣṇa as the Supreme Personality of Godhead. Even Śrīpāda

Śaṅkarācārya has accepted this truth. Yet Dr. Radhakrishnan is so deluded that he considers Lord Kṛṣṇa an ordinary *jīva,* or perhaps an extraordinary one.

There is no one who possesses more knowledge than Lord Caitanya. The knowledge of Kṛṣṇa consciousness, which is logical and scientific, must be received from Lord Caitanya. Has Dr. Radhakrishnan anywhere discussed Lord Kṛṣṇa on the basis of the precepts of Śrīla Jīva Gosvāmī, who is in the direct spiritual line of Lord Caitanya? We request Dr. Radhakrishnan to study the *Ṣaṭ-sandarbha* of Śrīla Jīva Gosvāmī. He was especially empowered by his spiritual masters to direct his writings toward the scholars and philosophers and make them understand this esoteric knowledge. Another philosopher of his stature is yet to be born; in fact, no one in the future will be able to surpass him in erudition. We hope that since Dr. Radhakrishnan is a philosopher, he will not reject Śrīla Jīva Gosvāmī's precepts.

From the writings of Dr. Radhakrishnan one can easily prove how he is perplexed in trying to fathom the science of Kṛṣṇa consciousness. He tries to present Lord Kṛṣṇa as an extraordinary human being and a historical figure of India, but the *Bhagavad-gītā* makes such a task impossible. In his "*Introductory Essay*" (page 30) he writes:

> In the *Gītā* Kṛṣṇa is identified with the Supreme Lord, the unity that lies behind the manifold universes, the changeless truth behind all appearances, transcendent over all and immanent in all. He is the manifested Lord, making it easy for mortals to know, for those who seek the imperishable Brahman reach Him no doubt but after great toil. He is called Paramātmān.
>
> How can we identify a historical individual with the Supreme God? The representation of an individual as identical with the universal Self is familiar to Hindu thought. In the *Upaniṣads,* we are informed that the fully awakened soul, which apprehends the true relation to the Absolute, sees that it is essentially one with the latter and declares itself to be so.

But the *jīva's* becoming "essentially one" with the Lord is not the last word in spiritual life. Of course, Śrīpāda Śaṅkarācārya propagated this idea so that atheists could at least come to this level of realization. But beyond this is the realm of the Supreme Absolute Personality of Godhead. Having entered the sphere of transcendence, if one does not perceive the supreme transcendental personality, one's spiritual practice remains incomplete due to contaminated intelligence, and one has to return to the realm of materialism. Though claiming that the world is an illusion—*jagan mithyā*—such an unsuccessful transcendentalist then becomes entangled in political, social, and altruistic affairs.

Dr. Radhakrishnan has never directly perceived the supreme transcendental personality, Lord Śrī Kṛṣṇa. Although Lord Kṛṣṇa is right in front of him, he cannot see Him, and thus out of delusion he calls Him a historical person. Genuine Indian religious philosophy teaches that there are both oneness with God and difference from Him. This concept of simultaneous oneness and difference has been termed *viśiṣṭādvaita, dvaitādvaita, śuddhādvaita,* and *acintya-bhedābheda-tattva.* If this esoteric concept were false, then Kṛṣṇa would not be worshiped throughout India, practically in every home. He is worshiped not as a historical figure but as the Supreme Lord. Kṛṣṇa's position as the Supreme Godhead is firmly established by the authoritative text *Śrīmad-Bhāgavatam,* which is the natural commentary on and essence of the *Vedānta-sūtra* and the Gāyatrī *mantra.* Many scholarly Māyāvādīs far more erudite than Dr. Radhakrishnan have tried to shake the faith of the general populace, but since time immemorial Kṛṣṇa temples have mushroomed by the millions—a slap in the face for the Māyāvādīs and atheists, who claim that Lord Kṛṣṇa is an ordinary mortal. In the future also, more Kṛṣṇa temples will be built to frustrate the agnostics and nonbelievers. All Viṣṇu temples are authorized by the scriptures and *ācāryas.* It hardly seems likely that, just for the sake of Dr. Radhakrishnan, the entire Indian population is going to strike a compromise with Māyāvāda philosophy.

Indian history is filled with accounts of many brilliant heroes who lit up the heavens with their fame. Why have the many sages and philosophers left aside these brilliant suns and chosen only Śrī Kṛṣṇa, Śrī Rāma, and Their expansions to worship as the Supreme Godhead? The spiritual preceptors who have delved into the scriptures to make an unbiased study of this phenomenon are scholars far more advanced than Dr. Radhakrishnan. Yet it is quite understandable that an ordinary mortal like Dr. Radhakrishnan is illusioned about Lord Kṛṣṇa, since even the residents of the heavenly planets are illusioned about Him. As stated in the *Śrīmad-Bhāgavatam* (1.1.1), *muhyanti yat sūrayaḥ:* "By Him even the great sages and demigods are placed into illusion." The earth planet is way down in the seventh position among the fourteen planets in this cosmic system, so its residents are endowed only with meager potency.

Among the countries of this meager planet earth, Bhāratavarṣa, or India, is the best because since the dawn of creation Indian sages have exhibited the most exceptional skill in pursuing the esoteric spiritual science. In days of yore, these sages could communicate with the higher planetary systems. But today India is in such a bad condition that we are not willing to follow the instructions of previous sages. We are willing to accept Kṛṣṇa as a historical figure, but by devious means we try to distort His instructions with confusing philosophical jargon. This is proof of India's undesirable state. India now has become eager to do away with the real God and replace Him with many fake Gods. This is the greatest misfortune for India.

Lord Kṛṣṇa Is the Supreme Personality of Godhead

It is strange but true that political leaders can never understand that the Absolute Truth cannot be impersonal or formless but must be the Supreme Personality of Godhead. The scriptures are filled with passages that describe incarnations such as the gigantic form of Lord Mahā-Viṣṇu lying on the Causal Ocean, but Lord Kṛṣṇa is the source of Mahā-Viṣṇu. Still the demented political leaders cannot comprehend the truth. But if out of His mercy Lord Kṛṣṇa wishes to bless such atheists, then their rocklike hearts will soften and they will see the two-handed form of Kṛṣṇa playing His flute in Vṛndāvana.

Those who try to understand Lord Kṛṣṇa without receiving His mercy, like Dr. Radhakrishnan, will certainly be deluded even if they are scholar-philosophers like him. The *Brahma-saṁhitā* says that Kṛṣṇa is easily manifest to the devotees but is beyond the reach of Vedic scholars. Śrīla Sārvabhauma Bhaṭṭācārya has proved this point by participating in a pastime of Lord Caitanya's in which the Bhaṭṭācārya exhibited his Vedic learning. In recent times, *paṇḍitas* such as Śrī Bankim Chattopadhyaya and Dr. Bhandarkar became equally deluded trying to approach this subject.

One who really wants to know Kṛṣṇa must follow the path He prescribes in the *Bhagavad-gītā* (18.55), *bhaktyā mām abhijānāti yāvān yaś cāsmi tattvataḥ.* "One can understand Me as I am, as the Supreme Personality of Godhead, only by devotional service." Except for devotional service, there is no way to understand Kṛṣṇa. When Lord Kṛṣṇa appeared in the form of Lord Caitanya Mahāprabhu, He gave the same instruction about attaining Kṛṣṇa through devotional service, so it is certain that Kṛṣṇa can be approached only in this manner. Following in the disciplic line of Lord Caitanya, the six Gosvāmīs of Vṛndāvana have written extensive literature with detailed explanations of Lord Kṛṣṇa. These confidential revelations are yet to be properly broadcast in the world. The Gosvāmīs' esoteric logic and profound analytical philosophy have not yet caught the attention of modern thinkers, and the burden of guilt for this discrepancy must indeed fall on us. The Gauḍīya Maṭha mission was founded to propagate the words of Śrīla Rūpa Gosvāmī and Śrīla Raghunātha dāsa Gosvāmī.

The gigantic universal form that Lord Kṛṣṇa exhibited to Arjuna is certainly not the quintessence of the Lord's divine mood. In fact, the two-handed human form of Kṛṣṇa playing the flute is the superexcellent manifestation of the Lord. But one must not make the mistake of thinking that because Lord Kṛṣṇa appears as a human, He *is* human. His form is eternal and full of knowledge and bliss, unlike an ordinary mortal's. He is not even an extraordinary human being. The human form may be a facsimile of the Supreme Lord's transcendental form, but that does not make God a man, or vice-versa. The Bible and other scriptures state that man was made according to the form of God, but that does not imply that God is a man.

There is substantial proof in the *Gītā* that those who thoroughly grasp the truth about God will, upon leaving the material body, enter into the spiritual realm and be with God. Only those who realize God as the eternal Supreme Personality can become immortal. This realization is the human being's prerogative alone, and one who attains it reaches the highest perfection. Once achieving perfection, the *jīva* never returns to this temporary world of birth, death, old age, and disease. Only those who discipline their lives so as to attain this objective fulfill the purpose of their human birth; others plunge into oblivion.

Māyā induces one to make plans so that this temporary life of birth, death, old age, and disease can be permanent. The greatest delusion is to plan a life of nonstop bliss in this material world. Which is the better plan: the one that leads to birth in lower animal species like hogs and dogs, or the one that transports the *jīva* back to Godhead? The *jīva's* spiritual existence in the abode of the Lord consists of service to Him in different mellows, such as servitude, friendship, parenthood, and conjugal love. Both Lord Kṛṣṇa and Lord Caitanya Mahāprabhu mercifully enacted pastimes to attract the *jīvas* and to teach them the meaning of the following words in the *Gītā:*

sarva-dharmān parityajya
mām ekaṁ śaraṇaṁ vraja
ahaṁ tvāṁ sarva-pāpebhyo
mokṣayiṣyāmi mā śucaḥ

> Abandon all varieties of religion and just surrender unto Me. I shall deliver you from all sinful reactions. Do not fear.

Who could be more deprived than those conditioned souls who do not try to understand this truth? In the words of Śrīla Narottama dāsa Ṭhākura, "One who has not tried to realize his relationship with the Lord has wasted his life; such a person is a miscreant and is worse than an animal.

Without proper understanding, Dr. Radhakrishnan has given his opinion about the descent of the Lord's incarnation. He writes, "An *avatār* is a descent of God into man and not an ascent of a man into God." What he means by "descent of God into man" is that the *avatāras,* or incarnations, possess physical bodies made up of the five gross elements. Of course, it remains to be clarified what he means by "not an ascent of man into God." Nowadays it is very much in vogue to designate a man as God. And it is not just a few who are said to be *avatāras:* many philosophers go as far as to say that *every* human being is God. For the present we do not wish to delve into this subject.

We would like to inform Dr. Radhakrishnan, however, that when the Supreme Lord empowers a *jīva* with His divine potency so that the *jīva* can carry out some specific work, then that *jīva* is known as a *śakty-āveśa avatāra*. But this is not the only type of incarnation. The scriptures describe innumerable incarnations of the Supreme Lord, such as *svayaṁ-rūpa, svayaṁ-prakāśa, āveśa, vilāsa, prābhava, vaibhava, yuga-avatāra, puruṣa-avatāra, guṇa-avatāra,* and *manvantara-avatāra*. If we calculate the duration of one *manvantara-avātara's* life, it comes to an incredible number of years—more than three hundred million. And there are other incarnations who live longer. The scriptures give details of the Lord's authorized incarnations—the purposes for their appearance, their forms, the places of appearance, their pastimes, and so on. There is no room for the *vox populi* whimsically choosing an ordinary mortal as an incarnation. And if despite the scriptural injunctions some people still accept a human being as an incarnation, it is easy to surmise the extent of their scriptural knowledge.

The goddess of learning, Sarasvatī, inspired Dr. Radhakrishnan to say "Man cannot become God." We would like to clarify this statement by saying "Even after becoming liberated, a man cannot become God." A liberated person can become a pure devotee of God, but he cannot become God or merge into God and lose his identity. There are innumerable instances in which a liberated soul, failing to become God, also refused to become God's devotee. The only option then open to him is aptly described in the *Śrīmad-Bhāgavatam* (10.2.32):

> *ye 'nye 'ravindākṣa vimukta-māninas*
> *tvayy asta-bhāvād aviśuddha-buddhayaḥ*
> *āruhya kṛcchreṇa paraṁ padaṁ tataḥ*
> *patanty adho 'nādṛta-yuṣmad-aṅghrayaḥ*

> O lotus-eyed Lord, although nondevotees who accept severe austerities and penances to achieve the highest position may think themselves liberated, their intelligence is impure. They fall down from their position of imagined superiority because they have no regard for Your lotus feet.

Attracted by material nature's external glare, such "liberated" souls have to come down to this earth and become wrapped up in some sociopolitical or altruistic work.

Besides the eternally conditioned *jīvas,* there are others, who are eternally liberated (*nitya-mukta*). They never come to this material world. Among the eternally conditioned *jīvas* (*nitya-baddha*) are those who make a big show of gaining liberation from this world. An analogy the Māyāvādīs often repeat is "All rivers flow into the ocean." This means that all *jīvas* merge into Brahman. But the truth that escapes them is that many large aquatics are permanent residents of the ocean and are never attracted to go and live in the river. The eternally liberated souls need not strive for liberation.

Dr. Radhakrishnan has used the expression "self-conscious man." We do not object to this term if it indicates a state of consciousness of the self in which a person realizes he is an eternal servant of God, Kṛṣṇa. Lord Caitanya came to teach this truth. Once the *jīva* realizes he is an eternal servant of Lord Kṛṣṇa, he ends his life of misery. He becomes liberated by that realization. And later he understands that liberation personified is standing nearby, waiting to serve him and all other eternal servitors of the Supreme Lord, Kṛṣṇa.

The authorized scriptures have declared that Kṛṣṇa is the original Supreme Lord and the source of all incarnations. In the *Bhagavad-gītā* (7.7), He says in His own words, *mattaḥ parataraṁ nānyat:* "O conqueror of wealth, there is no Truth superior to Me." Lord Kṛṣṇa came personally to teach that the highest Absolute Truth is not an impotent material concept. He is the full manifestation of absolute spiritual potencies. Those who cannot grasp this profound truth are fools spinning out endless speculations. That person who, although one, desires to expand and thus becomes many—can such a person be a human being or a formless impersonal entity? When this person decides to expand Himself manifold, is He doing so in order to destroy Himself? If the Lord were to lose His own identity by expanding Himself into many, that would mean destruction of Himself. Has the Supreme Lord committed such a foolish blunder? Or has the blunder been committed by those who misinterpret the Vedic statements and say that God expanded Himself into many entities and lost His identity? The Supreme Lord can do as He pleases: He can expand Himself as countless incarnations or as multifarious separated energies. And even after expanding Himself in this way, He remains complete and fully Himself, as He is. If this were not so, then how could He be the complete Absolute Whole?

Captivated by Māyā, the Jīva Has Forgotten Lord Kṛṣṇa

Lord Kṛṣṇa expands Himself into countless Viṣṇu forms as His *svāṁśa-vaibhava,* and He manifests Himself by His *vibhinnāṁśa-prakāśa* as countless billions of *jīvas.* All the Viṣṇu expansions are in the category of the Supreme Lord, but the *jīvas* are not: they are the Lord's marginal potency. This marginal potency, comprising the eternal *jīvas,* is a manifestation of the Lord's superior, spiritual energy, or *parā-śakti.* The conclusion of the *Bhagavad-gītā* is that the *jīva* is, was, and always will be eternally a manifestation of the Lord's spiritual energy; he will never enter the category of the Supreme Lord or the Viṣṇu forms. This separated energy of Kṛṣṇa's, known as *vibhinnāṁśa* or *jīva,* is an infinitesimal part of the Supreme Lord, much like the minute sparks of a large conflagration.

The fraction can never become the whole or equal to the whole. Thus the Māyāvādīs' claim that the fraction *can* become the whole is mischievous, even nefarious. This is the Vedic verdict. After overcoming his conditioned state, the fractional *jīva* enters the spiritual sky and participates in the Supreme Lord's transcendental, eternally blissful pastimes. The *jīva* permanently engages in the Lord's service in one of the many spiritual mellows and enjoys divine ecstasy.

The scriptures have clearly indicated that the ecstasy of devotional service to the Supreme Lord is far superior to the bliss of impersonal liberation, *brahmānanda.* Indeed, the happiness of merging into the Lord's existence (*sāyujya-mukti*) is like a puddle of water in a calf's hoofprint compared with the ocean of bliss derived from devotional service. The devotee never prays for the *jñānī's sāyujya-mukti,* for it is an impossible proposition. By *sāyujya-mukti* the impersonalists mean relinquishing one's identity, or individuality. This is nothing less than spiritual suicide. In this regard, I reproduce Dr. Radhakrishnan's comment on the Bible:

> The doctrine of the Incarnation agitated the Christian world a great deal. Arioes maintained that the Son is not

> the equal of the Father but created by Him. The view that they are not distinct but only different aspects of one Being is the theory of Sabellius. The former emphasized the distinctness of the Father and the Son and the latter their oneness. The view that finally prevailed was that the Father and the Son were equal and of the same substance; they were, however, distinct persons. ("*Introductory Essay,*" p. 35)

These words vaguely describe the philosophy of "simultaneously one and different," therefore we acknowledge it. Jesus, the son of God, is a *jīva,* a separated part of the Supreme Godhead. But the *jīva* is also spiritual, and hence Jesus is qualitatively the same as the Supreme Lord. But the son can never be equal to the Father in all respects; that is to say, the *jīva* is never on the same platform as the Supreme Lord. Also, all the *jīvas* are separate individuals. And just as each *jīva* is a unique personality, so God is also a unique personality, but the difference is that He is absolute. By describing the Lord as impersonal and formless, one loses sight of His perfect wholeness. We find the *Brahma-saṁhitā* (5.39) boldly declaring the Lord's Supreme Personality:

rāmādi-mūrtiṣu kalā-niyamena tiṣṭhan
nānāvatāram akarod bhuvaneṣu kintu
kṛṣṇaḥ svayaṁ samabhavat paramaḥ pumān yo
govindam ādi-puruṣaṁ tam ahaṁ bhajāmi

> I worship Govinda, the primeval Lord, who manifested Himself personally as Kṛṣṇa and the different *avatāras* in the world in the forms of Rāma, Nṛsiṁha, Vāmana, etc., as His subjective portions.

All these incarnations of the Supreme Lord are full-fledged divinities. They are not influenced by anyone's whims; they do not become impersonal or formless upon someone saying so. They are eternally present. When They deem it necessary, They appear in Their original transcendental forms, and then They disappear, just as the sun rises and sets. After Their appearance They perform manifest pastimes, and after Their disappearance They continue with Their unmanifest pastimes. According to the above mentioned *Brahma-saṁhitā* text, Lord Kṛṣṇa is the original Supreme Personality and all the incarnations are His partial expansions. But the Lord's incarnations are never in the category of the *jīvas.* Śrīla Vyāsadeva has also expounded this truth in the *Śrīmad-Bhāgavatam* (1.3.28): *ete cāṁśa-kalāḥ puṁsaḥ kṛṣṇas tu bhagavān svayam.* "All of the above mentioned incarnations are either plenary portions or portions of the plenary portions of the Lord, but Lord Śrī Kṛṣṇa is the original Personality of Godhead." In other words, not only do the incarnations appear, but Lord Kṛṣṇa, the source of all incarnations, also appears, both as Himself and as an incarnation. These esoteric subjects are understood by the Lord's devotees, not by others, even though they may be erudite scholars.

Therefore, when Dr. Radhakrishnan writes that Lord Kṛṣṇa is an ordinary mortal, or at best an extraordinary one, he is certainly confused. Lord Kṛṣṇa is the Supreme Personality of Godhead, the highest Absolute Truth, unsurpassable and perfectly divine. It is impossible to think of Him as impersonal and formless. He is indeed the transcendental, primeval Lord, the embodiment of eternity, absolute knowledge, and bliss. In the *Bhagavad-gītā* (10.12), Arjuna substantiates this truth about Lord Kṛṣṇa's absolute, supreme divinity. How is Dr. Radhakrishnan to appreciate Lord Kṛṣṇa's transcendental qualities and personality, since even the demigods fail to comprehend them? The word *ādi-deva,* meaning "the original, primeval Lord," indicates that Lord Kṛṣṇa is the origin of all the Viṣṇu expansions. The *Puruṣa-sūkta* prayers in the *Vedas* glorify Kāraṇodakaśāyī Viṣṇu, yet Lord Kṛṣṇa is the ultimate source of even this Viṣṇu expansion. Indeed, the *Brahma-saṁhitā* expressly declares that Kāraṇodakaśāyī Viṣṇu is merely a partial expansion of Lord Kṛṣṇa. Thus the Absolute Truth Dr. Radhakrishnan accepts as eternal and beginningless is, in fact, Lord Kṛṣṇa, but somehow this escapes him.

That Lord Kṛṣṇa is the original Supreme Personality of Godhead is accepted not only by Arjuna but by illustrious saints and sages like Vyāsadeva, Nārada, Devala, and Asita. All the previous spiritual preceptors, as well as present-day saints and countless millions of ordinary people, unanimously accept Lord Kṛṣṇa as the Supreme Godhead, but a famous *paṇḍita* like Dr. Radhakrishnan hesitates to accept Him as God! Why? Śrīla Yāmunācārya aptly explains in his *Stotra-ratna:*

tvāṁ śīla-rūpa-caritaiḥ parama-prakṛṣṭaiḥ
sattvena sāttvikatayā prabalaiś ca śāstraiḥ

prakhyāta-daiva-paramārtha-vidāṁ mataiś ca
naivāsura-prakṛtayaḥ prabhavanti boddhum

O my Lord, those influenced by demoniac principles cannot realize You, although You are clearly the Supreme by dint of Your exalted activities, forms, character, and uncommon power, which are confirmed by all the revealed scriptures in the quality of goodness and the celebrated transcendentalists in the divine nature.

In the *Bhagavad-gītā* (Chapter 4), Lord Kṛṣṇa speaks about the importance of receiving the transcendental knowledge of the *Gītā* in the proper disciplic succession. In this way one can avoid making the mistakes described above, which even powerful sages are prone to make. Yet there are those who still try to study the *Gītā* on their own and draw their own concocted conclusions, rejecting the authority and conclusions of the spiritual disciplic succession. We certainly commiserate with them, but at the same time it is hard not to laugh at them. From Chapter 4 of the *Bhagavad-gītā* we learn that after an interval of several million years, Lord Kṛṣṇa re-established the spiritual link with the disciplic succession right in the middle of the Battlefield of Kurukṣetra, explaining to Arjuna unequivocally and in detail the science of right action, knowledge, and devotional service. The *Bhagavad-gītā* is not a novel rendition of a new philosophy. Lord Śrī Kṛṣṇa is eternally the original Supreme Personality of Godhead. Similarly, the *Bhagavad-gītā* is eternally present as His instructions propounding the absolute, undifferentiated truth. The Supreme Lord is eternal, perennially young, and so are His immortal words: they are everfresh. Mundane scholars can always discover novel meanings in the *Bhagavad-gītā,* and in this way they may certainly exhibit their mundane erudition—but this is all just the play of *māyā.* The real essence of *Bhagavad-gītā* cannot be transmitted through such persons. The transcendental knowledge of the *Gītā* is available only through the transparent medium of the authorized disciplic succession. The devotees and saints are solely concerned with receiving the Lord's message in the *Gītā* as it is, while the mundane scholars fond of word jugglery look for secondary meanings.

To educate those who are enamored by empirical arguments and who do not receive transcendental knowledge through any bona fide disciplic succession—and who are thus going astray—we have compiled the essential knowledge of the *Bhagavad-gītā* in a nutshell:

1) Lord Śrī Kṛṣṇa is the Supreme Absolute Truth, the Supreme Personality of Godhead, the cause of all causes. The definition of God is given in this aphorism from the *Vedas:* "By Him and from Him is manifest this universe, and He controls its creation, sustenance, and annihilation." He is the mainstay of both this unlimited variegated cosmic manifestation and the immeasurable spiritual sky, the Vaikuṇṭhas. He is the eternally existing, transcendental Supreme Being with a spiritual form. The impersonal Brahman is but His bodily effulgence; He is the nondual Truth. The Supersoul (Paramātmā) is His plenary expansion who resides in everyone's heart and pervades the entire creation as well.

2) The *jīvas,* the living entities, are Lord Kṛṣṇa's minute parts. Although the *jīva* is qualitatively nondifferent from the Lord, he is quantitatively different from Him, since the Lord is infinite and *jīva* is infinitesimal. The *jīva* is situated in the Lord's marginal potency, which, inconceivably, is simultaneously one with and different from the Lord.

3) The *jīvas,* the marginal energy of the Lord, have the ability to reside eternally either in Vaikuṇṭha or in this material world. A *jīva* falls down to material nescience because of countless sinful activities, and in these alien surroundings he goes up and down, traveling through all the planetary systems, from Lord Brahmā's planet down to Pātālaloka. In the material world the *jīva* experiences birth, disease, old age, and death and is forced to accept three types of suffering, namely: those miseries stemming from his own mind and body, those inflicted by other living entities, and those hurled at him by the demigods.

4) The conditioned living entities are encaged in this many-faceted prison-house called the material world. The nature of this world is creation, sustenance, and destruction. During creation and sustenance this material nature is in a manifest state, and with destruction it again becomes unmanifest. Thus

this mundane, illusory realm is the Lord's inferior energy because it is sometimes manifest and at other times unmanifest.

5) Beyond this manifest and unmanifest external energy of the Lord exists another realm, which is transcendental and spiritually variegated. This is the unlimited spiritual sky, known as Vaikuṇṭha, which is everlasting. This realm is always manifest; it is never unmanifest. Thus it is not subject to creation and annihilation.

6) Those conditioned souls who identify with this illusory material nature and are proud of it, and who do not care to know about the Supreme Lord, are subjugated by the Lord's illusory potency, who is known variously as Mahā Kālī, Cāṇḍī, and Durgā, and who pierces them with her trident of the threefold miseries. These demoniac *jīvas* are forced into slavery by the illusory potency—Kālī, or Mahāmāyā. The *Bhagavad-gītā,* which is the essence of all the Vedic scriptures, was compiled for the deliverance of the conditioned souls. By studying the *Gītā* carefully, a *jīva* takes shelter of the Supreme Lord's lotus feet and attains liberation from the merry-go-round of repeated suffering in the material world.

7) The conditioned *jīva* suffers from the material disease—the threefold miseries of birth, death, old age and disease. When this suffering becomes unbearable, he looks for relief. Those who are less intelligent embrace the path of impersonal liberation and undertake severe austerities to achieve their goal. More elevated than these salvationists are the devotees of the Lord, who realize that their eternal nature is to be His servants. They do not try to extinguish this nature but rather practice and preach the eternal process of devotion so they can enter the Lord's eternal spiritual abode. All living entities have a right to practice this eternal process of devotional service.

8) The *mahat-tattva,* the material nature, manifests itself in twenty-four ingredients: 1) the unmanifest principle, 2) false ego, 3) intelligence, 4) mind, 5) ether, 6) air, 7) fire, 8) water, 9) earth, 10) sound, 11) touch, 12) form, 13) taste, 14) smell,

15) ears, 16) skin, 17) eyes, 18) tongue, 19) nose, 20) stomach, 21) hands, 22) feet, 23) anus, 24) genitals.

9) The undifferentiated Absolute Truth, the original Supreme Personality, Lord Śrī Kṛṣṇa, incarnates in this material world once in every day of Lord Brahmā—that is once every 8,640,000,000 solar years—to shower His mercy upon both His surrendered devotees and the atheistic nondevotees. He protects His devotees and slays the atheistic demons, thus giving the latter troublesome release, so to speak, in impersonal liberation. The *Bhagavad-gītā,* on the other hand, teaches liberation through devotional service to the Supreme Lord. The only way to obtain this devotional service is to take full shelter of the spiritual authority, the *guru,* who is coming in the line of a proper disciplic succession. Those who toil without worshiping the spiritual master will find that all their endeavors are futile.

10) Those foolish souls who refuse to take shelter of a bona fide *guru* are truly shelterless. Without the guidance of a *guru,* these rascals consider themselves knowledgeable, and on the basis of this misconception they make the mistake of worshiping God as a man and a mere mortal as God.

11) The Supreme Personality of Godhead is full in six opulences and is not the property of any particular sect, group, or country. He is available to everyone. He is the deliverer of all and the supreme father of all. He appears in this material world to liberate every living entity, and His message, the *Bhagavad-gītā,* is therefore applicable to every land and to all people. It is meant to be preached everywhere. Therefore those fortunate souls who are spreading the message of the Lord are most dear to Him.

12) Foolish, demoniac rascals in the grip of the Lord's illusory energy loudly brag about their materialistic plans. The *Bhagavad-gītā* alone can penetrate their hard shell of ignorance and awaken them to the truth.

13) With concerted, strong preaching, the devotees of the Lord must inform such foolish men that their so-called plans will surely be undermined because the platform they have

chosen to build their dream houses on is factually a mirage—a movie only. Reality is elsewhere. The information needed to transport one to that realm of reality and truth is available in the magazine called *Back to Godhead.*

14) Therefore, the real symptom of a true civilization is that its citizens are inspired by *Back to Godhead* to take up the process of devotion and go back to Godhead, where they will eternally reside in their actual home. Only in this way can they end all futile labor.

15) Just as the most sinful wretch lives in a ghostly body after death and moves about in the ether, having been denied a gross body, so the impersonalist, although rising to the point of liberation in the transcendental position, falls back down to the material world because of not having developed the mood of loving service to the Supreme Lord. Therefore the severe austerities and penances the impersonalist performs are not equivalent to the eternal religion of devotional service.

16) When monists are so attached to the formless, impersonal aspect of the Lord that they distinguish between Him and His transcendental body, their consciousness becomes contaminated by this blasphemy, and thus they are deprived of a place in the Lord's eternal abode. But if by some good fortune they come in touch with a pure devotee and hear from him with faith about the Lord's transcendental name, qualities, pastimes, and so on, then they will certainly be cleansed of their contamination and become inspired and attracted by the Lord's glorious character, and finally they will surrender to Him fully. Thus the *Bhagavad-gītā* is such an instructive text that for those who want to enter into the eternal pastimes of the Supreme Lord, its unequivocal message teaches the first stages of surrender, and this surrender is absolutely essential for reaching the ultimate destination. It is to be understood that the pure devotees have successfully passed this test of surrender according to the tenets of the *Bhagavad-gītā.*

Buddhi-yoga

The Highest Use of Intelligence

The Highest Use of Intelligence

The *Śrīmad-Bhāgavatam* (10.2.32) states:

ye 'nye 'ravindākṣa vimukta-māninas
tvayy asta-bhāvād aviśuddha-buddhayaḥ
āruhya kṛcchreṇa paraṁ padaṁ tataḥ
patanty adho 'nādṛta-yuṣmad-aṅghrayaḥ

O lotus-eyed Lord, although nondevotees who accept severe austerities and penances to achieve the highest position may think themselves liberated, their intelligence is impure. They fall down from their position of imagined superiority because they have no regard for Your lotus feet.

Thus the yogic process a surrendered servant of the Supreme Lord practices is altogether different from Patañjali's eightfold *yoga* system, beginning with sense control, yogic postures, and breath control. These practices are, in a sense, meant to increase physical prowess for better sense enjoyment. The devotee, on the other hand, follows the best *yoga* system of God-realization, which is enunciated in the *Bhagavad-gītā*. His activities are not selfishly motivated, aimed at realizing his own cherished dreams, but are directed toward fulfilling the will of God on earth. This *yoga* is known as *buddhi-yoga,* wherein lies the entire world's good fortune.

In the *Bhagavad-gītā* (6.46–47) Lord Kṛṣṇa states:

tapasvibhyo 'dhiko yogī
jñānibhyo 'pi mato 'dhikaḥ
karmibhyaś cādhiko yogī
tasmād yogī bhavārjuna

yoginām api sarveṣāṁ
mad-gatenāntar-ātmanā

śraddhā-vān bhajate yo māṁ
sa me yukta-tamo mataḥ

> A *yogī* is greater than the ascetic, greater than the empiricist, and greater than the fruitive worker. Therefore, O Arjuna, in all circumstances be a *yogī.* And of all *yogīs,* the one who with great faith always abides in Me, thinks of Me within himself, and renders transcendental loving service to Me—he is most intimately united with Me in *yoga* and is the highest of all. That is My opinion.

The devotee is placed in the highest position because his sole intention is to establish the will of the Supreme Lord in the world. Once everything in the world is conducted according to the Lord's desire, all activities will be spiritual and the Lord's presence will be felt everywhere and in everything. For the devotee, therefore, the purpose of *yoga* is not to attain such mean and miserly goals as liberation or sense enjoyment, but to re-establish his loving relationship of devotional service to the Lord and to spread this truth throughout the world. He knows that without being on the platform of Brahman, one cannot render the Lord pure devotional service, the highest stage of transcendence. Yet he also knows that Brahman realization is a concomitant of the highest stage of devotional surrender. Therefore, if through devotional service he can help create an atmosphere of spirituality that will pervade the earth and make everything blissful, then why should he strive for the meager, selfish joys of liberation?

Lord Caitanya declared that the constitutional position of every living entity is to be an eternal servant of Lord Kṛṣṇa. Therefore every *jīva* is inherently a liberated being. The *jīva's* present conditioned state is an illusion caused by his forgetting Lord Kṛṣṇa. Lord Kṛṣṇa says in the *Bhagavad-gītā* that the *jīva* is His separated part. The conditioned soul is enchained by the mind, senses, and so on, which are agents of *māyā,* the illusory energy. The *jīva* is now in captivity as a result of his previous sinful activities, but why should he remain so eternally? His imprisonment can be easily ended simply by the Lord's mercy. And if the Lord's mercy is not available, then on his own the *jīva* can never free himself. Conceited persons who think they can obtain liberation without the Lord's mercy, simply by performing strict penances and austerities, are totally mistaken; they fail.

Still, although receiving the Lord's mercy is the prime cause for attaining liberation, the Lord does not participate directly in the affairs of the conditioned soul. As the Lord states in the *Bhagavad-gītā* (5.14), referring both to the *jīva* and Himself:

na kartṛtvaṁ na karmāṇi
lokasya sṛjati prabhuḥ
na karma-phala-saṁyogaṁ
svabhāvas tu pravartate

> The embodied spirit, master of the city of his body, does not create activities, nor does he induce people to act, nor does he create the fruits of action. All this is enacted by the modes of material nature.

Although the above statement is true, it is under the Lord's guardianship that the *jīva* souls in the conditioned state experience the dualities of heat and cold, pleasure and pain, and so on, according to their activities. Since this is all indirectly controlled by the Lord, it is futile to complain about it. One should simply pray for His mercy, and all dualities will be eradicated. Therefore the Lord's devotees are never perturbed by dualities. The pious and intelligent person thinks that the sufferings inflicted upon him due to his previous sinful activities are only slight because of the Lord's mercy, and that by His mercy all suffering can be relieved in a moment. As Lord Brahmā states in the *Śrīmad-Bhāgavatam* (10.14.8):

tat te 'nukampāṁ su-samīkṣamāṇo
bhuñjāna evātma-kṛtaṁ vipākam
hṛd-vāg-vapurbhir vidadhan namas te
jīveta yo mukti-pade sa dāya-bhāk

> My dear Lord, one who earnestly waits for You to bestow Your causeless mercy upon him, all the while patiently suffering the reactions of his past misdeeds and offering You respectful obeisances with his heart, words and body, is surely eligible for liberation, for it has become his rightful claim.

Within their hearts, the broad-minded, pure devotees of the Lord are informed of the Lord's orders and the workings of the material nature. They are also aware that the fully independent Supreme Lord, who is eternally engaged in transcendental activities, chooses a particular land in which to unfold His earthly pastimes, and that this designated country is Bhārata-varṣa, or India. Therefore all Indians should execute the Supreme Lord's commands. As Śrīla Kṛṣṇadāsa Kavirāja Gosvāmī says in his *Caitanya-caritāmṛta* (*Ādi* 9.41):

bhārata-bhūmite haila manuṣya-janma yāra
janma sārthaka kari' kara para-upakāra

> One who has taken his birth as a human being in the land of India [Bhārata-varṣa] should make his life successful and work for the benefit of all other people.

It is indeed true that Indians are especially able to benefit others worldwide. But if the Indians do not meet this responsibility and instead get enticed and bedazzled by the illusory energy as it is manifest in the West in such variegated forms, then they will become known as misers and end their lives in disgrace. The sun is not visible at night because of the rotation of the earth, yet the sun is very much present in the sky, and the entire solar system is working under its influence. Similarly, the light of India's knowledge, contained in the sublime philosophy of the *Vedas,* the *Upaniṣads,* the *Vedānta-sūtra,* the *Purāṇas,* the *Gītā,* and their corollaries, is certainly available, but by divine will it is temporarily beyond our view due to the influence of ignorance and passion. Of course, by the Lord's will and by the mercy of His pure devotee, this knowledge will again spread everywhere. Lord Caitanya has made this prophecy:

pṛithivīte āche yata nagarādi-grāma
sarvatra pracāra haibe more nāma

> My holy name will be propagated in every town and village of this globe.

This prediction will very easily come true, for a pure devotee of the Lord can inundate the world with the tidal waves of love of Godhead, the religion preached by Lord Caitanya. Everything is possible if the Lord desires. And thus if the Lord desires, everyone can develop a loving mood of surrender to Him.

Indians must fearlessly preach the glories of the Lord far and wide. One who surrenders to the Supreme Lord, Nārāyaṇa, can easily face all dangers in the effort to propagate His message. As said in the *Śrīmad-Bhāgavatam* (6.17.28):

nārāyaṇa-parāḥ sarve
na kutaścana bibhyati
svargāpavarga-narakeṣv
api tulyārtha-darśinaḥ

Devotees solely engaged in the devotional service of the Supreme Personality of Godhead, Nārāyaṇa, never fear any condition of life. For them the heavenly planets, liberation, and the hellish planets are all the same, for such devotees are interested only in the service of the Lord.

When knowledge of the Absolute Truth, which is on the platform of pure goodness, is suppressed by the rampant influence of ignorance and passion, the sages and self-realized souls withdraw to a solitary place of worship and concentrate solely on elevating themselves spiritually. They also greatly benefit the few disciples who stay with them and serve them. But if the Lord desires, then these sages and *yogīs* come forward to benefit the world through missionary activities. For the ultimate good of the world, saintly kings like Janaka, Yudhiṣṭhira, and Kārtavīrya take up the burden of managing world affairs.

All the pastimes of the Supreme Lord in the spiritual world are eternal. His earthly pastimes are similarly transcendental and eternal. As the *Caitanya-bhāgavata* states, "Even at this very moment Lord Gaurāṅga is enacting His eternal, transcendental pastimes, but only the most fortunate souls can see them." When the sun sets, it goes out of our sight, but it continues to shine somewhere on this globe. Similarly, when the Lord winds up His earthly pastimes, He continues to manifest them in one or more of the uncountable millions of planets in the universe. As Lord Brahmā declares in the *Brahma-saṁhitā* (5.39):

rāmādi-mūrtiṣu kalā-niyamena tiṣṭhan
nānāvatāram akarod bhuvaneṣu kintu
kṛṣṇah svayaṁ samabhavat paramaḥ pumān yo
govindam ādi-puruṣaṁ tam ahaṁ bhajāmi

I worship Govinda, the primeval Lord, who manifested Himself personally as Kṛṣṇa and the different *avatāras* in the world in the forms of Rāma, Nṛsiṁha, Vāmana, etc., as His subjective portions."

The cycle of four *yugas,* or millenniums—namely, Satya, Tretā, Dvāpara, and Kali—goes around a thousand times in one day of Lord Brahmā. The *Bhagavad-gītā* (8.17) confirms this: *sahasra-yuga-paryantam ahar yad brahmaṇo viduḥ*. "By human calculation, a thousand ages taken together form the duration of Brahmā's one day." According to the Vedic calculation, one day of Brahmā sees the coming and going of fourteen Manus. Therefore, each Manu lives for seventy-one cycles of the four millenniums. At present we are in the period of Vaivasvata Manu, in the twenty-eighth cycle of the four millenniums, and it is the Kali-yuga. This Kali-yuga is very special, however, because Lord Caitanya appears in this age in His original form and propagates the esoteric science of pure love of Godhead. All this we learn from the scriptures. We have great expectations that this science of pure love of Godhead will be propagated worldwide in the immediate future.

During the Satya-yuga the mode of goodness is in abundance. Or one can say that when the quality of goodness increases in a person to the extent that he becomes situated in his original constitutional identity as a servant of the Lord, thus making his human life a complete success, at that time he enjoys the bliss and tranquillity of the Satya-yuga. The three modes—goodness, passion, and ignorance—are always present in this material nature. According to the predominance of a particular mode, the *yugas* change from Satya to Tretā to Dvāpara to Kali. The *jīvas* in Kali-yuga are predominantly in the mode of ignorance, and with the increase of this mode the threefold material miseries expand unlimitedly. Thus people today are afflicted by a short life-span, ill luck, warped intelligence, lethargy, disease, and many other sufferings.

Still, there is no reason to despise this age, for the most munificent incarnation of Godhead, Lord Caitanya, has appeared in Kali-yuga to shower His kindness upon the afflicted souls. The extent of the Supreme Lord's mercy is decidedly more generous in this age than in any other. In his play entitled *Vidagdha-mādhava,* Śrīla Rūpa Gosvāmī has described Lord Caitanya in this way:

anarpita-cariṁ cirāt karuṇayāvatīrṇaḥ kalau
samarpayitum unnatojjvala-rasāṁ sva-bhakti-śriyam
hariḥ puraṭa-sundara-dyuti-kadamba-sandīpitaḥ
sadā hṛdaya-kandare sphuratu vaḥ śacī-nandana

May that Lord who is known as the son of Śrīmatī Śacīdevī be transcendentally situated in the innermost chambers of your heart. Resplendent with the radiance of molten gold, He has descended in the Age of Kali by His causeless mercy to bestow what no incarnation ever offered before: the most sublime and radiant spiritual knowledge of the mellow taste of His service.

The present Kali-yuga is therefore very auspicious, for in this age one can attain the treasure of devotional service to the Lord that He Himself propagated. Our hope rests fully with the Lord's surrendered devotees, who are endowed with perfect knowledge of how to disseminate this transcendental science. Śrīla Śukadeva Gosvāmī, after describing the evil aspects of Kali-yuga, sums up this subject toward the very end of the *Śrīmad-Bhāgavatam* (12.3.51–52):

kaler doṣa-nidhe rājann
asti hy eko mahān guṇaḥ
kīrtanād eva kṛṣṇasya
mukta-saṅgaḥ paraṁ vrajet

kṛte yad dhyāyato viṣṇuṁ
tretāyāṁ yajato makhaiḥ
dvāpare paricaryāyāṁ
kalau tad dhari-kīrtanāt

My dear king, although Kali-yuga is an ocean of faults, there is still one good quality about this age: simply by chanting the Hare Kṛṣṇa *mahā-mantra,* one can become free from material bondage and be promoted to the transcendental kingdom. Whatever result was obtained in Satya-yuga by meditating on Viṣṇu, in Tretā-yuga by performing sacrifices, and in Dvāpara-yuga by serving the Lord's lotus feet can be obtained in Kali-yuga simply by chanting the Hare Kṛṣṇa *mahāmantra.*

The word *hari-kīrtana* used in these verses, which means "singing or chanting the glories of Kṛṣṇa," could very well apply to the *Bhagavad-gītā,* the song sung by God Himself. The promulgation of the *Bhagavad-gītā's* knowledge on a worldwide scale will establish a foundation upon which the edifice of the science of love of God will be constructed. This edifice will be the repository of the sublime treasure of devotional service as taught by Lord Caitanya in Kali-yuga, and it will serve as a shining monument to the transcendental endeavors of the Lord's pure devotees.

At present only a small portion of the knowledge contained in the *Vedas, Vedānta-sūtra,* and *Upaniṣads* is available to the general populace. What is noteworthy, however, is that the essence of all Vedic knowledge is available in the *Gītopaniṣad,* popularly known as the *Bhagavad-gītā*. Lord Kṛṣṇa milked the cow of the *Upaniṣads,* and Arjuna drank the milk thus obtained—the *Bhagavad-gītā*. If Arjuna found time to hear the *Bhagavad-gītā* in the middle of a battlefield at Kurukṣetra, then what urgent business is stopping us from hearing the *Gītā*? When knowledge of the *Gītā* spreads, everyone will easily be able to attain the platform of *yoga*. And as the pure devotees of the Lord become successful in their efforts to use their spiritual intelligence in the Lord's service, then the science of love of God taught by Lord Caitanya, the most magnanimous incarnation of Godhead, will be distributed everywhere. Judging from all the symptoms, the time is now ripe. Indians should now take shelter of their saintly preceptors, the pure devotees, and unitedly propagate the glorification of Kṛṣṇa via the medium of the *Bhagavad-gītā*. In this way the world will become prosperous and perfect. The present age has seen interest in spiritual matters markedly increase. *Yoga* and meditation societies have mushroomed expressly to transmit the knowledge of the *Bhagavad-gītā,* but how this will be accomplished is still a question. We are confident that Lord Caitanya's teachings on the process of loving devotional service will easily harmonize all conflicting concepts.

The most effective method for directing humanity toward a positive and favorable consciousness is available in India. Any person, under any circumstances, can reach an elevated state of consciousness by properly hearing the *Bhagavad-gītā,* and then, by constantly chanting the name of God, he can win God over. The present state of world affairs is full of foreboding, strife, and struggle. These are the effects of Kali-yuga. But our faith in the eternal nature of the *jīva* prompts us to believe that anyone can attain devotional service to Kṛṣṇa simply by hearing and chanting His name and thereby awakening his inherent dormant love for Him. We have full faith in the words of Śrīla Śukadeva Gosvāmī quoted above from the *Śrīmad-Bhāgavatam*—that simply by chanting the name of Kṛṣṇa one can reach His eternal kingdom.

Therefore all signs point toward auspicious changes in the global consciousness. But these changes must be initiated from within every individual's heart; they are impossible to accomplish through political lobbying or social adjustments. The devotional feelings that reach out from within the hearts of men find their culmination in the pure devotees' spiritual perfection. In the *Bhagavad-gītā* Lord Kṛṣṇa describes this spiritual perfection as *bhakti-yoga,* or *buddhi-yoga,* the *yoga* of devotional service. At a certain stage, all the systems of *yoga* become obsolete and have to be discarded—except for *buddhi-yoga.* The Lord says (*Bhagavad-gītā* 2.39–40) that a little progress on this path gives immense results:

eṣā te 'bhihitā sāṅkhye
buddhir yoge tv imāṁ śṛṇu
buddhyā yukto yayā pārtha
karma-bandhaṁ prahāsyasi

nehābhikrama-nāśo 'sti
pratyavāyo na vidyate
sv-alpam apy asya dharmasya
trāyate mahato bhayāt

> Thus far I have described this knowledge to you through analytical study. Now listen as I explain it in terms of working without fruitive results. O son of Pṛthā, when you act in such knowledge you can free yourself from the bondage of works. In this endeavor there is no loss or diminution, and a little advancement on this path can protect one from the most dangerous type of fear.

Real *yoga* is *buddhi-yoga,* the *yoga* of devotional service, which brings about direct perception of the Supreme Lord. When the devotee meets the Lord face to face, liberation takes the form of a woman and is at his beck and call, eager to serve him, and she is accompanied by personified material opulence, sense pleasure, and religiosity, all of whom wait upon the devotee like servants. The pure devotees of the Lord are all embodiments of perfection in *yoga;* thus the four Vedic goals are truly at their beck and call. And beyond these four goals is the supreme destination: superconsciousness, or God consciousness. This is the fifth and paramount Vedic goal. One who has reached the state of unalloyed Kṛṣṇa consciousness is an extremely rare personality—one in a million devotees, according to Lord Caitanya.

Such an elevated state of consciousness is the last word in *yoga.* None of the other *yoga* processes, such as *haṭha-yoga* or *rāja-yoga,* can bring one to this platform. *Buddhi-yoga* lies far above these *yoga* practices, which are mostly physical disciplines. *Buddhi-yoga,* however, is a spiritual discipline for self-realization. This realization is a full perception of the nondual Absolute Truth, whereby one sees everything resting in the Supreme Lord and the Supreme Lord in everything. As Lord Kṛṣṇa explains in the *Bhagavad-gītā* (7.7):

mattaḥ parataraṁ nānyat
kiñcid asti dhanañjaya
mayi sarvam idaṁ protaṁ
sūtre maṇi-gaṇā iva

O conqueror of wealth, there is no truth superior to Me. Everything rests upon Me, as pearls are strung on a thread.

This means that every living entity, from demons to demigods to human beings to lower creatures, is fully dependent on the Supreme Lord. One who perceives the Absolute Truth in this way can wholeheartedly surrender to the Supreme Personality of Godhead.

The vision of a pure devotee is described by Lord Kṛṣṇa in the *Bhagavad-gītā* (15.19–20):

yo mām evam asammūḍho
jānāti puruṣottamam
sa sarva-vid bhajati māṁ
sarva-bhāvena bhārata

iti guhyatamaṁ śāstram
idam uktaṁ mayānagha
etad buddhvā buddhimān syāt
kṛta-kṛtyaś ca bhārata

Whoever knows Me as the Supreme Personality of Godhead, without doubting, is the knower of everything. He therefore engages himself in full devotional service to Me, O son of Bharata. This is the most confidential part of the Vedic scriptures, O sinless one, and it is disclosed now by Me. Whoever understands this will become wise, and his endeavors will know perfection.

Once a person surrenders fully to the Lord's lotus feet, he sees the Lord's form everywhere, not this world of moving and nonmoving matter. Such surrender has six limbs:

ānukūlyasya saṅkalpaḥ
prātikūlyasya varjanam
rakṣiṣyatīti viśvāso
goptṛtve varanaṁ tathā
ātma-nikṣepa-kārpaṇye
ṣaḍ-vidhā śaraṇāgatiḥ

The six divisions of surrender are the acceptance of those things favorable to devotional service, the rejection of unfavorable things, the conviction that Kṛṣna will give protection, the acceptance of the Lord as one's guardian or master, full surrender, and humility.

The relationship between the Supreme Lord and His surrendered devotee is very intimate. Everything about the devotee is known to the Lord. The devotee has no separate interest that would involve him in speculative knowledge, fruitive activities, sense pleasures, lamentation, meditation, and so on. He simply engages fulltime in serving the Supreme Lord. His consciousness becomes purified of all contamination, and the fire of conditioned life is put out. Duality and illusion are eradicated from his heart, his devotion to Lord Kṛṣṇa becomes single-minded, and He throws himself at the Lord's lotus feet, feeling like a sold-out animal. At this stage the Supreme Lord Himself imparts all spiritual knowledge, or *buddhi-yoga*, to the devotee so that he can attain Him:

teṣām satata-yuktānāṁ
bhajatāṁ prīti-pūrvakam
dadāmi buddhi-yogaṁ taṁ
yena mām upayānti te

teṣām evānukampārtham
aham ajñāna-jaṁ tamaḥ
nāśayāmy ātma-bhāva-stho
jñāna-dīpena bhāsvatā

> To those who are constantly devoted to serving Me with love, I give the understanding by which they can come to Me. To show them special mercy, I, dwelling in their hearts, destroy with the shining lamp of knowledge the darkness born of ignorance. (*Bhagavad-gītā* 10.10–11)

When the devotee adopts such a mood of surrender and complete dependence, everything easily happens by the Lord's desire. Even if the process of surrender somehow remains incomplete, the devotee achieves the ends attainable through other yogic practices. As the Lord says, "A little advancement on this path protects one from the most dangerous type of fear." In other words, the Supreme Lord personally intervenes and arranges for His surrendered devotee's success in spiritual life. Is there any doubt that once the Lord's divine energy is active, all our artificial endeavors are most insignificant and futile? The Lord's inconceivable potency that descends to bless us with spiritual perfection shows the magnitude and glory of His potencies. Certainly there are other methods for spiritual advancement, such as *rāja-yoga,* by which one can become equipoised, or difficult *prāṇāyāma* exercises, severe austerities, and renunciation, and these practices are very powerful. But when the Lord's divine potency acts, they all seem extremely ineffectual compared to the process of surrender, which invokes that potency. All these other methods, though very potent, are human endeavors. So how can they compare with the Supreme Lord's divine potency? With this divine potency the Lord blesses particular persons in particular circumstances.

The first limb of surrender is to accept that which helps us invoke the Lord's mercy. This means to completely depend on the Lord's will. Such surrender is free from any conditions. It is untinged by the desire for sense pleasure, liberation, or mystic perfections. The devotee, unlike others, is never in anxiety. His only concern is to execute the will of the Lord. In this connection, Śrīla Vyāsadeva says,

> If a surrendered soul tries to arrange for food and shelter but does not succeed, or if, once having these things, he loses them, then despite such reverses he remains unperturbed and simply remembers the Supreme Lord, Hari.

It is true that when one prays sincerely at the Lord's lotus feet, the Lord generally fulfills one's wishes. But those who have completely surrendered to the Lord, throwing themselves at the His lotus feet, do not pray to Him for anything material. Yet the Lord automatically provides for all their needs. As Lord Kṛṣṇa assures us in the Gītā (9.22):

ananyāś cintayanto māṁ
ye janāḥ paryupāsate
teṣāṁ nityābhiyuktānāṁ
yoga-kṣemaṁ vahāmy aham

> But those who always worship Me with exclusive devotion, meditating on My transcendental form—to them I carry what they lack, and I preserve what they have.

The single-minded devotees are surrendered souls. They can perceive how the Lord's potencies are working. They feel no anxiety if sometimes the Lord's mercy does not manifest, even after long pleading and prayers, for they have unflinching conviction that the Lord will protect them under all circumstances. The mood of the present age is not spiritually conducive, and hence it is difficult to develop a high degree of faith in the Lord. Still, it is certain that faith in the Lord never goes in vain. In the beginning we may be somewhat hesitant to accept this fact, but in time we come to understand that the Supreme Lord is always protecting us.

At times, when doubts and restlessness assail us, we must remain fixed in our resolve. The best remedy for doubts is to seek the association of saintly persons. Saintly souls who are learned in the conclusions of the revealed scriptures and have realized the Supreme Lord can dissipate our doubts and calm our restless mind with unequivocal instructions and exemplary actions. When Kṛṣṇa conscious topics, which are both very potent and nectarean to the ears and heart, are heard and discussed in the association of saints, then faith in the Supreme Lord gradually increases, along with attraction and devotion to Him. Faith inspires initial surrender, and later, by the powerful influence of saintly association, one's faith deepens and becomes steady. Once faith becomes steady, all mental agitations and doubts clear up due to constant worship of the Lord. One then practices *bhajana* (chanting meditation) of a very esoteric and elevated nature, and this leads one to the stage of love of Godhead. To attain this state, saintly association is imperative; there is no substitute. Therefore it is said:

'sādhu-saṅga', 'sādhu-saṅga'—sarva-śāstre kaya
lava-mātra sādhu-saṅge sarva-siddhi haya

> The verdict of all revealed scriptures is that by even a moment's association with a pure devotee, one can attain all success. (Cc. *Madhya* 22.54)

And how the Lord feels about *sādhus* is revealed by the Lord Himself in the *Śrīmad-Bhāgavatam* (9.4.68):

sādhavo hṛdayaṁ mahyaṁ
sādhūnāṁ hṛdayaṁ tv aham
mad-anyat te na jānanti
nāhaṁ tebhyo manāg api

> The pure devotee is always within the core of My heart, and I am always in the heart of the pure devotee. My devotees do not know anything else but Me, and I do not know anyone else but them.

The Lord always resides in the heart of His pure devotees, and so they have the potency to purify the places of pilgrimage, which become heavily laden with the sins deposited there by all the pilgrims. These are some of the glories of the Lord's pure, surrendered devotees.

Lord Kṛṣṇa says in the *Bhagavad-gītā* (18.58), *mac-cittaḥ sarva-durgāṇi mat-prasādāt tariṣyasi:* "If you become conscious of Me, you will pass over all the obstacles of conditioned life by My grace." Therefore fruitive activity, the search for empirical knowledge, and mystic *yoga* all culminate in surrender to the Supreme Lord. As Lord Kṛṣṇa says in the *Gītā* (18.66):

sarva-dharmān parityajya
mām ekaṁ śaraṇaṁ vraja
ahaṁ tvāṁ sarva-pāpebhyo
mokṣayiṣyāmi mā śucaḥ

Abandon all varieties of religion and surrender unto Me. I will deliver you from all sinful reactions. Do not fear.

When the Supreme Lord has agreed to personally take responsibility for our protection, what is there to fear? When He who is omnipotent and the maintainer of the entire cosmic creation is willing to take charge of our life, then what objection can we have to surrendering to Him? If I am guaranteed the protection of the Supreme Personality, who creates, maintains, and destroys this limitless cosmic manifestation simply by His will, then what is left for me to desire? If we try in the proper way to realize the Supreme Lord's potencies, He will certainly reveal them to us as they are. How much can we accomplish with our puny physical and mental abilities? Real success in *yoga* comes only by fully surrendering to His lotus feet.

However, since it is not possible to attain such a mood of complete surrender in a moment, we should also not expect the Lord's mercy to manifest before us instantaneously. Although the Lord, and sometimes even His devotees, perform miracles, still we must not expect such extraordinary things to happen to us. Of course, it is certain that the degree of mercy the Lord bestows upon us is much greater than our degree of surrender to Him. Another danger is this: if we were to receive all His mercy at once, we would become corrupt and fallen, like many *yogīs* who attain mystic perfection. Better that we continue to perform our duties in a regulated way, with patience and enthusiasm; then undoubtedly we will receive the Lord's full mercy.

Both the *Vedas* and the *Śrīmad-Bhāgavatam* describe the conditioned soul with the same analogy: on the treelike human body reside two similar birds. One is the Supreme Soul, the Paramātmā feature of the Supreme Lord, and the other is the *jīva* soul. One bird, the *jīva,* is enjoying the fruits of material existence, while the other remains aloof, replete with all His transcendental potencies. The *jīva* soul must surrender to the Supreme Soul and relish the fruits given to him by the Lord.

The Lord says that His external potency—Mahā-māyā, or Kālī—serves Him in the form of the internal, spiritual potency. The *jīva* must allow this spiritual potency to influence him freely, without interference from the false ego, which makes him think that he is the doer. Thus surrendering to the Lord is the method prescribed to reach the highest stages of devotional service.

The *Śvetāśvatara Upaniṣad* says, *parāsya śaktir vividhaiva śrūyate:* "The Supreme Lord's potencies are multifarious." These potencies act in different capacities at different levels: on the platform of *jñāna,* empirical knowledge, they manifest in a particular way, different from any other. On the spiritual, transcendental platform, these potencies produce variegated spiritual manifestations. These potencies can be known if one attains perfection in Kṛṣṇa consciousness. On the platform of material nature, the senses are superior to the body as a whole, mind is superior to the senses, the intelligence is superior to the mind, and the soul is subtler and better than the intelligence. On the spiritual platform, when the pure soul is situated in his original, spiritual identity, he renders devotional service to the absolute embodiment of sweet transcendence, the Supreme Personality of Godhead. This devotional service is imbued with the partial expansion of *hlādinī-śakti,* the Lord's pleasure-giving potency.

Great thinkers and philosophers like Śrī Aurobindo describe this stage as *vijñānānanda,* "the pure bliss of realized knowledge." Jesus Christ called it "the kingdom of heaven." By contrast, when one tries to enjoy mundane pleasures on the material plane, spiritual bliss becomes smothered and lies dormant, in a slumbering state. Perfection in *yoga,* therefore, is marked by the awakening of spiritual bliss. And when one is strongly drawn to this blissful state, one attains to the transcendental abode of the Supreme Lord. Iron in constant touch with fire develops the properties of fire. Similarly, when the *jīva* in the material nature rises to the state of spiritual bliss by means of devotional service, his spiritual consciousness awakens and he becomes oblivious of this phenomenal world. In the *Bhagavad-gītā* (12.8–9) Lord Kṛṣṇa tells us how to increase the influence of His spiritual energy upon us:

mayy eva mana ādhatsva
mayi buddhiṁ niveśaya
nivasiṣyasi mayy eva
ata ūrdhvaṁ na saṁśayaḥ

atha cittaṁ samādhātuṁ
na śaknoṣi mayi sthiram
abhyāsa-yogena tato
mām icchāptuṁ dhanañjaya

> Just fix your mind upon Me, the Supreme Personality of Godhead, and engage all your intelligence in Me. Thus you will live in Me always, without a doubt. My dear Arjuna, O winner of wealth, if you cannot fix your mind upon Me without deviation, then follow the regulative principles of *bhakti-yoga*. In this way you will develop a desire to attain Me."

When a person fixes his mind on the eternal, exquisite form of Śyāmasundara, the blackish, beautiful Lord Kṛṣṇa, all distress and anguish are vanquished. In the initial stages, the attempt to fix the mind on Kṛṣṇa may be unsuccessful, but with regulated practice (*abhyāsa-yoga*) it becomes possible. *Abhyāsa-yoga* means sincere engagement in the ninefold process of *bhakti,* beginning with hearing and chanting the holy name, pastimes, and so on, of Lord Kṛṣṇa. Proper execution of *abhyāsa-yoga* culminates in the awakening of divine consciousness, or superconsciousness. This is true success.

The modern sage Śrī Aurobindo has explained that in the third stage of *yoga* practice, the *yogī* sees God everywhere. In the process of *jñāna-yoga,* or the cultivation of empirical knowledge, when the *yogī* attains impersonal Brahman realization he sees Brahman as all-pervasive and inactive. This realization is bereft of any understanding of the Lord's name, form, qualities, pastimes, or paraphernalia. But if these transcendental topics arrest one's attention, one very soon begins following the path of *bhakti-yoga*—the path enunciated in the *Vedas, Upaniṣads,* and *Bhagavad-gītā*. A transformation of vision takes place as one advances on this path. The rare soul who perfects this process can see the Supreme Lord in everything and everything in relation to the Supreme Lord. Quotes from various scriptures substantiate this point: in the *Bhagavad-gītā* (7.19) the Lord says, *vāsudevaḥ sarvam iti sa mahātmā sudurlabhaḥ:* "[The surrendered devotee knows] Me to be the cause of all causes and all that is. Such a great soul is very rare." And the *Upaniṣads* state, *sarvaṁ khalv idaṁ brahma:* "Everything is permeated by Brahman." A person attains the highest stage of this realization when he sees this cosmic creation as a transformation and manifestation of the Supreme Lord's divine energies. Śrī Nārada instructed Śrīla Vyāsadeva with the following words:

idaṁ hi viśvaṁ bhagavān ivetaro
yato jagat-sthāna-nirodha-sambhavāḥ
tad dhi svayaṁ veda bhavāṁs tathāpi te
prādeśa-mātraṁ bhavataḥ pradarśitam

The Supreme Personality of Godhead is Himself this cosmos, and still He is aloof from it. From Him only has this cosmic manifestation emanated, in Him it rests, and unto Him it enters after annihilation. Your good self knows all about this. I have given only a synopsis.

In this stage of realization, the eternal truth is no longer covered by the illusory, mundane pall of impersonal omnipresence, and what shines forth is the absolute spiritual personality. The fullest manifestation of that spiritual personality is Śrī Kṛṣṇa, the transcendental form of eternity, knowledge, and bliss, who is beyond the manifested and unmanifested material cosmos. As the *Brahma-saṁhitā* explains:

īśvaraḥ paramaḥ kṛṣṇaḥ
sac-cid-ānanda-vigrahaḥ
anādir ādir govindaḥ
sarva-kāraṇa-kāraṇam

Kṛṣṇa who is known as Govinda is the Supreme Godhead. He has an eternal blissful spiritual body [*sac-cid-ānanda-vigrahaḥ*]. He is the origin of all. He has no other origin and He is the prime cause of all causes.

The impersonal Brahman is the transcendental bodily effulgence of the Supreme Lord's *sac-cid-ānanda* form, and the illusory and transitory material nature is a transformation of His separated energy.

Although the *sac-cid-ānanda* Supreme Personality is a permanent resident of His own eternal abode, Goloka Vṛndāvana, He manifests Himself in His all-pervasive universal form and is present throughout this cosmic creation by means of His partial expansion, the Supersoul. As the *Brahma-saṁhitā* (5.37 and 43) states:

ānanda-cinmaya-rasa-pratibhāvitābhis
tābhir ya eva nija-rūpatayā kalābhiḥ
goloka eva nivasaty akhilātma-bhūto
govindam ādi-puruṣaṁ tam ahaṁ bhajāmi

goloka-nāmni nija-dhāmni tale ca tasya
devī-maheśa-hari-dhāmasu teṣu teṣu
te te prabhāva-nicayā vihitāś ca yena
govindam ādi-puruṣaṁ tam ahaṁ bhajāmi

I worship Govinda, the primeval Lord, residing in His own realm, Goloka, with Rādhā, resembling His own spiritual figure, the embodiment of the ecstatic potency possessed of the sixty-four artistic activities, in the company of Her confidantes [sakhīs], embodiments of the extensions of Her bodily form, permeated and vitalized by His ever-blissful spiritual rasa.

Lowest of all is located Devī-dhāma [mundane world], next above it is Maheśa-dhāma [abode of Maheśa]; above Maheśa-dhāma is placed Hari-dhāma [abode of Hari] and above them all is located Kṛṣṇa's own realm named Goloka. I adore the primeval Lord Govinda, who has allotted their respective authorities to the rulers of those graded realms.

Lord Govinda is the Supreme Personality, unsurpassable, the topmost being, the unlimited Godhead. He is known as Kṛṣṇa because He attracts everyone by His extraordinary transcendental pastimes. It is therefore unanimously accepted that all His other names and expansions are partial. As the *Śrīmad-Bhāgavatam* declares, *ete cāṁśa-kalāḥ puṁsaḥ kṛṣṇas tu bhagavān svayam:* "All these incarnations of Godhead are either plenary portions or portions of the plenary portions of the Lord, but Lord Śrī Kṛṣṇa is the original Personality of Godhead."

Thus Lord Śrī Kṛṣṇa is the original, beginningless, and supreme Personality of Godhead, and this material universe is simply part of His unlimited energy. We may now reject this material world as illusory, but one day, with Kṛṣṇa conscious vision, we will see its intimate connection with the Lord. In this stage of spiritual vision we will see material things as objects of neither exploitation nor rejection. Such transcendental vision is attained by the process of *buddhi-yoga,* or *bhakti-yoga.* We will then clearly see the truth of the following verse from the *Brahma-saṁhitā* (5.51):

agnir mahī gaganam ambu marud diśaś ca
kālas tathātma-manasīti jagat-trayāṇi
yasmād bhavanti vibhavanti viśanti yaṁ ca
govindam ādi-puruṣaṁ tam ahaṁ bhajāmi

> The three worlds are composed of the nine elements, viz., fire, earth, ether, water, air, direction, time, soul, and mind. I adore the primeval Lord Govinda from whom they originate, in whom they exist and into whom they enter at the time of the universal cataclysm.

Once one is fixed in transcendental realization, all distress, lamentation, illusion, fear, and so on, are immediately eradicated. The soul is assailed by these miseries as long as he harbors the delusion that something exists outside of Kṛṣṇa. Therefore when one is situated in transcendence, one feels happiness even in this world. The mundane conception of life is a product of the three modes of material nature, which affect the mind and senses. But when one's vision is transformed through *buddhi-yoga,* one sees everything as having a direct link with Kṛṣṇa. The material elements, such as fire, water, ether, and mind, along with the directions, the soul, and time—everything material and spiritual, personal and impersonal—all reflect Kṛṣṇa, the Supreme Being. When one reaches this state of realization, the dualities and illusion of sin and piety, happiness and distress, are dissolved by the ecstatic harmony of transcendence. In one *Upaniṣad* there is a statement that once a person experiences the happiness derived from Brahman realization, he no longer has anything to fear. A verse from the *Īśopaniṣad* (7) conveys a similar mood:

yasmin sarvāṇi bhūtāny
ātmaivābhūd vijānataḥ
tatra ko mohaḥ kaḥ śoka
ekatvam anupaśyataḥ

> One who always sees all living entities as spiritual sparks, in quality one with the Lord, becomes a true knower of things. What, then, can be illusion or anxiety for Him?

Self-realization leads to the understanding that everything is situated in the Supreme Lord. At that time there is no more illusion or lamentation, and everything is wonderfully harmonized. One sees the whole material universe as a manifestation of unity in diversity. On this platform everything is full of happiness, knowledge, and eternity. This is the platform of Brahman realization.

In this realized state, we perceive Lord Nārāyaṇa's presence not only in all living beings but also in all nonliving things. When the darkness of ignorance cloaking our consciousness is dissipated by the merciful light of knowledge emanating from the spiritual master, we gain spiritual vision and can see that every object is directly linked with the Supreme Lord.

There are various stages of elevation the *jīva* goes through, which are like different shells (*koṣas*) covering him. They are the coverings of food (*anna-maya*), life air (*prāṇa-maya*), mind (*mano-maya,* or *jñāna-maya*), and transcendental knowledge (*vijñāna-maya*). When the final shell is penetrated, the soul attains pure consciousness, enters the state of complete bliss (*ānanda-maya*), and experiences *sac-cid-ānanda* as universal. First the soul has covered consciousness, then he reaches the stage of budding consciousness, then blossoming consciousness, and finally fully blossomed consciousness. And all the while he experiences a gradual expansion of bliss—but only in relation to Lord Kṛṣṇa and His devotional service. At the final stage, flowers, fruits, plants, trees, clay—all objects and elements—become spiritualized by being used in Lord Kṛṣṇa's service. In other words, nothing is seen to be separate from the Lord. As the *Īśopaniṣad* (1) explains, *īśāvāsyam idaṁ sarvam:*

"Everything animate or inanimate that is within this universe is controlled and owned by the Lord."

To see God everywhere and in every living entity is not the final word in self-realization; one needs to see Him in all events, in every activity, in every thought influencing everyone's life, including one's own. Two things are indispensable for acquiring such a vision: first we must offer the results of all our activities to Lord Kṛṣṇa, and second, every action we perform must be done exclusively as devotional service to Him. We must constantly meditate on the fact that Lord Kṛṣṇa is the only enjoyer and proprietor of every action. As the Lord says in the *Bhagavad-gītā* (9.24, 27):

ahaṁ hi sarva-yajñānāṁ
bhoktā ca prabhur eva ca
na tu mām abhijānanti
tattvenātaś cyavanti te

yat karoṣi yad aśnāsi
yaj juhoṣi dadāsi yat
yat tapasyasi kaunteya
tat kuruṣva mad-arpaṇam

> I am the only enjoyer and master of all sacrifices. Therefore, those who do not recognize My true transcendental nature fall down. Whatever you do, whatever you eat, whatever you offer or give away, and whatever austerities you perform—do that, O son of Kuntī, as an offering to Me.

Considering everything material, some people make a show of renunciation and reject even those things that can be used in the Lord's service. This is futile. All objects in the material world are meant not for our enjoyment or gratification but for the Lord's service. This is the mood of one in transcendental consciousness, or superconsciousness. And all activities performed in this consciousness constitute true renunciation, or *yukta-vairāgya,* as opposed to false renunciation, or *phalgu-vairāgya.* By instructing Arjuna to act in this way, the Supreme Lord has ordered us to do so as well. It is our duty to execute His instruction. Whatever the result may be, we must be convinced that all such activities are all-auspicious. As the Lord says in the *Bhagavad-gītā* (9.28):

śubhāśubha-phalair evaṁ
mokṣyase karma-bandhanaiḥ
sannyāsa-yoga-yuktātmā
vimukto mām upaiṣyasi

> In this way you will be freed from bondage to work and its auspicious and inauspicious results. With your mind fixed on Me in this principle of renunciation, you will be liberated and come to Me.

Real perfection in *yoga* comes when we forget our personal demands and determine what service the Lord wants from us. Personal interest must be sacrificed, along with our conceptions of good and bad, right and wrong, necessary and unnecessary, and so on. We must emulate that great warrior Arjuna and try to find out what service the Supreme Lord wants from us. Such Kṛṣṇa conscious activities alone will lead us to the full consummation of all our duties, and the results will be all-auspicious. This degree of fixed faith is indispensable to progress. In the *Caitanya-caritāmṛta* (*Madhya* 22.62), Śrīla Kṛṣṇadāsa Kavirāja defines this faith:

'śraddhā'-śabde—viśvāsa kahe sudṛḍha niścaya
kṛṣṇe bhakti kaile sarva-karma kṛta haya

> By rendering transcendental loving service to Kṛṣṇa, one automatically performs all subsidiary activities. This confident, firm faith, favorable to the discharge of devotional service, is called *śraddhā.*

We need to accept one fact: the energy of the omnipotent Supreme Lord, which carries out the work of creation, maintenance, and annihilation, is in no respect inferior to our puny potency. Therefore, God does not have to consult anyone about His or our difficulties or advantages. The question is, What is our duty? In the *Bhagavad-gītā* (4.16–17) the Lord says,

kiṁ karma kim akarmeti
kavayo 'py atra mohitāḥ
tat te karma pravakṣyāmi
yaj jñātvā mokṣyase 'śubhāt

karmaṇo hy api boddhavyaṁ
boddhavyaṁ ca vikarmaṇaḥ
akarmaṇaś ca boddhavyaṁ
gahanā karmaṇo gatiḥ

Even the intelligent are bewildered in determining what is action and what is inaction. Now I shall explain to you what action is, knowing which you shall be liberated from all misfortune. The intricacies of action are very hard to understand. Therefore one should know properly what action is, what forbidden action is, and what inaction is.

The confidential truth about what constitutes good action is almost impenetrable. Some hold that good action consists of executing one's social responsibilities. This is what common men generally understand by good action. But a few verses after the ones quoted above, Lord Kṛṣṇa uses the phrase *brahma-karma* to describe good action, and the word *brahma* points to Brahman. Therefore some say work done on the platform of Brahman is good action. Others say that good action includes works beneficial for the self, the society, the nation, and humanity at large. When a person acts with such lofty intentions, he is surely known as a good man. Indeed, his actions are certainly noble compared with those of persons with warped mentalities. This kind of action is not *buddhi-yoga,* however, because such philanthropic works can at best replace one set of people's mundane desires with a new set, but they can never completely root out these unwanted desires from within the heart. Philanthropic activities cannot prepare us for unalloyed devotional service, which is uncontaminated by empirical knowledge and fruitive action.

Individual material cravings are less harmful to the world than mass movements for sense gratification. If the material desires of an individual are unfulfilled, he certainly becomes depressed, but when the mass of people remain dissatisfied, the distress is much greater and gives rise to social conflict. In any case, mundane yearnings bring suffering, both individual or collective. Even if a person starts out not intending to enjoy the fruits of his actions, once those fruits come he is forced to enjoy them because he thinks of himself as the doer, influenced as he is by the three modes of nature—goodness, passion, and ignorance. These fruits are not without the bitter seeds of anxiety, entanglement, frustration, and disruption. Therefore, neither the execution of social responsibilities nor philanthropic work is ultimately good action. Devotional service to the Supreme Lord, which is beyond the three modes, must be accepted as the only good action.

The noble Arjuna thoroughly analyzed what was good and bad, what was his duty and not his duty, and decided not to take up arms to fight. Then Lord Kṛṣṇa, understanding that Arjuna was motivated by self-gratificatory social sentiments and sheer selfish interests, gave him two kinds of instructions: the first dealt with the process by which the conditioned *jīva* attains liberation; the second taught Arjuna how the liberated soul can surrender to the Lord and render pure devotional service. Authorized scriptures like *Bhagavad-gītā* contain the transcendental teachings of the Lord Himself or of self-realized personalities. These scriptures are free from the four human frailties, that is, illusion, mistakes, limited senses, and the cheating propensity. Thus the scriptural injunctions have always remained pristine, despite childish attempts by imperfect men to distort them. Such scriptural instructions not only teach self-control and the elevation of consciousness, but they also help rid us of false ego, bring us to the stage of goodness, and offer us ultimate liberation.

Uncorrupted by any kind of discrepancy or mistake, the *Vedas* stand out as the most ancient religious texts in the world. Every human being has a right to follow their edicts, along with the instructions contained in other books of Vedic literature. The Vedic literature consists of the *śruti* (the *Vedas* and *Upaniṣads*) and the *smṛti* (the *Vedānta-sūtra*, the *Purāṇas, Itihāsas* like the *Mahābhārata* and *Rāmāyaṇa,* the *Pañcarātras,* and finally the *Śrīmad-Bhāgavatam*). The *Śrīmad-Bhāgavatam* is the natural commentary on the *Vedānta-sūtra* and offers solid education on how to conduct life perfectly. In recent ages the *smṛti* texts have become prominent and influenced human thought and action. All these scriptures fully support the *varṇāśrama* system of four social and four religious orders. But what is today being labelled *varṇāśrama* is an atheistic concept totally unsupported by the scriptures. Real *varṇāśrama* is based not on birth but on people's qualities and activities. One cannot reach the goal of the scriptures by practicing today's demoniac caste system.

Only the introduction of *daivī-varṇāśrama,* the transcendental *varṇāśrama* system, will serve the purpose of the scriptures. This will move humanity toward liberation.

It is not at all difficult to compromise the real purport of the magnificent scriptural edicts by selfish motivations and a cheating mentality. When this happens, people aspire for show-bottle religiosity, material gain, sense enjoyment, and impersonal liberation. On the other hand, sincere observance of the scriptural injunctions leads to all-round success in life.

It is not enough to take only the first steps toward liberation. We must strive to reach the final goal within this very life-time. To achieve this end, it is imperative that we approach a spiritual master well-versed in the *Vedas* and Vedic literature, and take instruction from him on how to follow the scriptural rules. These rules are meant for the conditioned souls, not the liberated souls who are fully surrendered to the Lord's lotus feet; they have transcended the rules and regulations of the scriptures and can be called *paramahaṁsas*—self-realized, pure devotees.

In the *Bhagavad-gītā* (3.27) Lord Kṛṣṇa says:

prakṛteḥ kriyamāṇāni
guṇaiḥ karmāṇi sarvaśaḥ
ahaṅkāra-vimūḍhātmā
kartāham iti manyate

> The spirit soul bewildered by the influence of false ego thinks himself the doer of activities that are in actuality carried out by the three modes of material nature.

Success in any activity depends on five essential factors: the place, the doer, the tools or senses, the endeavor, and finally the sanction of the Supreme Lord. Of these, the Supreme Lord's blessing is the most important. This sanction is enacted through the Supreme Lord's favorable supervision of His material energy, for it is by the Lord's will that material nature acts. Material nature acts according to one's consciousness: when the living entity is under the influence of the three modes of nature, his actions are conducted by the Lord's external energy, the material nature. But when he is in transcendental consciousness, the *śuddha-sattva* state, his actions are conducted by the Lord's internal, spiritual potency. The living entity can choose to have his activities conducted by either the Lord's external energy or His internal energy. This is the extent of the *jīva's* minute independence.

The moment the spirit soul surrenders completely at the lotus feet of the Supreme Lord and prays to Him for engagement in His loving devotional service, the soul is freed from the bondage of fruitive reactions. In this stage he proves the truth of the scriptural injunction *jīvera svarūpa haya kṛṣṇera nitya-dāsa:* "In his original spiritual identity, the spirit soul is an eternal servant of Kṛṣṇa." This position gives the soul immense bliss. It is wrong to equate the position of an eternal servant of Kṛṣṇa with that of a slave of *māyā,* the illusory potency of Kṛṣṇa. In other words, the feelings of power and pleasure gained by lording it over matter are insignificant compared to the ecstasy one feels in the Lord's service. Even the eight kinds of mystic perfections are puny compared with the bliss of being an eternal servant of Kṛṣṇa. And surrender is the only means to attain this state; no artificial method can be applied. The awakening of pure Kṛṣṇa consciousness, which is the perfection of the living entity, is obtained only by surrendering to the Lord, the propensity for which is eternally inherent in the *jīva.* Hence Lord Caitanya says in the *Caitanya-caritāmṛta* (*Madhya* 22.107):

nitya-siddha-kṛṣṇa-prema 'sādhya' kabhu naya
śravaṇādi-śuddha-citte karaye udaya

Pure love for Kṛṣṇa is eternally established in the hearts of living entities. It is not something to be gained from another source. When the heart is purified by hearing and chanting, the living entity naturally awakens.

In the *Bhagavad-gītā* (18.61) Lord Kṛṣṇa states:

īśvaraḥ sarva-bhūtānāṁ
hṛd-deśe 'rjuna tiṣṭhati
bhrāmayan sarva-bhūtāni
yantrārūḍhāni māyayā

The Supreme Lord is situated in everyone's heart, O Arjuna, and is directing the wanderings of all living entities, who are seated as on a machine, made of the material energy.

The Lord is present in everyone's heart by His inconceivable spiritual potency. He also directs the movements of the *jīvas* by means of His material energy, consisting of the three modes of nature. After placing the *jīvas* in a material body, the Lord controls their wanderings. The intelligence of those *jīvas* who surrender to the Lord is fixed in devotional service, and so they are never again attracted to mundane activities. Transcending the three modes, they dispassionately observe all activities within the realm of the three modes.

In the early stages of devotional service one may be apprehensive because of reactions to sins and pious deeds. All this is due to previous habits. But if one fully surrenders to the Supreme Lord, the Lord Himself burns to ashes all reactions to pious and impious deeds. As stated in the *Śrīmad-Bhāgavatam* (2.7.42):

yeṣāṁ sa eṣa bhagavān dayayed anantaḥ
sarvātmanāśrita-pado yadi nirvyalīkam
te dustarām atitaranti ca deva-māyāṁ
naiṣāṁ mamāham iti dhīḥ śva-śṛgāla-bhakṣye

But anyone who is specifically favored by the Supreme Lord, the Personality of Godhead, due to unalloyed surrender unto the service of the Lord, can overcome the insurmountable ocean of illusion and can understand the Lord. But those who are attached to this body, which is meant to be eaten at the end by dogs and jackals, cannot do so.

Lord Kṛṣṇa encourages all living entities with these words in the *Gītā* (9.31), *kaunteya pratijānīhi na me bhaktaḥ praṇaśyati:* "O son of Kuntī, declare it boldly that My devotee never perishes." Here the Lord clearly intends to relieve all our fears. One can understand the Supreme Lord as He is only by His mercy, which can elevate one from a second-class devotee to a first-class, pure devotee. As said in the *Śrīmad-Bhāgavatam* (10.14.29):

athāpi te deva padāmbuja-dvaya-
prasāda-leśānugṛhīta eva hi
jānāti tattvaṁ bhagavan-mahimno
na cānya eko 'pi ciraṁ vicinvan

My Lord, if one is favored by even a slight trace of the mercy of Your lotus feet, he can understand the greatness of Your

> personality. But those who speculate to understand the Supreme Personality of Godhead are unable to know You, even though they continue to study the *Vedas* for many years.

For the fully surrendered pure devotee, not only is he himself transcendentally situated, but he sees this material nature as untainted by the three material modes. He then employs these material *guṇas*—the qualities of ignorance, passion, and goodness—in the Lord's service. For example, he uses his anger to chastise the enemies of the Lord's devotees.

Lord Kṛṣṇa makes the following statement in the *Bhagavad-gītā* (14.26):

> *māṁ ca yo 'vyabhicāreṇa*
> *bhakti-yogena sevate*
> *sa guṇān samatītyaitān*
> *brahma-bhūyāya kalpate*

> One who engages in full devotional service, unfailing in all circumstances, at once transcends the modes of material nature and thus comes to the level of Brahman.

Such a pure devotee sees the material quality of goodness as the Lord's bodily effulgence. For him the quality of ignorance is transformed into peacefulness and equanimity. And he uses lust, a product of the mode of passion, to love and serve the supremely beautiful Lord. He meditates on how to serve the Supreme Lord, and then with enthusiasm and patience he performs all kinds of devotional service. In the devotional mellow of *śānta,* or neutrality, such devotional enthusiasm may be absent, but because such a mood of devotion attracts the Lord's love, it is fully spiritual.

Here is another thought for meditation: the Supreme Personality of Godhead is unlimited, and any service rendered to Him is also unlimited because the Lord's unlimited energy is the dynamic force behind such service. When this supernatural energy is reposed in us, all our thoughts and feelings, our physical body, our mind, our knowledge, and so on, are energized by it. Every endeavor then simply merges into this flow of energy, and we become like a lotus growing from the mud—in the world but uncontaminated by it. This is how the nondual principle comes alive: our mind, heart, consciousness, and activities become nondifferent from the Supreme Lord, the Absolute Truth. We consider ourselves the Lord's property, surrendered at His lotus feet, His unalloyed, eternal slaves. Rejecting all mental speculation and mundane desire, with a serene mind we experience incessant spiritual bliss in rendering Him loving service. In the *Bhagavad-gītā* (3.30) the Lord describes the process of surrender in this way:

mayi sarvāṇi karmāṇi
sannyasyādhyātma-cetasā
nirāśīr nirmamo bhūtvā
yudhyasva vigata-jvaraḥ

> Therefore, O Arjuna, surrendering all your works unto Me, with full knowledge of Me, without desires for profit, with no claims to proprietorship, and free from lethargy, fight.

To achieve such a state of surrender, one has to be free from selfish desires, unaffected by dualities, and devoid of all false prestige. Dualities are born of false ego, the worst enemy of surrender. One who transcends false ego, and with it the effects of duality, is very easily freed from material desires, and then he vanquishes hate, greed, anger, fear, and so on. In the stage of full surrender to the Lord, even negative qualities like mundane desire and envy, along with dualities like hunger and thirst, heat and cold, joy and sorrow, loss and gain, sin and piety, and honor and dishonor, are converted into spiritual energy by being brought into contact with the Supreme Lord. Saintly, blissful personalities who are devoid of undesirable characteristics like lust and envy are found especially in India. One can conquer duality, illusion, and so on only by spiritual elevation to the state of directly perceiving the Supreme Lord and seeing everything in relation to Him. The only method of achieving this state of consciousness is *buddhi-yoga.*

For the devotee of the Lord, this kind of vision develops easily. Conversely, the empirical philosophers, fruitive workers, and gross materialists cannot possibly attain this stage. The devotees are inspired by Him to develop spiritual perception, and thus the dualities fade into inconsequence. Such a state is the ultimate result of their devotional surrender and love for the Lord. In the *Bhagavad-gītā* (18.54) Lord Kṛṣṇa describes the neophyte stage of such divine consciousness:

brahma-bhūtaḥ prasannātmā
na śocati na kāṅkṣati
samaḥ sarveṣu bhūteṣu
mad-bhaktiṁ labhate parām

> One who is thus transcendentally situated at once realizes the Supreme Brahman and becomes fully joyful. He never laments or desires to have anything. He is equally disposed toward every living entity. In that state he attains pure devotional service unto Me.

The living entity becomes bound up by the ropes of ignorance, duality, and illusion as soon as he sees this material world through the colored crystal known as "me and mine." To nullify such false ego and contaminated consciousness, one must follow the process of *buddhi-yoga,* which is uncontaminated by the three modes of nature (ignorance, passion, and goodness). Otherwise superconsciousness is unattainable.

The state of pure goodness is marked by pure knowledge of the Absolute. But when this knowledge is pervertedly reflected in the material world, it becomes mundane and empirical, and the *jīva* is thrown into the whirlpool of dualities, which condition him. The mode of passion increases attachment, sense gratification, and material desires, and the *jīva* becomes entangled in fruitive activities. The mode of ignorance induces illusion, covering the *jīva's* intelligence; then he slides down to the lowest consciousness, spending time only in sleeping and laziness. And the material mode of goodness also turns the *jīva* away from the Absolute Truth and makes him conditioned. With an increase of the mode of passion, goodness and ignorance decrease. When the mode of goodness increases, passion and ignorance decline. In this way the material modes wax and wane in varying degrees. The mode of goodness promotes mundane knowledge and elevated material consciousness, the mode of passion produces untiring energy for work and insatiable desire for results, and the mode of ignorance drags the *jīva* down to nescience, laziness, sleep, and delusion. The *jīva* in goodness moves up to more elevated consciousness, one in passion remains suspended in the mediocre state, and one in ignorance descends to the depths of depravity.

Therefore, it is a hazardous path of elevation that depends on personal characteristics within the jurisdiction of the three modes of nature. Without transcending these three material modes, a person will find himself securely in their clutches, and thus deluded, he will think that all his activities are divinely inspired. He will then broadcast this false concept, considering himself an advanced devotee and everyone else inferior. Impressed with his own knowledge, he will try to see God by dint of this knowledge instead of acting in such a way that God will want to see him. Intoxicated by false ego, he will see his activities, which are motivated by passion, as divine. Those who are proud of their knowledge do not surrender to the Lord; instead, they try to attain the Supreme Lord's mercy by the inductive method and thus exhibit an obnoxious mentality. One should constantly remember the Lord and pray to Him for mercy. The Lord, situated in the devotee's heart, responds to such a prayer and illumines his heart with knowledge, which dissipates the darkness of ignorance.

Lord Caitanya has taught:

tṛṇād api sunīcena
taror iva sahiṣṇunā
amāninā māna-dena
kīrtanīyaḥ sadā hariḥ

> One should chant the holy name of the Lord in a humble state of mind, thinking oneself lower than the straw in the street. One should be more tolerant than a tree, devoid of all sense of false prestige, and should be ready to offer all respect to others. In such a state of mind one can chant the holy name of the Lord constantly.

Often people do not understand the transcendental message of this verse. Although they are forced to act by the influence of the three modes, they make an artificial show of humility, pretending to be weak, lowly, and penniless beggars. This sort of cheating mood is most undesirable. Realizing the truth of the Vedic statement *ahaṁ brahmāsmi* ("I am Brahman") is one meaning of humility. The essence of this teaching is to understand that matter and spirit are diametrically opposed.

When we are inspired by devotional service to the Lord, our original identity begins to manifest in us and ultimately brings us to God-realization. The devotees work hard to induce people from the materialistic masses to take up devotional service, all the while trying not to disturb their minds. Such spiritual efforts are never to be confused with the mundane endeavors of fruitive workers, empirical philosophers, or outright sense gratifiers. As the Supreme Lord says in the *Gītā* (3.24), *utsīdeyur ime lokāḥ na kuryāṁ karma ced aham:* "If I did not perform prescribed duties, all these worlds would be put to ruination."

Those who are not enthusiastic to execute the Supreme Lord's transcendental orders will automatically be forced by the mode of passion to perform useless action, which is really the state of inactivity. Arjuna asked Lord Kṛṣṇa about the symptoms and behavior of one who has transcended the material modes. The following verses from the *Gītā* (14.26–27) summarize the Lord's response to this question:

māṁ ca yo 'vyabhicāreṇa
bhakti-yogena sevate
sa guṇān samatītyaitān
brahma-bhūyāya kalpate

brahmaṇo hi pratiṣṭhāham
amṛtasyāvyayasya ca
śāśvatasya ca dharmasya
sukhasyaikāntikasya ca

> One who engages in full devotional service, unfailing in all circumstances, at once transcends the modes of material nature and thus comes to the level of Brahman. And I am the basis of the impersonal Brahman, which is immortal, imperishable and eternal and is the constitutional position of ultimate happiness.

Bhakti-yoga can be divided into three stages: 1) to take the first step toward complete surrender by accepting things favorable to the execution of devotional service; 2) to serve the Supreme Lord after realizing one's true nature; 3) to become situated on the elevated stage, in which one sees the Supreme Lord in everything and everything in the Supreme Lord. In this way, initial faith increases and leads to full surrender to the Lord.

Once a person resolves to accept only those things conducive to devotional service, the Lord's internal potency helps him reach the goal. Our sole duty is to constantly remember the Lord and pray for His sanction in everything. The instructions we receive from a spiritual master firmly situated in Kṛṣṇa consciousness help us properly engage in the devotional processes of hearing, chanting, and constant remembrance of the Lord. If we are inspired by our remembrance of the Lord and by His will, then we will never be misdirected. We will not be intimidated by the horrible hallucinations of this illusory material energy. By following the spiritual master's orders with single-minded determination, we will remain undeterred in executing the Lord's service and will make quick progress.

The mood of surrender during the stage of *vaidhi-bhakti* (devotional service under strict rules and regulations) is different from that in the stage of *rāgānuga-bhakti* (spontaneous devotional service). In the spontaneous stage, the mood of surrender is the natural expression of the self. When the process of surrender is followed step by step, one patiently executes the Lord's orders and gradually becomes enthusiastic. Such a devotee follows the regulative principles of hearing, chanting, remembering, and so on, and emulates previous saintly preceptors. In the association of devotees he becomes more and more proficient in rendering devotional service. Gradually his service becomes easier. Thus constant remembrance of the Lord comes simply by developing enthusiasm and patience in devotional activities.

One deviates from the path of *yoga* because of forgetfulness. In devotional service there is no such apprehension, because the Supreme Lord always protects the *bhakti-yogī.* Even if the *bhakti-yogī* falls down, he can regain his former position by receiving strength from the Lord. Because of his remembrance of the Lord, all obstacles on his path are cleared away. Therefore the process of surrender leads to real perfection in *yoga;* it is the easiest path to follow and is also the most direct.

We learn from the book *Sanat-sujātīya* that four things are required in attaining perfection in *yoga* practice: 1) the scriptures; 2) enthusiasm; 3) a bona fide spiritual master; 4) sufficient time. The scriptures recommend the path of surrender described in this book. Enthusiasm means to constantly remember the Lord and to pray for His mercy. The spiritual master in the heart of the surrendered devotee is the Supreme Lord Himself. He manifests as the beloved initiating spiritual master and the instructing spiritual masters. It is the Supreme Lord who, acting as the spiritual master in the heart, enlightens us with *buddhi-yoga,* or divine consciousness. And this consciousness helps us understand the Supreme Lord as He is.

The sages say that when we surrender to the Lord we will clearly see how He personally makes arrangements for us, even in small matters. Then we will easily see how with His omnipotent supreme intelligence He is assisting us out of love. So it is unnecessary to waste time in further speculation. We have to vanquish illusion, develop equanimity and spontaneity, and practice *bhakti-yoga.* Then a supremely powerful force will gradually transform our material existence into spiritual existence. All our misconceptions, accumulated over millions of lifetimes, will be rectified in a short time. Hence we need not become anxious because of a lack of time. The eightfold *yoga* practice—*yama, niyama, āsana, prāṇāyāma,* and so on—gives quick results, and one feels that he is doing something substantial. However, although such efforts may certainly make one materially proficient, they are nevertheless simply human endeavors. They are totally distinct from the activities carried out by the Lord's potency. The Supreme Lord's energy often works in subtle ways, but where it ultimately takes us is inconceivable to the human mind.

The mundane processes for elevation are, after all, initiated by intelligent human brains. They are like man-made canals: useful for easy transportation from one place to another, but otherwise of limited utility. Human efforts are imperfect, and therefore they keep us in the material world. As the Lord says in the *Bhagavad-gītā* (8.16):

ā-brahma-bhuvanāl lokāḥ
punar āvartino 'rjuna
mām upetya tu kaunteya
punar janma na vidyate

From the highest planet in the material world down to the lowest, all are places of misery wherein repeated birth and death take place. But one who attains to My abode, O son of Kuntī, never takes birth again.

The energy of the Lord is like a fathomless ocean that remains undisturbed in all circumstances. It is shoreless, without beginning or end; therefore the process which directly manifests from this energy is omnipotent and can transport one to any heights or levels. The necessities for ocean travel are a ship, a navigator, a rudder, and a favorable wind. One must clearly understand that this human body is the most suitable ship to take us across the ocean of nescience, the spiritual master is the best navigator, the scriptures are the rudder, and the Lord's mercy is the perfect wind. If we do not take advantage of this excellent arrangement and cross over the material ocean of nescience, then we are our own worst enemy. We must always fix our attention on the favorable wind of the Lord's mercy, which incarnates as the spiritual master. Therefore one must approach a spiritual master, take shelter of his lotus feet, and learn from him the science of devotional service. This is what the *Upaniṣads* enjoin—*tad-vijñānārthaṁ sa gurum evābhigacchet.*

The saintly, pure devotees, the *guru,* and the scriptures all represent the same Absolute Truth. The pure devotees are in fact all *gurus* because they never swerve from the spiritual principles enunciated in the scriptures: they see only through the lense of the scriptures. Spiritual practices are impossible to execute without the authority of these three ruling principles—the saintly devotees, the *guru,* and the scriptures. One must vehemently denounce the Western mentality of defying spiritual tradition and the scriptures. Such a mentality reveres mundane philosophies based on speculation and concocted logic, considering these practices signs of superior intelligence. The only weapon the proponents of such philosophies have is mundane argument, but often they exhibit a lack of mastery even of this art. Recent trends show that without probing deeply into a subject, these Westerners uselessly debate direct and indirect meanings *ad infinitum.* Each of these sophists surely realizes that he must one day accept defeat at the hands of a greater sophist, for there is always someone more intelligent. Therefore the process of debate leads nowhere.

There is a wide gulf between superficial dabbling in philosophy to impress people with a few stock phrases, and a sincere search for knowledge of the Absolute. Through the speculative process it is impossible to fathom the inconceivable topics concerning the Absolute Truth, for they can be understood only through the science of devotion. As Śrīla Rūpa Gosvāmī writes in his *Bhakti-rasāmṛta-sindhu,* quoting from the *Mahābhārata:*

> *acintyāḥ khalu ye bhāvā*
> *na tāṁs tarkeṇa yojayet*
> *prakṛtibhyaḥ paraṁ yac ca*
> *tad acintyasya lakṣaṇam*

> Anything transcendental to material nature is inconceivable and thus cannot be grasped through mundane arguments. Therefore one should not try to understand transcendental subjects in this way.

Without the mercy of the Supreme Lord, such esoteric subjects are incomprehensible, even if one spends many years researching them. Beyond the sensual realm lie indirect, subtle perceptions, which need to be properly understood. But they can be understood properly only if one sees their relationship to the inconceivable, transcendental Absolute Truth. Without seeing this connection, one will find all discussion of these subtle perceptions to be like beating the chaff for grain—a mere exercise in futility that brings only frustration and distress. Such empty sophistry may show off some mundane erudition, but it cannot help one make spiritual progress. In fact, these dry empirical debates often create big hurdles. So it is better to avoid them.

It is strongly recommended that one simply follow in the footsteps of spiritual stalwarts who act according to the scriptural injunctions and the spiritual guidelines given by saintly souls and the *guru.* One should not raise too many doubts and questions. As the Lord states in the *Bhagavad-gītā* (4.34), *tad viddhi praṇipātena paripraśnena sevayā:* "Just try to learn the truth by approaching a spiritual master. Inquire from him submissively and render service unto him." This process, which strictly follows the *Vedas,* will bring us to a realization of the inconceivable truth. Once we are on this path, many realizations dawn on us, and it is imperative that we pursue them in order to progress further. The faint illumination of knowledge that appears at first is certain to lead to full enlightenment, but we have to be patient. We must carefully avoid letting pride enter our hearts because of some initial perceptions of the inconceivable Absolute; rather, we must eagerly approach the *guru,* or the pure devotee, and ask how to proceed. We must reject the narrow and bigoted idea that there is nothing more to know. The most important point is to always fully depend on the mercy of the supreme spiritual master residing in the heart.

In recent times we have heard two words being loudly voiced: Māyāvāda (impersonalist) and Advaita-vāda (monist). I deem it proper to write a few words about them. Śrīpāda Śaṅkarācārya was a *brāhmaṇa* who propagated the impersonalist philosophy. But if he were to hear the pathetic version of his theory being espoused today, complete with nonbrahminical Western logic and mundane concepts, he would surely be struck dumb. Śrīpāda Śaṅkarācārya taught and exhibited ideal brahminical behavior. He propounded irrefutable arguments that destroyed materialistic views. Furthermore, his erudition, realization, and renunciation were of an extremely high caliber. Yet when his so-called followers dilute and mutilate his philosophy, we are moved simultaneously to tears and laughter.

Through logic and sophistry one can never understand how the Supreme Lord created this unlimited cosmos, but the demoniac atheists will never tire of using these methods. Lord Kṛṣṇa describes their mentality in the *Bhagavad-gītā* (16.8): *asatyam apratiṣṭhaṁ te,* "They say that this world is unreal, with no foundation, no God in control." In fact, the very brain that thinks these childish thoughts is also a most insignificant creation of the Supreme Lord. Hence to expect that such pea-brains can grasp the mysteries behind the Supreme Lord's extraordinary plans is to hope for the impossible. Śrīpāda Śaṅkarācārya assessed the prevailing trends of his time and concluded that the monistic view, or the impersonal philosophy, was best suited for his contemporaries. But that was not his final conclusion. He went on to say, *bhaja govindaṁ mūḍha-mate:* "O fools, simply worship Govinda." From his use of the word *bhaja,* "worship," we understand him to mean that one should worship Lord Govinda's name, form, qualities, pastimes, and so on. The state of transcendence discussed here is far beyond impersonal realization, the ultimate goal of the monists. Indeed, those who worship Govinda enter into Śrī

Vṛndāvana in Śrī Mathurā, the highest spiritual realm, where Śrī Śrī Rādhā and Kṛṣṇa enact Their quintessential pastimes.

The Supreme Lord is one, yet He has *prābhava* (fully potent) expansions and *vaibhava* (partially potent) expansions. The Supreme Lord is endowed with at least six unlimited opulences—absolute wealth, power, beauty, knowledge, fame, and renunciation. With His countless mouths Śrī Ananta Śeṣa is unable to fully describe these opulences. Therefore the Lord is also said to be indescribable, all-pervading, and unmanifest. The *Upaniṣads* describe the Supreme Lord as *asamaurdhva*, "one without a second." We have already established this truth. Similarly, Lord Kṛṣṇa Himself says in the *Bhagavad-gītā* (Chapter 10) that He is the Aśvattha tree, fire, Śrīla Vyāsadeva, Arjuna, and so on. These facts have also been firmly substantiated. To perfectly comprehend the absolute pastimes of the absolute Supreme Godhead is impossible through any of the "isms," such as empiricism, impersonalism, or sophism. Only by the Lord's mercy can one fathom the Supreme Godhead. That same Supreme Personality benignly reveals the truth about Himself in the *Bhagavad-gītā*. This text is the essence of all the Vedic scriptures and is the synthesis of all conflicting "isms." Lord Caitanya is the unchallenged spiritual stalwart who propagated the process of surrender to Kṛṣṇa, the conclusion of all of the *Bhagavad-gītā's* teachings. Those who follow in His footsteps are the real *yogīs* and devotees.

The Supreme Lord's pastimes are eternal. Those who doubt this are impersonalists. When one tries to gauge the omnipotent Supreme Godhead with a limited measuring principle, one is drawn to the impersonal concept. One must carefully avoid this all-devouring philosophy. When Śrī Nārada Muni saw how Lord Kṛṣṇa had expanded Himself in His original form and was dancing with many *gopīs* simultaneously, he realized that Lord Kṛṣṇa was the Supreme Personality of Godhead, the source of everything. Lord Kṛṣṇa is always being served and worshiped by Śrīmatī Rādhārāṇī, yet He expands Himself unlimitedly. Just as a candle can light other candles yet remain unchanged, so the Supreme Lord, though "one without a second," can expand Himself in unlimited forms, including the all-pervading, universal soul. This is direct proof of the Supreme Lord's absolute divinity.

The Lord is different from all, yet the same as all. This is due to His inconceivable potency of being simultaneously one with and different from everything. One has to hear this philosophy from a pure devotee of the Lord; otherwise it is impossible to understand whether the Absolute Truth is a person or an impersonal substance. If the Supreme is omnipotent, He should be simultaneously personal and impersonal. One who rejects either of these aspects of the Lord tries to limit the absoluteness of the Supreme. Such logic is described as "the logic of half a hen," by which a fool wishes to profit from the egg-laying half of the hen without having to feed the front half. Those who have been blessed by the spiritual master and the Supreme Lord can easily see through this foolish concept and abstain from futile, time-wasting debates. The process of surrender gradually reveals the wonderful glories of the Supreme Lord. Puny human attempts to comprehend such topics will merely end in confusion. The Supreme Lord manifests Himself to the devotee in proportion to the devotee's service attitude and surrender. Arguments and debates are totally inadequate means for understanding the Supreme Absolute Truth.

The objective of life is not simply a subject of debate or speculation. The ultimate aim of life is to realize that supreme object, the Personality of Godhead. *Buddhi-yoga,* or Kṛṣṇa consciousness, means to become absorbed in serving the Supreme Lord and His name, qualities, form, pastimes, etc. In other words, it means becoming an instrument for His satisfaction. We have to become infused with His spiritual potency; thus strengthened, we then have to make the propagation of His transcendental glories our prime duty in life. By means of such potent missionary activities, innumerable *jīvas* can experience endless spiritual joy.

Neither spiritual retreats, churches, mosques, temples, *karma-yoga, jñāna-yoga,* dry empirical philosophy, nor imitation devotees can save humanity from the jaws of death. They are inadequate for purifying the consciousness because what they offer as spiritual succor is limited by their sectarian vision, a set of do's and dont's, and a rigid approach that simply further entangle humanity in the material energy. What is needed are exemplary spiritual actions and the espousal of the genuine path of self-realization, but these have not been properly instituted. Just as Bhagirātha brought down the Gaṅgā and liberated his forefathers, similarly, we must bring a deluge of love of Godhead that can extricate the conditioned souls from the clutches of gross materialism. At least for some time, we must create Satya-yuga, the age of reason and piety. We can easily accomplish this herculean task simply by reintroducing Lord Caitanya's *saṅkīrtana* movement of the congregational chanting of Lord Kṛṣṇa's name and thus flooding the world with *kṛṣṇa-prema.* All living entities—the human beings, who are afflicted by Kali-yuga, as well as sub-human beings—must be drowned in the floodwaters of *kṛṣṇa-prema.*

By studying the *Vedas,* the *Vedānta-sūtra,* and the *Upaniṣads,* one may find processes for purifying the consciousness and elevating oneself to the transcendental platform. But for the conditioned souls of Kali-yuga, such means are beyond reach. Lord Caitanya alone can liberate the conditioned souls of this age. In His younger days Lord Caitanya was known as Nimāi Paṇḍita because He was an erudite scholar. Indeed, He became famous as a master of logic. Yet for the sake of the *jīvas* afflicted by the Kali-yuga, He presented Himself as illiterate. Such pastimes are possible only for the Supreme Lord. When the famous Māyāvādī *sannyāsī* Prakāśānanda Sarasvatī met Lord Caitanya in Benares, he spoke as follows to the Lord: "I see You are a *sannyāsī,* yet You are in the company of sentimentalists, and like them You are dancing and singing. The real business of *sannyāsīs* is to study the *Vedas* and meditate on Brahman. But You have rejected these duties and are acting like a sentimentalist. I am impressed with Your effulgent form, which resembles that of Lord Nārāyaṇa Himself, but why do You act below Your status?"

The Māyāvādī *sannyāsīs* study the *Vedas* simply to gain liberation. Lord Caitanya did not advent merely to teach such an insignificant goal. He propagated the congregational chanting of the holy name and the scientific method of devotional service. His main aim was to establish the authorized religious principle for this age—*saṅkīrtana*—and thereby liberate all living entities. His reply to Prakāśānanda Sarasvatī was very simple, as if coming from an ordinary mortal. The Lord said,

> Respected Swamijī, please listen to the reason why I act as I do. My *guru* saw that I was ignorant, and so he instructed Me as follows: "You are foolish and have no proper understanding of Vedānta philosophy. So simply chant this Hare Kṛṣṇa

mantra, which is the essence of all mantras. This *mantra* will deliver You from the entanglement of material existence and award You the shelter of Kṛṣṇa's lotus feet. In the Age of Kali there is no religious principle except chanting Kṛṣṇa's name. It has been ascertained from all the scriptures that Kṛṣṇa's holy name is the essence of all *mantras.*" He then made Me learn a verse, which I will repeat to you for your consideration:

"harer nāma harer nāma
harer nāmaiva kevalam
kalau nāsty eva nāsty eva
nāsty eva gatir anyathā"

"If one wants to make spiritual progress in this Age of Kali, there is no alternative, there is no alternative, there is no alternative to the holy name, the holy name, the holy name of the Lord."

By chanting Kṛṣṇa's holy name, one cleanses all the dust from the mirror of one's consciousness. The blazing fire of material existence is then extinguished. This fire is especially severe in the present materialistic civilization, which is full of conflict, the hallmark of Kali-yuga. But extinguishing the fire of material existence is far from the final result of chanting. Indeed, it is only a preliminary consequence. Gradually, the knowledge that love of Godhead is the absolute necessity of life becomes clearer, the dark veil of ignorance is lifted, and one gets a glimpse of absolute knowledge. As the devotee realizes this transcendental knowledge, he feels ever-increasing spiritual ecstasy overwhelming his heart. This spiritual joy expands at every moment. Let the all-auspicious chanting of the holy name of Kṛṣṇa be ever-victorious!

Those who seek the smaller values of life and thus take up *yoga* for selfish motives are not very noble, and even if they achieve success, they still remain inferior. But those who practise *yoga* for the benefit of others are truly worthy, for even if they personally do not attain perfection, they are very elevated souls. Devotees of the Lord practise the *yoga* called *buddhi-yoga,* or Kṛṣṇa consciousness. This *yoga* is meant to bless all humanity, as well as bring the practitioner to the perfection of life. The *Śrīmad-Bhāgavatam* (1.5.17) aptly describes the great value of such *yoga:*

tyaktvā sva-dharmaṁ caraṇāmbujaṁ harer
bhajann apakvo 'tha patet tato yadi
yatra kva vābhadram abhūd amuṣya kiṁ
ko vārtha āpto 'bhajatāṁ sva-dharmataḥ

One who has forsaken his material occupations to engage in the devotional service of the Lord may sometimes fall down while in an immature stage, yet there is no danger of his being unsuccessful. On the other hand, a nondevotee, though fully engaged in occupational duties, does not gain anything.

Appendixes

General Index

Numerals in boldface indicate references to verses fully quoted.

CENTRES OF THE INTERNATIONAL SOCIETY FOR KRISHNA CONSCIOUSNESS

ISKCON is a world wide community of devotees of Krishna dedicated to the principles of bhakti-yoga. Classes are held in the evenings during the week, and a special feast and festival is held every Sunday afternoon. Write, call, or visit for further information.

AUSTRALASIA

AUSTRALIA

Adelaide—74 Semaphore Rd., Semaphore, S.A. 5019/ (08) 493 200

Bambra—New Nandagram , 'Oak Hill' Dean's Marsh Road, Bambra, VIC 3241/ (052) 887383

Brisbane—95 Bank Rd., Graceville, QLD 4075, (mail: PO Box 83, Indooroopilly, 4068)/ (07) 379-5455

Melbourne—197 Danks St., Albert Park, VIC 3206, (mail: PO Box 125, Albert Park, VIC 3206)/ (03) 699-5122

Millfield—New Gokula, Lewis Lane (off Mt. View Rd.), Millfield, near Cessnock/ (049) 981 1852

Murwillumbah—New Govardhana , Tyalgum Rd., Eungella via Murwillumbah, NSW 2484, (mail: PO Box 687, Murwillumbah, NSW 2484)/ (066) 72-1903

Perth—144 Railway Parade (cnr. The Strand), Bayswater (mail: P.O. Box 102, Bayswater, W.A. 6053)/ (09) 370 1552

Sydney—112 Darlinghurst Rd., Darlinghurst, NSW 2010, (mail: PO Box 159, Kings Cross, NSW 2011)/ (02) 357-5162

NEW ZEALAND AND FIJI

Auckland, New Zealand—New Varshana, Highway 18, Riverhead, (next to Huapai Golf course) (mail: RD 2 Kumeu, Auckland)/ (9) 412-8075

Christchurch, New Zealand—83 Bealey Ave., Christchurch, (mail: PO Box 25-190, Christchurch)/ (3) 61-965

Labasa, Fiji—Delailabasa (mail: Box 133, Labasa)/ 82912

Lautoka, Fiji—5 Tavewa Ave., Lautoka (mail: PO Box 125, Lautoka)/ 61-633 ext.48

Raki Raki, Fiji—Rewasa (mail: Box 204, Raki Raki)/ 94243

Suva, Fiji—7 1/2 miles Nasinu (mail: PO Box 6376, Nasinu) / 39-1282

Wellington, New Zealand—6 Shotter St., Karori, Wellington, (mail: PO Box 2753, Wellington)/ (4) 76 4445

NORTH AMERICA

CANADA

Ashcroft, B.C.—Saranagati Dhama, Box 99, Ashcroft, B.C. V0K 1A0

Montreal, Quebec—1626 Pie IX Boulevard, H1V 2C5/ (514) 521-1301

Ottawa, Ontario—212 Somerset St., E., K1N 6V4/ (613) 233-1884

Regina, Saskatchewan—1279 Retallack St., S4T 2H8/ (306) 525 1640

Toronto, Ontario—243 Avenue Rd., M5R 2J6/ (416) 922-5415

Vancouver, B.C.—5462 S.E. Marine Dr., Burnaby, V5J 3G8/ (604) 433-9728

U.S.A.

Arcata, California—P.O. Box 4233, Arcata, CA 95221/ (707) 826 9219

Atlanta, Georgia—1287 Ponce de Leon Ave., N.E., 30306/ (404) 377-8680

Baltimore, Maryland—200 Bloomsbury Ave., Catonsville 21228/ (301) 744-9537

Berkeley, California—2334 Stuart St., 94705/ (415) 644-1113

Boise, Idaho—1615 Martha st., 83706/ (208) 344 427

Boston, Massachusetts—72 Commonwealth Ave., 02116/ (617) 247-8611

Carriere, Mississippi (New Talavan)—Route 2, Box 449, 39426/ (601) 798-8533

Chicago, Illinois—1716 W. Lunt Ave., 60626/ (312) 973-0900

Cleveland, Ohio—11206 Clifton Blvd., 44102/ (216) 651 6670

Dallas, Texas—5430 Gurley Ave., 75223/ (214) 827-6330

Denver, Colorado—1400 Cherry St., 80220/ (303) 333-5461

Detroit, Michigan—383 Lennox Ave., 48215/ (313) 824-6000

Gainesville, Florida (New Raman-reti)—Box 819, Alachua, Florida 32615/ (904) 462-9046

Gainsville, Florida—1417/1419 N.W. 1st Ave., 32601/ (904) 375-2884

Gurabo, Puerto Rico—Rt. 181, Box 215-B, Bo.Sta. Rita, 00658/ (809) 737-5222

Hillsbourough, North Carolina (New Gokula)—Rt.6, Box 701,27278/ (919) 732-6492

Honolulu, Hawaii—51 Coelho Way, 96817/ (808) 595-3947

Huston, Texas—1320 W. 34th. St., 77018/ (713) 686-4482

Laguna beach, California—285 Legion St., 92651/ (714) 494-7029

Lansing, Michigan—1914 E. Michigan Ave., 48912/ (517) 332-1823

Long Island, New York—197 S. Ocean Ave., Freeport, 11520/ (516) 378-6184

Los Angeles, California—3764 Watseka Ave., 90034/ (213) 836-2676

Miami Beach, Florida—2445 Collins Ave., 33140/ (305) 531-0331

Mulberry, Tennessee (Murakri-sevaka)—Murari Project. Rt. No. 1., Box 146-, 37359/ (615) 759-7331

New Orleans, Louisiana—2936 Esplanade Ave., 70109/ (504) 488-7433

New York, New York—305 Schermerhorn St., Brooklyn, 11217/ (718) 855-6714

Philadelphia, Pennsylvania—51 W. Allens Lane, 19119/ (215) 247-4600

Philadelphia, Pennsylvania—529 South St., 19147/ (215) 238-1753

Port Royal, Pennsylvania (Gita-nagari)—R.D. No. 1, Box 839, 17082/ (717) 527-4101

San Diego, California—1030 Grand Ave., Pacific Beach, 92109/ (619) 483-2500

San Francisco, California—84 Carl st., 94117/ (415) 753-8647

Seattle, Washington—1420 228th Ave., S.E., Issaquah, 98027/ (206) 391 3293

St. Louis, Missouri—3926 Lindell Blvd., 63108/ (314) 535-8085

Tallahassee, Florida—1323 Nylic St., 32304/ (904) 681-9258

Topanga, California—20395 Callon Dr., 90290/ (213) 455-1658

Towaco, New Jersey—(mail P.O. Box 109, 07082)/ (201) 299-0970

Walla Walla, Washington—314 E. Poplar, 99362/ (509) 529-9556

Washington, D.C.—10310 Oaklyn Dr., Potomac, Maryland 20854/ (301) 299-2100

EUROPE

GREAT BRITIAN AND IRELAND

Belfast, Northern Ireland—140 Upper Dunmurray Lane, Belfast/ 621757

Birmingham, West Midlands—84 Stanmore Rd., Edgebaston

Dublin, Ireland—3 Temple Lane, Dublin 2/ (01) 679 5887

Hare Krishna Island, N. Ireland—Derrylin, County Fermanagh, BT 92 96N, N. Ireland/ (3657) 21512

Leicester, England—21 Thoresby St., North Evington,/ (0533) 762587

Liverpool, England—135 Northumberland St., L8 8AY/(051) 709 9188

London, England (city)—10 Soho St., London W1/ (01) 437-3662

London, England (country)—Bhaktivedanta Manor, Letchmore Heath, Watford, Hertfordshire WD2 8EP/ (09276) 7244

Manchester, England—20 Mayfield Road, Whalley Range, Manchester M168FT/ (061) 2264416

Newcastle upon Tyne, England—21 Leazes Park Rd., /(091) 222 0150

Scotland—Karuna Bhavan, Bankhouse Road, Lesmahagow, Lanarkshire/ (0555) 894790

ITALY

Bergamo—Villaggio Hare Krishna, Via Galileo Galilei, 41, 24040 Chignola D'isola (BG)/ (035) 490706

Bologna—Via Nazionale 124, 40065-Pianoro (BO) (51) 774-034

Catania—Via San Nicolo al Borgo 28, 95128 Catania, Sicily/ (95) 522-252

Florence (Villa Vrndavana)—Via Communale degli Scopeti 108, S. Andrea in Percussina, San Casciano Val di Pesa (FI) 50026 (55) 820-054

Naples—Via Torricelli 77, 80059 Torre del Greco (NA)/ (81) 881-5431

Padua—Via delle Granze 107, 35040 Loc. Camin (PD) (49) 760-057

Rome—Via di Tor Tre Teste 142, 00169 Roma

OTHER COUNTRIES

Amsterdam, Holland—Krsna Dham, 225 Ruysdaelkade, 1072 AW (020) 751 404

Antwerp, Belgium—184 Amerikalei 2000/ (03) 237 0037, 237 0038

Athens, Greece—Poseidonos 27, Ilioupoli, 16 345/ 1-993-7068

Barcelona, Spain—c/de L'Oblit, 67-08026/ (93) 347-9933

Bavarian Forest (Bayrisher Wald), W. Germany (Nava-Jiyada-Nrsimha-Ksetra)—(contact ISKCON Heidelberg)

Belgrade, Yugoslavia—Vaisnavska vjerska zajednica, Sumatovacka 118, 11000 Beograd/ (011) 434 183

Bellinzona, Switzerland—New Nandagram, al Chiossascio, 6594 Contone TI/ (092) 622747

Berlin, Germany—Bhakti Yoga Zentrum, Friedrichstrasse 31, 1000 Berlin 61/ (030) 251 4372

Brihuega, Spain (New Vraja Mandala)—(Santa Clara) Brihuega, Guadalajara/ (11) 280018

Brussels, Belgium—49 rue Marche auz Poulets-1000 Bruxelles/ (02) 513 86 05/04
Budapest, Hungary—M.K.T.H.K., J. Kalmar, Marton U. 52, 1038 Budapest
Copenhagen, Denmark—Kongens Tvaeruej 11, 2000 Copenhagen f/ (01) 86-85-81
Durbuy, Belgium—Chateau de Petit Somme, Durbuy 5482/ 086-322926
Gothenburg, Sweden—Hare Krishna Center, Grimmeredsvagen 103.42169 Vastra Frolunda/ 031-290966
Grodinge, Sweden—Korsnas Gard, 14032 Grodinge/ 0753-29151
Heidelberg, W. Germany—Kurfursten Anlage 5, 6900 Heidelberg/ 06221-15101
Helsinki, Finland—Eljaksentie 9, 00370 Helsinki
Horup, Germany—Neuhorup 1, D-2391 Horup
Jarna, Sweden—Almviks Gard, 15300 Jama (46) 755-52068
Lisbon, Portugal—Rua Fernao Lopes, 6, Cascais 2750 (mail: Apartado 2489, Lisboa 1112)/ (11) 286 713
Lugano, Switzerland—The Gokula Project, La Pampa, 6981 Sessa (Malcantone) TI/ (091) 73-25-73
Malmo, Sweden—Center for Vedisk Kultur, Remegentsgata 14, S-211 42 Malmo/ (040) 127181
Moscow, USSR—Contact ISKCON Office of Soviet Affairs, Almviks Gard, 15300 Jama, Sweden/ (46) 0755-52068
Munich, Germany—Brodstrasse 12, D-8000 Munchen 82
Osafiya, Israel—Hare Krishna, Osafiya 30900/ 4-391150
Oslo, Norway—Senter for Krishnabevvissthet, Skolestien 11, 0373 Oslo 3
Paris, France—31 Rue Jean Vacquier, 93160 Noisy le Grand/ (01) 45921018; 43043263
Prague, Czechoslovakia—Hare Krishna, Na Hrazi 5, 18000 Praha 8/ (2) 821438
Pregrada, Yugoslavia—Davor Bateli, Goricka 5/6, Pregrada/ (049) 49 73176
Stockholm, Sweden—Fridhemsgatan 22, 112 40 Stockholm/ 08-549002
Turku, Finland—ISKCON, Sairashuokeenkatu 8A1, 20140 Turku 14/ (9) 21 308981
Valencay, France (New Mayapur)—Lucay-Le-Male, 36 600 / (54) 40-26-88
Valencia, Spain—c/de Almirante cadarso #12, Vedat de Torrente/ (961)55962
Vienna, Austria—Center for Vedic Studies, Liechtensteinstrasse 23/11, 1090 Vienna/ (0222) 310-10-33
Warsaw, Poland—Towarzystwo Swiadomosci Kryszny--Bhakti Yoga W PRL, 02-770 Warasawa 130, skr. pocztowa 257
Zurich, Switzerland—Bergstrasse 54, 8032 Zurich/ (01) 69-32-79
Zurich, Switzerland—Preyergrasse 16, CH-8001 Zurich

AFRICA

Abeokuta, Nigeria—Ibadan Rd., Obantoko, behind NET (mail: P.O. Box 5177)
Abidjan, Ivory Coast—01 BP 8366, Abidjan
Accra, Ghana—582 Blk. 20, Odokor, Official Town (mail: P.O. Box 01568, Osu)
Buea, Cameroon—Southwest Province (mail: c/o Yuh Laban Nkesah, P and T, VHS)
Cape Town, South Africa—17 St. Andrews Rd., Rondebosch 7700/ (21) 689 1529
Durban (Natal), S. Africa—Chatsworth Circle, Chatsworth 4030 (mail: P.O. Box 56003)/ (31) 435-815
Freetown, Sierra Leone—13 Bright St., Brookfields (mail: P.O. Box 812, Freetown)
Harare, Zimbabwe—46 Crowhill Rd., (mail: P.O. Box 2090)/ 8877801
Johannesburg, South Africa—14 Goldreid St., Hillbrow, Johannesburg 2001/ (11) 666-2716
Kitwe, Zambia—3121 Gandhi Close, Buyantanshil/ 8877801
Lagos, Nigeria—No.2 Murtala Mohammed International Airport Expressway, Mafaluku (mail: P.O. Box 8793, Lagos)
Lusaka, Zambia—Plot 4/288 Chingololo Rd., Makeni (mail: P.O. Box 35658, Lusaka)/ 210 578
Mauritius (ISKCON Vedic Farm)—Hare Krishna Rd., Beau Bois, Bon Acceuil/ 418 3955
Mombasa, Kenya—Hare Krishna House, Sauti Ya Kenya and Kisumu Rds., (mail: P.O. Box 82224, Mombasa)/ 312248
Nairobi, Kenya—Muhuroni close, off West Nagara Rd., (mail: P.O. Box 28946, Nairobi)/ 744365
Nkawkaw, Ghana—P.O.Box 69, Nkawkaw
Phoenix, Mauritius—Hare Krishna Land, Pont Fer, (mail: P.O. Box 108, Quatres Bornes/ (230) 696 5804
Port Harcourt, Nigeria—2 Eligbam Rd., (corner of Obana Obhan St), G.R.A ll (mail: P.O. Box 4429, Trans Amadi)
Tokoradi, Ghana—64 Windy Ridge (mail: P.O. Box 328)
Warri, Nigeria—1 Ogunu St., Bendel Housing Estate, Ugborikoro (P.O. Box 1922, Warri)/ 053-230-262

ASIA

INDIA

Agartala, Tripura—Assam-Agartala Rd., Banamalipur 799001

Ahmedabad, Gujarat—7, Kailas Society, Ashram Rd., 380 009/ 449935

Bamanbore, Gujarat—N.H. 8-B Surendranagar/ 79

Bangalore, Karnataka—Hare Krishna Hill, 1 'R' Block Rd., Rajajinagar, 560 010/ 359 856

Baroda, Gujarat—Hare Krishna Land, Gotri Rd., 390 015/ 326299

Bhayandar, Maharashtra—Shivaji Chowk, Station rd., Bhayandar (West) Thane 401 101/ 698 2987

Bhubaneswar, Orissa—National HIghway No. 5. Nayapali, 751 011/ 53125

Bombay, Maharashtra—Hare Krishna Land, Juhu 400 049/ 626 860

Calcutta, W.Bengal—3 Albert Rd., 700 017/ 47 3757

Chamorshi, Maharashtra—78 Krishnanagar Dham, District Gadhachiroli, 442 603

Chandigarh, Punjab—Hare Krishna Land, Dakshin Marg, Sector 36-B, 160 036/ 44634

Coimbatore, Tamil Nadu—Padmam 387, VGR Puram, Alagen Rd.–1, 641 001/ 4597

Gauhati, Assam—Post Bag No. 127, Gauhati 781 001

Guntur, A.P.—Opp. Sivalayam, Peda Kakani 522 509

Hardwar, U.P.—Pahala Mala, Brittany cottage, Kharkhari 249 401 (mail: P.O. Box 14)

Hyderabad, A.P.—Hare Krishna Land, Nampally Station Rd., 500 001/ 551018

Hyderabad, A.P.—P.O. Dabilpur Village, Medchal Taluc, Hyderabad District, 501 401

Imphal, Manipur—Hare Krishna Land, Airport Road, 795 001/ 21587

Madras, Tamil Nadu—59 Burkit Rd., T. Nagar, Madras-17/ 443266

Mayapur, W. Bengal—Shree Mayapur Chandrodaya Mandir, P.O. Shree Mayapur Dham (Dist. Nadia)/ (034733) 220/218

Moirang, Manipur—Nongban Ingkhon, Tidim Road

Nagpur, Maharashtra—70 Hill Road, Ramnagar, 440 010/ 33513

New Delhi—M-119 Greater Kailash 1, New Delhi 110 048/ 6412058

New Delhi—14/63 Punjabi Bagh, 110 026/ 541 0782

Pandharpur, Maharashtra—**Hare Krishna Asrama, across Chandrabhaga River,** Dist. Sholapur, 413 304

Patna, Bihar—Rajendra Nagar Road No. 12, 800 016/ 507615

Pune, Maharashtra—4 Tarapoor Rd., Camr., 411 001/ 60124 and 64003

Secunderabad, A.P.—9-1-1 St. John's Rd., 500 026/ 825232

Silchar, Assam—Ambikapatti, Silchar, 788004, Cachar District

Siliguri, W. Bengal—Subash Pally, Siliguri

Surat, Gujarat—Rander Rd., Jahangirpura, Surat, 395 005/ 84215

Tirupati, A.P.—K.T. Road, Vinayaka Nagar 517 501/ 2285

Trivandrum, Kerala—T.C.24/1485, WC Hospital Rd., Thycaud, 695 014/ 68197

Udhampur, Jammu and Kashmir—Prabupada Nagar, Udhampur 182 101/ 496 P.P.

Vrndavana, U.P.—Krishna-Balaram Mandir, Bhaktivedanta Swami Marg. Raman Reti, Mathura/ 178

OTHER COUNTRIES

Bali, Indonesia—(Contact ISKCON Jakarta)

Bangkok, Thailand—P.O. Box 15, Prakanong, Bankok

Cagayan de Oro, Phillippines—30 Dahlia St,. Ilaya Carmen, 900 Cagayan de Oro (c/o Sepulveda's Compound)

Cebu, Phillippines (Hare Krishna Paradise)—231 Pagsabungan Rd., Basak, Mandaue City/ 83254

Chittagong, Bangladesh—Caitanya Cultural Society, Sri Pundarik Dham, Mekhala, Hathazari 108 (city office and mail: 23 Nandan Kanan, Chittagong)/ 20-2219

Colombo, Sri Lanka—188 New Chetty St., Colombo 13/ 33325

Hong Kong—27 Chatam Road South, 6/F, Kowloon/ 3-7396818

Iloilo City, Phillippines—13-1-1 Tereos St., La Paz, Iloilo/ 73391

Jakarta, Indonesia—Yayasan Kesadaran Krsna Indonesia, JL Kamboja 10-12, Toman Raya/ 599 301

Kathmandu, Nepal—Vishnu Gaun Panchayat Ward No. 2, Budhanilkantha/ 4-10368

Kuala Lumpur, Malaysia—Lot 9901, Jalan Awan Jawa, Taman Yari, off 5 1/2 Mile, Jalan Kelang Lama, Petaling/ 730 172

Manila, Phillippines—170 R. Femandez, San Juan, Metro Manila/ 707410

Taipei, Taiwan—(mail: c/o ISKCON Hongkong)

Tehran, Iran—Keshavarz- Dehkedeh Ave., Kamran St., No. 58/ 658870

Tel Aviv, Israel—(17B) Gordon St., P.O. Box 48163, Tel Aviv 61480/ 03-238-239

Tokyo, Japan—2-41-12 Izumi, Suginami-ku, Tokyo T168/ (3) 327-1541

LATIN AMERICA

BRAZIL

Belem, PA—Av. Gentil Bittencourt, 1002 (entre Generalissimo e Quintino Bocaiuva)/ (091) 222-1886

Belo Horizante, MG—Rua St. Antonia, 45, Venda Nova, CEP 31510

Brasilia, DF—HIGS 706-Bloco C, Casa 29/ (061) 242-7579

Campo Grande, MS—Rua Calos Chagas, 32-Caicara

Caruaru, Pernambuco—Distrito de Murici (mail: Rua do Norte, 61, Sala 3, Centro)

Curtiba, PR—Rua Jornalista Caio Machado, 291, B. Sta. Quiteria CEP 80320

Florianopolis, SC—Rua 14 de julho, 922, Estreito, CEP 88075

Fortaleza, CE—Rua Jose Laurenco, 2114, Aldeota/ (085) 244-7068

Golania, GO—Rua C-60, Quadra 123, Lt-11, Setor Sudoeste, CEP 74305

Manaus, AM—Avenida 7 de Setembro, 1599 Centro, CEP 69003

Pitajui, SP—Av. Brazil, 306, CEP 16600

Pindamonhangaba, SP (New Gokula)—Bairro Riberao Grande (mail: Caixa Postal 108, CEP 12400/ (0122) 42-5002

Porto Alegre, RS—Rua Tomas Flores, 331, Bomfim, CEP 90210

Recife, PE—Rua Reverendo Samuel Falcao, 755, Madalena, CEP 50710

Rio de Janeiro, RJ—Rua Armando Coelho de Freitas, 108, Barra da Tijuca, CEP 33620

Salvador, BA—Rua Alvaro Adormo, 17, Brotas/ (071) 244-1072

Santos, SP—Rua Nabuco de Araujo, 151-Embare/ (0132) 21-3596

Sao Paulo, SP—Avenida Angelica, 2583, Consolacao, CEP 01227/ (011) 59 7352

MEXICO

Guadalajara—Pedro Moreno 1791, Sector Juarez, Jalisco/ 26-12-78

Mexico City—Gob. Tiburcio Montiel 45, San Miquel Chapultepec, Mexico, D.F. 18/ (905) 271-0132

Mexico City—Govinda's Cultural Center, Insurgentes Sur 2384-1, Mexico City 01000D.F./ 548-9323

Monterrey—Zaragoza 1007, nte. Zona centro/ 74-69-76

Morelia—Ticateme No. 52 pte., Col. Selix Ireta 58070, Morelia, Mich.

Tulacingo, Hidalgo (Nueva Gauda-Mandala Bhumi)—(contact ISKCON Mexico City)

Vera Cruz—Calle 3, Carebelas No. 784, Fraccionamienito Reforma/ 50759

PERU

Arequipa—Jerusalen 402/ 229523

Cuzco—San Juan de Dios 285. 222353

Hare Krishna- Correo De Bella Vista—DPTO De San Martin

Lima—Pasaje Solea 101 Santa Maria-Chosica/ 910891

Lima—Schell 615 Miraflores

Lima—Av. Garcilazo de la Vega, 1670-1680/ 259523

OTHER COUNTRIES

Asuncion, Paraguay—Centro Bhaktivedanta, Alberdi 1603 esq. 4ta., Asuncion/ 595 21 70066

Bahia Blanca, Argentina—Centro de Estudios Vedicos, F. Sanches 233, (8000) Bahia Blanca

Bogota, Colombia—Calle 63A, #10-62 Chapinero/ 249-5797

Buenos Aires, Argentina (Bhaktilata Puri)—(contact Centro Bhaktivedanta, Buenos Aires)

Buenos Aires, Argentina—Centro Bhaktivedanta, Andonaegui 2054, (1431)

Cali, Colombia—Avenida 2 EN, #24N-39/ 68-88-53

Caracas, Venezuela—Avenida Berlin, Quinta Tia Lola, La california Norte/ (58-2) 225463

Cochabamba, Bolivia—Av. Heroinas E-0435 Apt. 3 (mail: P.O. Box 2070, Cochabamba)

Colombia (Nueva Mathura)—Cruzero del Guali, Municipio de Caloto, Valle del Cauca/ 612688 en Cali

Concepcion, Chile—Nonguen, 588/ 23150

Cordoba, Argentina—Montevideo 950, Paso de los Andes/ (051) 262229

Crabwood Creek, Guyana—Grant 1803, Sec. D, Corentyne, Berbice

Cuenca, Ecuador—Entrada de las Pencas 1-Avenida de las Americas/ (593-7) 825211

Essequibo Coast, Guyana—New Navadvipa Dham, Mainstay, Essequibo Coast

Georgetown, Guyana—24 Uitvlugt Front, West Coast Demerara

Guatemala, Guatemala—1a Avenida 9-59, Zona 1/ (51) 5290

Guayaquil, Ecuador—6 de Marzo 226 y V.M. Rendon/ (593-4) 308412 y 309420

Guayaquill, Ecuador (Nuevo Nilacala)—(contact ISKCON Guayaquill)

Guyana—Seawell Village, Corentyne, East Berbice

La Paz, Bolivia—Calle 16 Obrajes 460 (mail: P.O. Box 10278)/ 783556

Montevideo, Uruguay—Centro de Bhakti-yoga, Pablo de Maria 1427, Montevideo/ 598 2484551

Panama, Republic of Panama—Via las Cumbres, entrada Villa Zaita, frente a INPSA No. 10 (mail: P.O.Box 6-29-54, Panama)/ 31-2057

Pereira, Colombia—Carrera 5a, #19-36/ 42769

Quito, Ecuador—Carron 641 Amazones/ 520466

Rosario, Argentina—Centro de Bhakti-yoga, Paraguay 556, (2000) Rosario 2000/ 54-41-252630

San Jose, Costa Rica—Centro Cultural Govinda, Av. 7 Calles 1 y 3, 235 mtrs. norte del Banco Anglo, San Pedro (mail: Apdo, 166, 1002)/ 23 5238

San Jose, Costa Rica—Granja Nueva Goloka Vrindavana, Carretera a Paralso, de la entrada del Jardin Lancaster (por Calle Concava), 200 metros as sur (mano derecha) Cartago (mail: Apdo. 166, 1002)/ 51-6752

San Salvador, El Salvador—Avenida Universitaria 1132, Media Quadra al sur de la Embajada Americana, San Salvador (mail: P.O. Box 1506)/ 392734

San Salvador, El Salvador—Carretera a Santa Ana, Km.34, Canton Los Indios, Zapotitan, Dpto. de La Libertad

Santiago, Chile—Manuel Carvallo 771, Nunoa/ 392734

Santo Domingo, Dominican Republic—Calle Cayetano Rodriquez No. 254

Trinidad and Tobago, West Indies—Orion Drive, Debe/ 647 739

Trinidad and Tobago, West Indies—Prabhupada Ave., Longdenville, Chaguanas